A HANDBOOK FOR SCHOOL BOARD MEMBERS

RONALD W. REBORE, SR.
University of Missouri–St. Louis

PRENTICE-HALL, INC., Englewood Cliffs, New Jersey 07632

Library of Congress Cataloging in Publication Data

Rebore, Ronald W.
  A handbook for school board members.

  Includes bibliographies and index.
    1. School boards—United States.   I. Title.
LB2831.R39   1984   379.1'531'0973   83-13897
ISBN 0-13-381228-6

Editorial/production supervision and
    interior design: Virginia M. Livsey
Cover design: Ray Lundgren
Manufacturing buyer: Ronald Chapman

To Harriet Rebore

Printed in the United States of America

10   9   8   7   6   5   4   3   2   1

ISBN 0-13-381228-6

Prentice-Hall International, Inc., *London*
Prentice-Hall of Australia Pty. Limited, *Sydney*
Editora Prentice-Hall do Brasil, Ltda., *Rio de Janeiro*
Prentice-Hall Canada Inc., *Toronto*
Prentice-Hall of India Private Limited, *New Delhi*
Prentice-Hall of Japan, Inc., *Tokyo*
Prentice-Hall of Southeast Asia Pte. Ltd., *Singapore*
Whitehall Books Limited, *Wellington, New Zealand*

CONTENTS

                                                                          iii

SEVEN   THE ROLE OF THE SCHOOL BOARD IN DISTRICT   **141**
PROPERTY MANAGEMENT

EIGHT   THE ROLE OF THE SCHOOL BOARD
IN DEVELOPING THE INSTRUCTIONAL PROGRAM
AND IN PUPIL RELATIONS

NINE   THE ROLE OF THE SCHOOL BOARD IN DISTRICT   **185**
PERSONNEL MANAGEMENT

PREFACE

The proper and effective governance of school districts is the most important issue facing public education in the United States. In fact, from the very beginnings of our public school system, the issue of governance has always been of central importance because the decisions of school board members have such a pervasive effect upon the educational experience of the children living within their respective jurisdictions.

There are few resources dealing with school district governance that contain a comprehensive, technical, yet practical treatment of the subject. Most state school board associations that have handbooks address statutes and state board of education procedures applicable to particular school boards in their state. Additional material put out by these associations deals with those personal characteristics that are desirable in all board members for effective boardsmanship. Consequently, if a board member wished to find a comprehensive, practical answer to a technical question about school finance, he or she might have to research many different sources. This book consolidates many of these sources and can therefore serve as a ready and continual resource for all school board members.

There are four major trends in public education that have surfaced over the last ten years and will occupy the attention of board members for decades to come. Current information about school governance will be an asset to school board members as they confront these trends.

First, the general state of the economy and the taxpayers revolt has resulted in the failure of tax levy elections and decreased state aid to school districts. Thus revenues are not keeping pace with inflation and school boards have been faced with reevaluating the scope and content of programs that were assumed to constitute a free public education.

Second, the development of new technologies has forced school boards to attempt to incorporate these advances into the curriculum. Without such attempts students will be improperly prepared to make use of calculators, microcomputers, videodiscs, and cable television.

Third, personnel issues continue to occupy a central place in the making of school board policy. Declining enrollment has caused some boards to take a second look at the performance evaluation of teachers in addition to reduction-in-force and early retirement incentive programs. Other boards of education are vitally concerned with collective bargaining and affirmative action issues.

Fourth, social problems remain a constant concern of many school boards. For instance, desegregation, pupil discipline, one-parent families, and drug abuse have caused boards to deal with the effects of these problems on instructional programs.

This book is intended to meet the needs of three categories of individuals: first, school board members who wish to acquire a well-rounded understanding of the educational enterprise; second, superintendents of schools and other school district teachers, administrators, and staff members who wish to update their knowledge about school district governance and management; finally, this book should be of interest to professors of educational administration who have the responsibility of teaching courses in an administrator degree program. This book could serve as a supplemental textbook for a variety of courses in educational administration and could be a primary textbook for courses in central office administration.

Chapters one through four are concerned with the fundamentals of school district governance while chapters five through ten concentrate on the relationship between governance and school district operations. Each chapter is written from a practical perspective and identifies those processes, procedures, and techniques necessary to effectively carry out the governance function. In addition, each chapter contains extensive exhibits and appendices that highlight the concepts presented in the book.

The emphasis throughout the book is on presenting current information and ideas that will be valuable not only to newly elected board members but also to the "old hats" who are interested in updating their knowledge about the educational enterprise.

A final note is in order concerning the contents of chapters one, nine, and ten. While the presentation is unique to this book, the essence of these chapters has been gleaned from a previous book by this author, also published by Prentice-Hall, entitled: *Personnel Administration in Education: A Management Approach,* (1982).

Ronald W. Rebore

CHAPTER ONE
THE STRUCTURAL
FRAMEWORK
OF PUBLIC
EDUCATION

The mission of public schools is to impart knowledge to children and the youth of our country for the purpose of preserving our free democratic heritage.

THE GOVERNANCE STRUCTURE

Philosophical Foundations

America's system of free and universal elementary and secondary education is a unique and distinguishing characteristic. It is generally considered to be our greatest safeguard of freedom and the best guarantee of economic and social welfare for our citizens.

The school as an institution receives its mandate from the society it serves. It is, however, only one of many institutions. Government, home, church, and other social entities also play a role in society. These institutions have complementary purposes. Each provides for the advancement of society and for the individual citizen. The educational programs of the school would be ineffective without the support of government, family, and churches. A hallmark, however, of modern society and these institutions is change. The National School Public Relations Association makes a dramatic point concerning this phenomena.

Calculators, cable television, microcomputers, video discs, satellites, tele-conferencing—the list of new technologies arriving on the scene almost daily is growing and becoming more important to our lives. Only a decade ago, the idea of computers being as common in the home as the television was looked

1

upon as an idea as far-fetched as man walking on the moon was in the middle of this century.

No one will deny that the . . . (present) is the age of technology, an age as dramatic as the industrial revolution in its capacity to change the way we live. Students today will have their future, and much of their present, dominated by electronic wizardry. And unless they have an understanding of and the ability to use the new technology, they will be as illiterate as persons who cannot read or write.[1]

This statement highlights communicative and technological advancement, but in the complex strata of any given society, infinite streams of change occur simultaneously. The family, church, school, and government, with all their subcomponents, are not static institutions but rather evolving entities.

Change is not only continual but also accelerative, and is further complicated by the fact that it occurs unevenly. Technology may be undergoing mutations faster than educational programs can be changed to reflect the expansion of knowledge, often leaving an individual years behind in learning about new advances.

Our perception of reality and how it is related to societal and individual needs determines the content of educational programs. Although fundamental principles such as individual freedom, individual responsibility, and democratic government place a continuous obligation upon the schools, the accelerating rate of change demands that our schools be flexible enough to adjust to new developments and conditions. Education cannot be static in the dynamic milieu of reality.

At various times in the history of our nation, educators and professional organizations have formally stated the objectives and purposes of American education. Three of the most repeated statements are listed in Table 1-1. Note the high degree of similarity between the various declarations. In themselves these statements are hardly subject to improvement and should be studied by all who are concerned with education. Nevertheless, these objectives must be understood within the context of the continual evolution of society.

Responsibilities of Federal and State Government

Carrying out the objectives of American education is the responsibility of individual states. The United States Constitution is conspicuous in its omission of any provision or specific reference to education. The Tenth Amendment to the Constitution, ratified in 1791, states that "the powers not delegated to the United States by the Constitution, nor prohibited by it to the States, are reserved to the States respectively, or to the people." Education has thus consistently been considered a state function.

Experience shows, however, that the federal government has always been involved to some degree. Through the legislative branch, Congress provides funds to

[1]National School Public Relations Association, "New Challenge for Schools: Age of Information," *Education USA,* Vol. 24, No. 19 (January 4, 1982), p. 141.

TABLE 1-1 Educational Aims and Imperatives

1952 "TEN IMPERATIVE NEEDS"[a]	1960 "FOUR DIMENSIONS OF THE TASK OF THE SCHOOL"[b]	1966 "IMPERATIVES IN EDUCATION"[c]

1. Family life	D. Productive dimensions
	  15. Home and family
		2. To make urban life
		    satisfying

2. Health	C. Personal dimensions
	  9. Physical: bodily health
	    and development
	  10. Emotional: mental health
	  11. Ethical: moral integrity
	  12. Esthetics: cultural and
	    leisure pursuits
		3. To strengthen the moral
		    fabric of society
		4. To deal constructively
		    with psychological ten-
		    sions

3. Ability to think
   and communicate
   clearly
4. Arts (esthetics)
5. Science
	A. Intellectual dimensions
	  1. Possession of knowledge:
	    concepts
	  2. Communication of know-
	    ledge: skills
	  3. Creation of knowledge:
	    habits
	  4. Desire for knowledge:
	    values
		1. To discover and nurture
		    creative talent

6. Use of leisure		6. To make the best use of leisure time

7. Occupational skill
8. Ability to consume
   wisely
	D. Productive dimensions
	  13. Vocation: selective
	  14. Vocation: preparative
	  16. Consumer: personal buy-
	    ing, selling, investment
		7. To prepare people for
		    the world of work
		8. To keep democracy

9. Civic understanding	B. Social dimensions
	  6. Man to state: civic
	    rights and duties
	  7. Man to country
		5. To make intelligent use
		    of resources

10. Human relations	B. Social dimensions
	  5. Man to man: cooperation
	    in day-to-day relations
	  8. Man to world: relation-
	    ships of peoples
		9. To work with other peoples
		    of the world for human
		    betterment

[a]Educational Policies Commission, National Education Association, EDUCATION FOR ALL AMERICAN YOUTH: A FURTHER LOOK, Washington, D.C.: The Association, 1954.

[b]L. M. Downey, THE TASK OF PUBLIC EDUCATION, Chicago: Midwest Administration Center, The University of Chicago, 1960.

[c]American Association of School Administrators, IMPERATIVES IN EDUCATION, Report of the AASA Commission on Imperatives in Education, Arlington, Va.: The Association, 1966.

local school districts for special services and programs. Through the United States Office of Education, the executive branch of the government exercises authority over educational matters. The many Supreme Court decisions affecting education testify to the influence of the judicial branch on our schools.

In 1965, the American Association of School Administrators issued a document entitled *The Federal Government and Public Schools.* In it, five reasons were listed explaining the Association's interest in education at the national level.

1. When the nation fights poverty and unemployment, the public schools are one of its principal weapons.
2. When the nation promotes economic growth, its investment in education brings unique dividends.
3. When the nation provides for the common defense, it calls on the schools to play a crucial role.
4. When the nation builds unity out of diversity by delicately blending the cultures of people from many lands, it looks first and foremost to the schools.
5. When the nation refers its complex problems to the people for final decision, it needs more than ever an informed electorate.[2]

In an ever shrinking world and nation, the objectives of American education are of deep concern to both federal and state governments. This involvement of the federal government, however, should not supplant the jurisdiction of state governments but rather should complement and enrich their efforts. Note the accommodating relationship between the objectives outlined in Table 1-1 and the position of the American Association of School Administrators on federal involvement in education.

The authority of the state to create and govern public schools is embodied in state constitutions and exercised through state legislatures. In turn, the latter have delegated certain aspects of their authority to local units, which are boards of education. To ensure some control over local school boards, state legislatures have established minimum educational program requirements, teacher certification requirements, and have provided state funds to help finance education.

The administrative arm of a state legislature is the State Department of Education, which is usually governed by a board and administered by a commissioner or state superintendent. Figure 1-1 presents the relationship between the state and local educational agencies.

The National Council of Chief State School Officers has properly emphasized the state's educational responsibility and its relationship to local and federal agencies:

"Our system of constitutional government makes the states responsible for the organization and administration of public education and for general supervision of nonpublic schools. Each state has in practice delegated authori-

[2] American Association of School Administrators, *The Federal Government and Public Schools* (Washington, D.C.: The Association, 1965), p. 3.

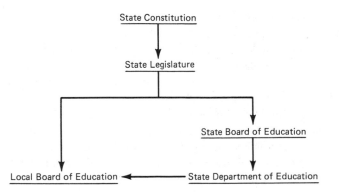

FIGURE 1-1   Jurisdictional Flow Chart

ty to organize and operate schools to various types of local administrative units of its own creation (Boards of Education). Within its general unity, our system of education leaves room for diversified programs among states and local administrative units.

"Local, state and federal governments all have a vital interest in education. Each can contribute most effectively only if there is appropriate allocation of responsibility among them and only if relations among them are properly defined. Initiative and responsibility must be encouraged in the local units which operate most of the schools. The states must ensure organization, financial support and effective administration of education programs of suitable quality and make certain these programs are available to every child. The federal government has an obligation to provide supplementary assistance to the states in accord with the national interest in universal education.

"Local school boards and other state education authorities represent the public in the administration of education. Working with their professional staffs, these authorities are responsible for carefully planned programs of education and for obtaining the participation of the people in planning the kinds of schools and education they need and want."[3]

Responsibilities of the Board
of Education

School districts are perhaps the most democratically controlled agency of government. Citizens of a given community elect school board members, who are charged with formulating policies for the organization and administration of local schools. State departments of education exercise some regulatory authority, assuring that a minimum educational program is provided in every school district, but the citizens of the local district maintain control of the schools through locally elected boards.

As the duties and responsibilities of school boards are described, it is essential to keep in mind that education is a state function. The courts have consistently up-

[3] The National Council of Chief State School Officers, *Our System of Education* (Washington, D.C.: The Council, 1950), pp. 5-6.

held this principle. By virtue of the authority delegated to school boards from the state legislature, boards represent the state, even though its members are locally elected. Board members, as individuals, exercise no authority outside a legally constituted meeting. Policies can be agreed upon only in an official meeting, and individual members cannot commit the board to any definite action except as authorized by the board at a legal meeting.

In exercising authority to govern schools, the board of education should carefully formulate and adopt policy statements. This very difficult task cannot be successfully accomplished without guidance from the professional educational staff and, at times, an attorney. In contemporary society, there are many more factors influencing board decisions than there were just five years ago. Many techniques can be used to formulate a policy. Chapter three will address the specifics of policy construction and will establish the importance of this responsibility to school board operations. After the board of education establishes its policies, it is the responsibility of the superintendent of schools and his or her staff to establish administrative procedures that implement board policies.

THE ADMINISTRATIVE STRUCTURE

Theoretical Foundations

Administration is an indispensable process in all social institutions. However, it is often taken for granted and, in contemporary times, has become the scapegoat for many social problems.

The need for administration has been evident whenever a task had to be performed by two or more people. Ancient records of significant events describe administrative activities—from building the pyramids in Egypt to supervising medieval feudal domains to governing colonies in distant hemispheres—all demanded the skill and understanding of people acquainted with the administrative process.

Our understanding of the nature of administration has evolved over time. The earliest concepts about administration centered around the "action" model—administrators were those who took charge of an activity and accomplished a task. However, the formal study of administration is a recent phenomenon. It is practiced mainly in the business world and is devoted to the effective execution of managerial leadership roles. The need for the formal study of administration in public education was originally rooted in the increasing complexity of urban school districts. The prevailing assumption that anyone with a good general education could become an effective administrator was quickly shattered by this situation.

Knezevich defines administration as "a social process concerned with identifying, maintaining, stimulating, controlling, and unifying formally and informally organized human and material energies within an integrated system designed to accomplish predetermined objectives."[4] The school administrator fulfills this definition by developing and establishing administrative processes, procedures, and techniques that harness human and material energies. The importance of administrative leadership stems from its potential for directing these energies within an organization toward the fulfillment of educational objectives.

This definition also views administration as an executive activity, distinct from policy making. Administration is primarily concerned with the implementation, and not the making of policy. In education, the administrator of a district is responsible for carrying out the policies of the board of education.

The systems approach to administration has gained steadily in popularity ever since President Johnson mandated its implementation in federal agencies, and the continual outcry for accountability in the public sector further encouraged its use. Using the systems approach, a school system is viewed as a network of interrelated subsystems. Emphasis is placed on formulating short- and long-range objectives that can be translated into operational activities that can be implemented and then evaluated.

Although I have adopted the concept underlying the systems approach, I do not use the precise language and style of the advocates for this approach. Rather, administration is viewed as a process composed of various functions. Three of the most critical functions in a school system center on personnel administration, instructional programs administration, and support services administration. Here, support services include transportation, food service, and financial management. Each of these functions has goals that are implemented through administrative processes, procedures, and techniques. Functions are performed by administrators within a given organizational framework. The remaining portion of this section delineates and clarifies the role of the superintendent of schools and major central office administrators.

The Organization of Central Office

Historically and, in most states, by statutory mandate school boards have delegated the responsibility for implementing policies to a chief executive officer, the superintendent of schools. The superintendent assumes full control of all operations. As school districts grow in complexity, it becomes necessary to develop specialized functions, and the central office staff comes into being. However, all employees, professional and other, report ultimately to the superintendent and are subordinate to him or her. The superintendent is the only employee who regularly and directly deals with the board of education.

The superintendent's role description falls into the following three major categories:

[4] Steven J. Knezevich, *Administration of Public Education* (New York: Harper & Row, Publishers, Inc., 1975), p. 12.

Chief advisor. The superintendent is the main consultant and advisor to the school board on all matters concerning the school district. The superintendent is expected to contribute to the board's deliberations by furnishing reports, information, and recommendations, both upon request of the board and upon self-directed initiative. The superintendent's duties and functions as the board's chief advisor include:

1. Formulating and recommending personnel policies necessary for the efficient functioning of the school staff.
2. Providing information to the school board on vital matters pertaining to the school system.
3. Preparing and submitting to the board a preliminary budget.
4. Recommending all candidates for employment. (The board may reject specific candidates recommended, but all personnel should be employed upon the superintendent's recommendation.)
5. Submitting an annual report of the operations of the school system to the board.

Executive officer. Once a policy decision has been established by the board of education it becomes the responsibility of the executive officer of the board and the district's staff to execute those decisions. The administration should implement board policies via rules and regulations. As the chief executive officer of the district, the superintendent sets the tone for the entire system. In performing this function the duties and responsibilities of the superintendent are to:

1. Carry out policies, rules, and regulations established by the board. (In matters not specifically covered by board policies the superintendent should take appropriate action and report the action to the board not later than the next board meeting.)
2. Prepare regulations and instruct school employees as necessary to make the policies of the board effective.
3. Direct all purchases and expenditures in accordance with the policies of the board.
4. Formulate and administer a program of supervision for the schools.
5. Develop a program of maintenance and improvement or expansion of buildings and site facilities.

Educational leader. As the educational leader within the community, the superintendent will be called upon to keep the public informed as to the activities, achievements, needs, and directions of the school system. The superintendent's leadership role should be exercised not only with other professional educators within the district but with regional, state, and national professional educators, organizations, and agencies as well. The superintendent should also exercise a leadership role with the board by keeping the members informed of new trends in education and their implications for the local district.

A leadership role must also be assumed among the staff members of the school district. Without the support and understanding of the employees, the goals and objectives set by the district cannot be achieved.[5]

The two most recent trends in school administration, particularly in the superintendency, emphasize (1) management techniques rather than instructional leadership, and (2) the administrative team approach to central office and building level management. In most districts the administrative team is a cluster of similarly educated administrators who reinforce the efforts of the superintendent.[6] They usually hold the title of deputy, associate, or assistant superintendent. In most school districts, personnel holding the title of director or coordinator are not members of the administrative team, but serve, rather, as support personnel to the team.

Formal designation of membership on the administrative team consists of being appointed to the superintendent's cabinet, which is a strategy-planning and decision-making body. The heads of personnel administration, instructional programs administration, and support service administration (the three major functions) are typically included in the cabinet.

This formal organization of the superintendent's cabinet does not imply that the superintendent confines the "team" effort to only the highest levels of school district administration. Rather, the cabinet is an attempt to share the administrative policy-making process with key administrators. The issues and problems of school systems are so far reaching today that the superintendent must have continual and effective counsel in making decisions.

Because there is a need in all school districts to identify various echelons in the administrative organization, it is recommended that the title of director or coordinator be attached to administrative positions subordinate to an assistant superintendent in charge of a particular function. Although it is in no way meant to be inclusive, Figure 1-2 represents a possible central office organization that incorporates a line of authority from superintendent to assistant superintendents (cabinet positions) to directors and coordinators. The number of central office administrators listed suggests that this could be the organizational structure for a school district with a pupil population of ten to twenty thousand. It was designed as a model exemplifying the scope of possible central office administrative positions. Smaller districts would consolidate central office responsibilities into fewer positions. For example, a school district with two thousand students might be administered by a superintendent and an assistant superintendent who share all of the responsibilities.

[5] Iowa Association of School Boards, *The Iowa School Board Member: A Guide to Better Boardmanship* (Des Moines, Iowa, 1980), pp. 37–40.
[6] American Association of School Administrators, *Profiles of the Administrative Team* (Arlington, VA.: The Association, 1971), p. 11.

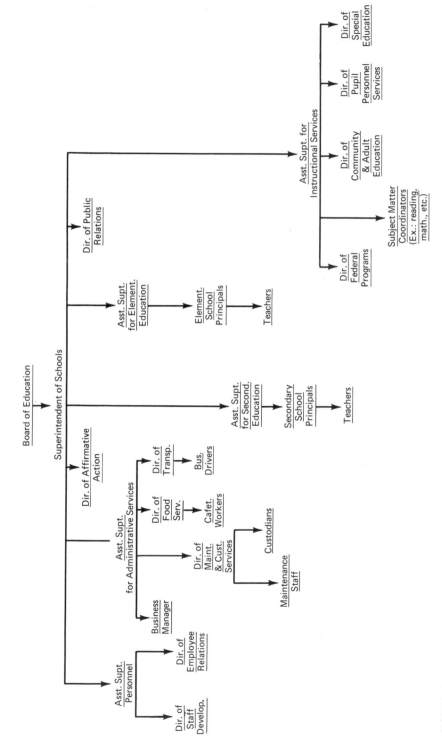

FIGURE 1-2

Individual School
Building Organization

During the early years of our country's development, one-room school houses were staffed by a teacher who was responsible not only for instruction but also for performing all tasks related to the maintenance and upkeep of the building. This situation gradually changed in the 1800's with the recognition of education as a profession, promulgating a better-defined role for the teacher. Finally, in the 1900's, education advanced to the point where instructional materials, teaching techniques, licensing requirements, and job descriptions clearly established the expertise of the teacher. One aspect of that expertise was and is now understood to be the capability of taking a body of knowledge and organizing it into instructional units or lessons. A second aspect is having the skill to transmit the lessons in such a way that students learn their content. More about the learning and instructional process will be discussed in chapter eight.

Specialization of the teacher's role was the catalyst that lead to the creation of the modern-day principalship. During the evolutionary period of the teacher's role, many precursors of the building principal appeared. As schools expanded and employed more teachers, one was usually chosen as the headmaster or headmistress. This title was brought over from England and, as the word itself indicates, the "head" or "lead" teacher was placed in charge of the school.

The contemporary public school is composed of an administrative, instructional, professional support, and classified employee staff. Each of these categories provides a vital service in the accomplishment of the school's mission, which is to educate children and young people.

The elementary school. Figure 1-3 is an organizational chart for an elementary school with four to seven hundred pupils. The pattern of grade level organization could be kindergarten through grade five, through grade six, or through grade eight, depending on the organizational pattern of the secondary school program. The curriculum organization might be nongraded or traditional, with team teaching or with undivided classroom teacher units. The school building, in like manner, could have an architectural design utilizing the open space concept or self-contained classroom model.

The professional staff is the appropriate source of information for the board of education when advantages and disadvantages of these grade level patterns and curriculum organization are being weighed. The role and function of the elementary school staff is the immediate concern in any kind of organizational structure because it is through this line that questions and issues about the curriculum and grade level patterns are addressed and ultimately resolved by a decision of the school board. This decision should be based upon the recommendation of the superintendent and formulated with input provided by the professional staff operating through an organizational structure.

The principal is the administrative executive in the elementary school building. Like all executives, it is his or her responsibility to provide the leadership neces-

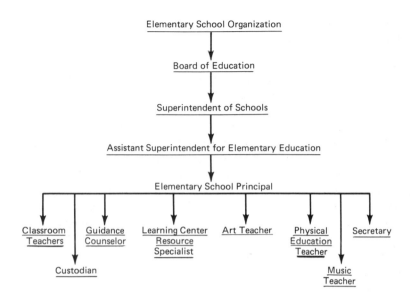

FIGURE 1-3

sary for the effective execution of the school's mission, which is to educate the children in this particular building. The principal must be able to manage the human and material resources available in such a manner that the school's objective is realized. The role of the elementary school principal, therefore, revolves around performing the following tasks:

1. To formulate building level policies and procedures which will elucidate the duties and responsibilities of the professional staff, classified employee staff, students, and parents in the school's attendance area;
2. To develop a personnel planning forecast which will ensure that the right number of staff members with the most appropriate credentials are available to carry out the mission of the school;
3. To conduct an ongoing projection of pupil enrollment which will be the basis of personnel planning, budgeting, and facility management;
4. To develop a building level budget for supplies, materials, and equipment;
5. To create an ongoing facility maintenance and operations plan which will ensure that the building is energy efficient and in proper condition.

The concept of a principal acting as a school executive is rather new in many school districts but has become a necessity, given the complexity of our contemporary society. This concept does not nullify the traditional role of the principal but rather expands the scope of his or her responsibilities. Traditionally, the principal evaluated teacher performance, handled chronic pupil disciplinary problems, and was the main line of communication with parents. Under number one above, the building level policies and procedures should clearly identify these to still be a

12

primary function of the building principal. However, the principal will be more effective in dealing with teachers, students, and parents if he or she is truly the chief executive officer of a particular elementary school.

The instructional staff is, of course, responsible for teaching basic skills to students. In the elementary school program, the expertise of a teacher lies in the ability to assimilate and organize the material to be taught, and to present it to children in such a way that learning occurs. Academic freedom in the elementary school consists of the right to organize and present the curriculum in the manner which the teacher finds to be most effective with children at a given point in time. Determining *what* is to be taught is the prerogative of the board of education, which consults the central office curriculum specialists as a resource. The elementary school teacher should be well versed in child development theory and the psychology of learning, because it is upon this base that lessons are planned and presented.

Other professional staff members are charged with helping the teacher in the instructional process. In the model presented in Figure 1-3, these professionals include the guidance counselor, learning center resource specialist, fine arts, and physical education teachers. All of these professionals, along with the classroom teachers and building principal, are responsible for pupil discipline and effective communications with parents. Appropriate education can occur only within an atmosphere of openness and mutual respect between all employees, students, and parents.

Classified employees, which include building secretaries and custodians, are also a vital part of every elementary school. The tasks that they perform relieve the professional staff so that it can concentrate its efforts on the learning-instructional process. In addition, parents and students are constantly interacting with classified employees, making these individuals valuable public relations agents of the school district.

The Secondary Schools. Figure 1-4 is an organizational chart for a junior high school, middle school, or high school. The enrollment could be from fifteen hundred to two thousand students. The pattern of grade level organization might be (a) junior high school (grades 7-9) and high school (grades 10-12) or (b) middle school (grades 6-8) and high school (grades 9-12). Middle schools have become the subject of much research within the last decade and have proven to be an effective framework for organizing the curriculum. Child development theory appears to substantiate the idea that sixth grade students are closer in maturity to seventh and eighth grade students than to fifth graders. In like manner, ninth grade students are closer in maturity to tenth graders than they are to eighth grade students. The emphasis in a middle school, like that in an elementary school, should be on learning as it relates to child development and on the acquisition of basic skills rather than on mastering the rudiments of a discipline such as history or chemistry.

Junior high schools are structured to provide the student with a transition period to high school and more closely resemble a high school in curriculum and instructional philosophy. However, it is important to guard against a junior high

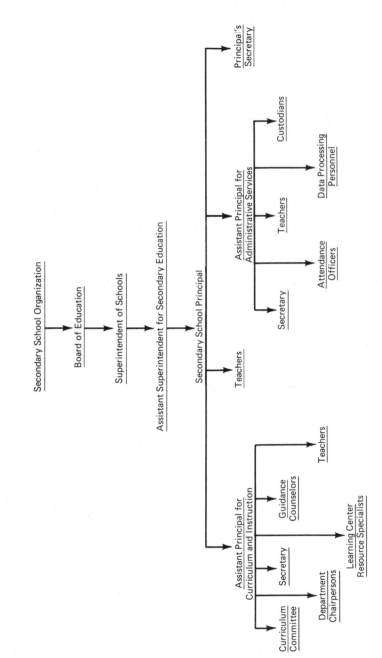

Secondary School Organization

Board of Education

Superintendent of Schools

Assistant Superintendent for Secondary Education

Secondary School Principal

Teachers

Principal's Secretary

Assistant Principal for Administrative Services
- Secretary
- Attendance Officers
- Teachers
- Data Processing Personnel
- Custodians

Assistant Principal for Curriculum and Instruction
- Curriculum Committee
- Department Chairpersons
- Secretary
- Learning Center Resource Specialists
- Guidance Counselors
- Teachers

FIGURE 1-4

school becoming a miniature senior high school. The emphasis should only be on *preparing* the student for his high school experience.

Much of what has been said about the role and function of the building principal, instructional staff, professional support staff, and classified employee staff can be applied to secondary school personnel. The principal, as the chief executive administrator of the building, is responsible for developing policies and procedures, for personnel planning, for projecting pupil enrollment, for budget preparation, and for facility management. The major difference lies in the reality that the principal usually shares this responsibility with an administrative team composed of assistant principals who are assigned to specific areas of management. Figure 1-4 assigns administrative services to one assistant while curriculum and instruction are assigned to a second. Pupil discipline and communicating with parents are, of course, the responsibility of all employees. Teacher evaluation is such an important responsibility and involves such a time-consuming process that most principals will divide the number of teachers to be evaluated equally among themselves and the assistant principals.

The instructional staff will be organized into departments, with a chairperson assuming much of the responsibility for helping the appropriate assistant principal in scheduling and budgeting for his or her department. While child development and the psychology of learning are important in all learning situations, the thrust of the instructional program in a high school will be on content mastery. Other building-level professionals such as guidance counselors, learning center resource specialists, as well as district-wide professionals such as social workers and psychometrists, will assist secondary school teachers with problems and issues that might affect classroom instruction.

The classified staff is more extensive in the secondary school and includes not only secretaries and custodians but also attendance officers and data processing specialists. Their services are essential if the contemporary secondary school is to be effective.

SUMMARY

Our system of free and universal public education is a characteristic unique to American society. The school as an institution receives its mandate to exist from the society it serves. Change is an integral part of this society. The content of our educational programs must address the fundamental principles of individual freedom, individual responsibility, and democratic government but must also have the flexibility to deal with new developments and conditions.

Implementing society's educational objectives is the responsibility of individual states. The authority of the state to create and govern public schools is embodied in state constitutions. The state legislature is the avenue through which this authority is exercised. The administrative arm of the state legislature is the department of education, which is usually governed by a board and administered by a commissioner or state superintendent. A state legislature also delegates certain aspects of its authority to local units, boards of education. However, the state maintains some control over local boards by establishing minimum educational program requirements, teacher certification requirements, and by providing funds to help finance education.

The federal government has increased its influence on education through congressional acts that provide funds for special programs, through the regulations of the United States Office of Education, and through Supreme Court decisions. However, the federal government's power and influence should be viewed as an adjunct to the authority of the state in education.

School districts are perhaps the most democratically controlled agency of government. The citizens of a local community elect school board members who are charged with the adoption of policies for the organization and administration of the schools. The implementation of board policies is the responsibility of the administrative staff.

Administration is the process by which human and material resources are organized and directed toward the accomplishment of educational objectives formulated as board of education policies. Therefore, administration is an executive activity distinct from policy making. It is composed of various functions including personnel administration, instructional programs administration, and support services administration. Each of these functions has objectives that are implemented through administrative processes, procedures, and techniques.

Functions are performed by administrators within a given organizational framework. The superintendent, as the chief executive officer of the school board, has full control of all school operations. These operations are so complex that the superintendent's efforts must be supported by a central office administrative team. This team is usually composed of assistant superintendents who administer the major functions of the school system. These assistant superintendents form a cabinet that helps the superintendent formulate strategies, and shares in the decision-making process. Directors and coordinators perform administrative tasks that support the major functions of the system, and report directly to assistant superintendents.

The individual schools in our contemporary society are composed of an administrative, instructional, professional support, and classified employee staff. Each of these categories of employees performs a vital service in the accomplishment of the school's mission, which is to educate children and young people.

In addition to having the traditional responsibilities of evaluating teacher performance, handling chronic pupil disciplinary problems, and communicating with parents, the building principal is the chief executive officer of the individual school. Thus the role of principal is expanded in scope to include formulating policies and procedures for managing the building, developing personnel planning forecasts, conducting pupil enrollment projections, preparing a building budget, and managing the school plant facilities.

The instructional staff is responsible for teaching the curriculum. As a professional activity teaching includes organizing the material and deciding on the most appropriate method of instruction based upon child development theory and the psychology of learning. Other professional personnel including counselors and learning center resource specialists provide valuable services that support the efforts of the classroom teacher. Maintaining good pupil discipline and open communication with parents is the responsibility of the building principal and the entire professional staff.

Classified personnel, which includes secretaries and custodians, perform tasks that relieve professionals, allowing them to concentrate on the learning-instructional process.

Finally, all school employees are public relations agents for the individual school and for the entire school district.

IMPLICATIONS FOR SCHOOL BOARD MEMBERS

There are three implications for boards of education that emerge from this treatment of the structural framework of public education.

First, boards of education must keep informed about the changes in our society that will affect the type of curriculum students must have to become educated members of our community.

Second, the chief executive officer of the school board is the superintendent of schools. The board of education should not become involved in the administration of the school district, which is solely the responsibility of the superintendent.

Third, the board of education should become thoroughly familiar with the administrative organization of central office and individual buildings. Only with this knowledge will the board be able to effectively evaluate the recommendations of the professional staff and create policies that are realistic enough to effectively govern the school district.

APPENDIX A
CODE OF ETHICS OF THE
EDUCATION PROFESSION[7]

Adopted by 1975 Representative Assembly

PREAMBLE

The educator, believing in the worth and dignity of each human being, recognizes the supreme importance of the pursuit of truth, devotion to excellence, and the nurture of democratic principles. Essential to these goals is the protection of freedom to learn and to teach and the guarantee of equal educational opportunity for

---

[7]National Education Association, *Code of Ethics for the Education Profession* (Washington, D.C.: The Association, 1975).

all. The educator accepts the responsibility to adhere to the highest ethical standards.

The educator recognizes the magnitude of the responsibility inherent in the teaching process. The desire for the respect and confidence of one's colleagues, of students, of parents, and of the members of the community provides the incentive to attain and maintain the highest possible degree of ethical conduct. The Code of Ethics of the Education Profession indicates the aspiration of all educators and provides standards by which to judge conduct.

The remedies specified by the NEA and/or its affiliates for the violation of any provision of this Code shall be exclusive and no such provision shall be enforceable in any form other than one specifically designated by the NEA or its affiliates.

PRINCIPLE I

Commitment to the Student

The educator strives to help each student realize his or her potential as a worthy and effective member of society. The educator therefore works to stimulate the spirit of inquiry, the acquisition of knowledge and understanding, and the thoughtful formulation of worthy goals.

In fulfillment of the obligation to the student, the educator—

1. Shall not unreasonably restrain the student from independent action in the pursuit of learning.
2. Shall not unreasonably deny the student access to varying points of view.
3. Shall not deliberately suppress or distort subject matter relevant to the student's progress.
4. Shall make reasonable effort to protect the student from conditions harmful to learning or to health and safety.
5. Shall not intentionally expose the student to embarrassment or disparagement.
6. Shall not on the basis of race, color, creed, sex, national origin, marital status, political or religious beliefs, family, social or cultural background, or sexual orientation, unfairly:
   a. Exclude any student from participation in any program;
   b. Deny benefits to any student;
   c. Grant any advantage to any student.
7. Shall not use professional relationships with students for private advantage.
8. Shall not disclose information about students obtained in the course of professional service, unless disclosure serves a compelling professional purpose or is required by law.

PRINCIPLE II

Commitment to the Profession

The education profession is vested by the public with a trust and responsibility requiring the highest ideals of professional service.

In the belief that the quality of the services of the education profession directly influences the nation and its citizens, the educator shall exert every effort to raise professional standards, to promote a climate that encourages the exercise of professional judgment, to achieve conditions which attract persons worthy of the trust to careers in education, and to assist in preventing the practice of the profession by unqualified persons.

In fulfillment of the obligation to the profession, the educator—

1. Shall not in an application for a professional position deliberately make a false statement or fail to disclose a material fact related to competency and qualifications.
2. Shall not misrepresent his/her professional qualifications.
3. Shall not assist entry into the profession of a person known to be unqualified in respect to character, education, or other relevant attribute.
4. Shall not knowingly make a false statement concerning the qualifications of a candidate for a professional position.
5. Shall not assist a noneducator in the unauthorized practice of teaching.
6. Shall not disclose information about colleagues obtained in the course of professional service unless disclosure serves a compelling professional purpose or is required by law.
7. Shall not knowingly make false or malicious statements about a colleague.
8. Shall not accept any gratuity, gift, or favor that might impair or appear to influence professional decisions or actions.

SELECTED BIBLIOGRAPHY

CARLISLE, HOWARD M., *Situational Management.* New York: American Management Associations, 1973.

DALE, ERNEST, *Management: Theory and Practice* (3rd ed.). New York: McGraw–Hill Book Company, 1973.

DRUCKER, PETER F., *Management: Tasks, Responsibilities, Practices.* New York: Harper & Row, Publishers, Inc., 1974.

HANSON, E. MARK, *Educational Administration and Organizational Behavior.* Boston: Allyn and Bacon, Inc., 1979.

MORPHET, EDGAR, ROE L. JOHNS, and THEODORE L. RELLER, *Educational Organization and Administration: Concepts, Practices, and Issues* (4th ed.). Englewood Cliffs, N.J.: Prentice-Hall, Inc., 1982.

SERGIOVANNI, THOMAS J., MARTIN BURLINGAME, FRED D. COOMBS, PAUL W. THURSTON, *Educational Governance and Administration.* Englewood Cliffs, N.J.: Prentice-Hall, Inc., 1980.

CHAPTER TWO
THE DYNAMICS
OF SCHOOL BOARD
OPERATIONS

The constituents of a school district have a right to expect that individual board members will put aside personal ambitions and will conduct school district business in an organized, open, and efficient manner.

Who is the typical school board member? What is the age, sex, religious affiliation, and educational level of this individual? There is no such person; no typical school board member exists. In addition, people make decisions to run for the board of education for a variety of reasons, all of which are so personalized that they defy classification. For this present treatment none of the above, however, is important. Once an individual is elected to the board of education, he or she immediately assumes a mandate to govern the educational experience of children and young people, the effects of which are eminent and pervasive. It is an understatement to say that membership on a school board is the most important governmental position in our community, state, and nation. Our American culture has always understood that freedom and the economic system of capitalism demand an educated citizenry.

THE DYNAMICS OF SCHOOL
BOARD DECISION MAKING

When the members of a school board assemble to conduct business, there are numerous issues which underlie the proceedings. Because all actions of a school board involve a potential change in school district policy, the dynamics of change, in addition to the possible *hidden agendas* of members, coupled with the decision making process are variables interacting at board meetings.

Change is a phenomena which, in human experience, probably causes the most disruption to a school district. It does not matter if the change produces an improved situation; the fact of the change itself is cause enough for people to be dissatisfied with the actions of a school board. There is no easy or right way for a school board to proceed in bringing about change; however, the following aspects of the change process, if taken into consideration, will lessen the unwanted reaction of the school district community.

—Change is more acceptable when it is understood than when it is not.

—Change is more acceptable when it does not threaten security than when it does.

—Change is more acceptable when those affected have helped create it than when it has been externally imposed.

—Change is more acceptable when it results from an application of previously established impersonal principles than when it is dictated by personal fiat.

—Change is more acceptable when it follows a series of successful changes than when it follows a series of failures.

—Change is more acceptable when it is inaugurated after prior change has been assimilated than when it is inaugurated during the confusion of other major changes.

—Change is more acceptable if it has been planned than if it is implemented only to see what its effects will be.

—Change is more acceptable to people new on the job than to people who have been on the job for a long period of time.

—Change is more acceptable to people who share in the benefits of change than to those who do not.

—Change is more acceptable if the organization has been trained to accept change.[1]

Consequently, change as a phenomena can and should be a consideration of the school board when issues are brought before it for a decision. Timing is a legitimate variable which may dictate that a change, even though beneficial, should be forestalled until the people most affected are prepared and ready for it. Closing a school because of declining enrollment is a classic example. Unless the parents, teachers, and students of a particular school understand the need to close their school; unless they have been given ample time to speak their mind and participate in the accumulation of data to support the closing; and unless they understand where the children will attend school the following year, this type of change has the potential of creating deep-seated resentment of school board members.

---

[1] R. M. Besse, "Company Planning Must Be Planned," *Dun's Review and Modern Industry,* Vol. 74, No. 4 (April, 1957), pp. 62–63.

A second variable at work when a board of education meets to conduct business and make decisions concerning school district issues is the hidden agendas of school board members. All groups operate on two levels, the surface level and the hidden agenda level. Inexperienced school board members are often confused by the actions and decisions of fellow board members when this aspect of human experience is overlooked. Every member of the school board must face this fact and must deal with it individually and as a corporate body. Some hidden agendas are even beneficial to the school district. For example, a school board member may vote against a new teacher evaluation policy because it is opposed by a local teacher union, in order to gain the support of that group in working for an upcoming tax levy election.

The following suggestions on how to handle hidden agendas were not formulated with school boards in mind, but are certainly relevant:

—Remember that the group is continuously working on two levels at once: the surface level and the hidden agenda level. Consequently, the group may not move as fast on the surface tasks as the participants might expect.
—Look for the hidden agendas that are present. Recognition is a first step in a diagnosis of group difficulty.
—Sometimes a participant can make it easier for a group to bring its hidden agendas to the surface. The participant may say, for example, "I wonder if we have said all that we feel about the issue. Maybe we should take time to go around the table so that any further thoughts can be opened up."
—Some hidden agendas can be presented and talked about and should then become easier to handle. But many hidden agendas would hurt the group more if they were talked about openly. Group participants need to be sensitive to the possible dangers and should try to recognize what a group can and cannot face at a given point.
—Do not scold or pressure the group when hidden agendas are recognized. They are present and legitimate and must be worked on in much the same manner as the surface task. At different times, hidden agendas should be given different amounts of attention, depending upon their influence on the surface task and the nature of the group and its participants.[2]

A final consideration in terms of the dynamics which are operationalized as boards of education confront school district business and issues is *how* decisions are reached, particularly when the board is dealing with a serious problem. There are two aspects to the decision making process: first, those logical steps that should be taken to insure that the best solution has been reached and secondly, those considerations which should be addressed within an organization when problems are being confronted by the school board.

Much has been written about the most effective way of handling issues and reaching solutions to problems. Even using the insights gained by experience, there is no one way of acting, that will minimize the potential for making the wrong de-

[2]William Pfeifer and John E. Jones, *A Handbook of Structured Experiences for Human Relations Training* (Iowa City, Iowa: University Associates Press, 1969), pp. 36–46.

cision. The following steps provide a framework that can be used by individual board members as they develop their own personal approach to solving problems.

1. Consider the problem in its totality from every angle possible but also carefully consider its particular components.
2. Target those aspects of the problem that, if addressed, will lead to a quick and effective solution.
3. Identify what data would help in clarifying the problem and its components.
4. Gather the necessary data from the most credible sources.
5. Develop a list of ideas that could constitute a solution to the problem.
6. Select the most feasible solution to the problem.
7. Implement the solution.
8. Follow up to ascertain if the solution agreed on actually solved the problem.

Figure 2-1, Guidelines for Decision Making, addresses those variables about decision making which should be considered by a board of education as it goes through the steps of the decision making process. Attention to these guidelines will minimize the disruption to the school district as an organization. A common criticism leveled against school boards is that they make decisions in isolation from the school district as a unit and hence run the risk of making decisions that are difficult and at times impossible to implement.

SCHOOL BOARD PROCEDURES AND OPERATIONS

The laws of most states are very clear about the fact that school boards are corporate entities and, therefore, the board as a board exists only when its members are meeting in a legally constituted session. The board of education as a corporate entity—not as a group of individuals—is charged with governing the school district. It goes without saying that this jurisdiction extends only to the educational experience of children living within the legally constituted boundaries of the school district.

The role and function of the school board in governing the school district center upon two major areas: first, creating policies that will give the district's administrative staff the guidance necessary to carry out the mission of the school district; second, evaluating, through administrative staff, the programs of the school district and the personnel charged with implementing the programs. Both areas are complementary; that is, it will be impossible for a school board to create effective policies if the members of the school board are not informed about the progress of the district's programs and about the performance of school district personnel.

The policy making process will be addressed further on in this chapter. Policies are not formulated in a vacuum but rather at board meetings, as is the case with program and personnel evaluation. Program and personnel appraisal will be treated

FIGURE 2-1 Guidelines for Decision Making[3]

—The combined consideration of appropriate personnel should be applied to the solution of problems.

—Decisions should be followed by action.

—A follow-up of the effectiveness and wisdom of both the decision and its implementation should be scheduled to determine its continuation or alteration.

—A decision should be made as near the task as possible.

—The unique abilities of each staff member should be utilized.

—Decisions regarding significant problems will be those which have the least wrong with them (hopefully).

—Delegation of authority should be commensurate with the function to be performed.

—Responsibility can be delegated but not avoided.

—Decisions will be influenced by the history of similar circumstances.

—All people affected by a decision should be kept informed as to status.

—Protection from reaction to necessary but unpopular decisions must be provided.

—A balance between responsiveness to popular or current demands and stability must be maintained.

—The inevitable gray area between legislative and executive function requires interaction of fair-minded, reasonable people.

—Both horizontal and vertical lines of communication must be kept open.

—The importance of timing in communication should be understood.

—A recognition of what should be communicated is vital.

—Common practice should be a balance between "consideration" and "organizational structure."

—Realization of institutional goals should form the basic pattern for decisions.

—Avoid making decisions under stress and in situations that are volatile.

in later chapters. The present treatment centers on those procedures which will insure that the policy making and appraisal functions are addressed in an orderly way by the board of education.

The School Board Meeting

For the effective governance of a school district it is imperative that the board of education meet on a regular basis, probably once a month. There should be a board policy establishing the time and place of the regular meetings and a pro-

[3]Missouri School Boards Association, *A Manual for Missouri School Board Members* (Columbia, Mo.: The Association, 1981), p. H–11.

cedure for reminding board members of regularly scheduled meetings facilitated through the superintendent's office.

Special meetings may need to be called from time to time for the purpose of handling problems and issues that cannot wait until the regular meeting or that would be better dealt with apart from the regularly scheduled meeting. Special meetings are usually called by the president of the school board or when a majority of the school board members request a special meeting. The mechanics of notifying board members concerning the purpose, time, and place of special board meetings are the responsibility of the superintendent of schools.

The board of education should always meet in a school district facility—either at the central administrative office building or in a school building. The meeting place should be large enough to accommodate visitors who wish to be in attendance. The room should be set up in such a way that visitors readily understand that they cannot participate in the proceedings unless invited to do so. A common practice in school districts with a permanent board of education meeting room is to have the board members and the superintendent seated at tables on a raised platform with the central office administrators and the recording secretary seated at a table off to one side of the platform. Visitors can then be seated in rows of chairs in front of the platform. Because it is also common practice for the president of the board to ask visitors if they wish to address the board at a set time during the meeting, a table can be placed in front of the platform before the rows of chairs from which a presentation can be made.

Most state statutes have provisions that allow public bodies to meet in a closed executive session on certain issues. While the variety of provisions makes classification difficult, the following constitute appropriate reasons for holding an executive session: (1) the hiring, terminating, or promotion of personnel; (2) a proceeding involving scholastic probation, expulsion, or graduation; (3) litigation involving the school district; (4) the lease, purchase, or sale of property.

The School Board Meeting Agenda

Board meetings will more than likely become disorderly and unproductive unless a formal agenda that includes explanatory materials is prepared and sent to the board members before the meeting. As the chief executive officer of the school board, the superintendent is usually charged with preparing the agenda, which ensures that the ordinary business of the school district, such as paying invoices and approving contracts, can be timely addressed. In addition, school board members can request the superintendent to add items to the agenda for discussion and action by all members. In fact, it is a good practice for the superintendent to contact each board member before the agenda is prepared for this very purpose. The agenda with the minutes from the preceding meeting, accompanied by pertinent reports and explanatory materials, should be received by each board member at least three days before the meeting, to give members sufficient time to prepare for the meeting. Board members should be encouraged to contact the superintendent before the meeting if clarification or additional information is needed concerning items on the agenda.

The agenda should be constructed in such a manner that it can also serve as the "order of business" to be followed at the board meeting. The order of business will be dictated by the items to be dealt with at the meeting, but the following order should suffice at most meetings:

1. *Call to Order.* The president of the board calls the meeting to order. If the president and vice-president are both absent, the secretary should preside. Finally, the treasurer in the secretary's absence. A *quorum* is necessary to transact business, and is usually defined as two-thirds of the members of the board.

2. *Scheduling Visitors' Presentations.* It has become common practice in recent years for boards of education to allow visitors a place on the agenda to address the board about issues and other concerns. The board may and should limit the number of individuals allowed to speak, and set a time limit on presentations to facilitate the transaction of business.

3. *Approval of the Agenda.* The members present may also change the agenda by adding or deleting items. Even if there are no changes in the agenda and if there are no visitors who wish to address the board, the agenda must be formally adopted through the normal *motion* process.

4. *Approval of the Warrants.* The board of education must approve the checks that are issued to pay the bills of the district and the payroll. The *warrants* are a listing of the check numbers, and state to whom and for what purpose the checks are written. Once the board approves the warrants, the checks may be signed and mailed. It is common practice to require the signature of two board members on the checks, usually the president and treasurer of the board. A facsimile plate and check signing machine may be used and will facilitate the signing of checks. Through a resolution, the board may authorize the paying of certain bills in advance of the board meeting, such as utility bills, but checks for such expenses must be included on the warrants for the purpose of information. Payroll checks can also be handled in the same manner when a contract exists between an employee and the board because the contract itself is authorization to issue the checks.

5. *Unfinished Business.* If the board of education did not complete a previous board agenda or requested additional information from the superintendent about an item at a previous meeting before taking action, this is the appropriate place to address such an issue or issues.

6. *New Business.* The superintendent, upon the request of the president, may make preliminary remarks about the items to be discussed and acted upon. There is no appropriate order to placing items under this section. However, it might be more beneficial to place noncontroversial items before those items which will take considerable time in order to accomplish as much business as possible without carrying items over to the next board meeting.

7. *Superintendent's Report.* The superintendent can use this section of the agenda to inform the school board about certain programs and issues that are not only important but that should be made public. The actual report may be given by other administrators, teachers, or staff members. A budget operating summary is a very important report that should be a regular part of this section. Other reports could include an explanation of curriculum programs, the district's standardized testing program, and any other aspect of school district operations.

8. *Adjournment.* This procedure as well as all other aspects of the board meeting should be accomplished through parliamentary rules and regulations.

Minutes of the Board Meetings

All official actions of a school board must occur at a board meeting for them to be legally binding. The minutes of the board meetings, therefore, are essentially the formal and legal medium through which the board of education communicates and documents its decisions and actions. Courts have traditionally admitted only the minutes of board meetings in reviewing the actions of school boards when such actions are relevant to litigation. It goes without saying that minutes must be absolutely accurate in reflecting the intent and actions of the board of education.

The minutes of board meetings are public documents and must be open to scrutiny by all interested citizens. It is customary to keep the minutes in the central office in a container, vault, or room that is fireproof, secure, and safe from vandalism. The minutes may be kept in loose-leaf form and may be bound into volumes of one complete year or according to some other procedure that will insure the orderly storage of these records. Some school districts microfilm the minutes and keep the microfilm in a different place from the original records, significantly reducing the risk of loss of the minutes from fire or theft.

The minutes should be available to the public during the regular working hours of central office personnel. Copies of the minutes could be made available by charging a nominal fee to offset duplication costs.

It is also desirable that the director of community relations summarize the minutes after they are approved by the school board and to send this summary to internal and external interest groups such as teacher unions and the press.

Most state statutes have provisions that permit the minutes of executive sessions to be a closed record, exempt from public inspection. Therefore, such minutes must be bound under a separate cover and kept in a secure place.

The contents of the minutes for all school board meetings should include the following:

> First, identification data that includes the time and place of the meeting; the board and staff members in attendance; the approval of minutes from the preceding meeting; and the purpose of the meeting if it is a special meeting or executive session.
>
> Second, identification of who made the motions at the meeting; who seconded the motions; a record of how each member voted (by name) unless it was a unanimous vote; and a statement that the motion passed or failed.
>
> Third, identification of all other matters brought before the school board and the disposition of these matters if the board did not take action.

Figure 2–2 sets forth certain procedures for keeping minutes that can act as a guide to a school board as it addresses this very important concern.

Parliamentary Procedures

Because the board of education is a legislative body with the authority to organize its procedures and to transact business, it is essential to the orderly conducting of this business that definite parliamentary procedures be adopted and/or

FIGURE 2-2 Procedures for Keeping Minutes[4]

1. *Duplication of minutes.* Copies should be furnished in sufficient number for each member of the board.

2. *Circulation of minutes.* Copies of the minutes may be mailed to members of the board following the meeting or at least several days in advance of the next meeting. Members will have opportunity to study carefully the action which was taken at the previous meeting.

3. *The prereading of the minutes.* If minutes have been circulated and read by all members of the board in advance of the meeting, much board time can be saved by making it unnecessary to read in detail all minutes of the previous meeting.

4. *Disposition of the minutes.* Before any items of business are considered, the secretary should read the minutes of the previous meeting unless copies were sent to the members prior to the meeting. Corrections should be made, if necessary, and approval of the minutes must be recorded. The president and the secretary should sign the approved minutes as soon as they are put in final form.

5. *Number of resolutions.* The minutes will be more usable and the record of board actions more accessible if resolutions are numbered consecutively and clearly indexed.

6. *The practice of marginal headings* is highly desirable. If the marginal index contains the date the action was taken, it will facilitate the compiling of a motions history.

7. *Motions history.* Any complete minute book will have available a complete and carefully numbered motions history. This is particularly recommended.

8. The minutes should be typed and kept in permanent form in the board record book provided for that purpose.

adapted to the needs of each school board. With no standards for conducting business, the board of education would be subject to an informality which would surely result in a waste of time and energy. On the other hand, definite procedures will provide a framework that will allow for the courteous and efficient handling of issues.

There is a danger, however, that a school board will formulate very complex and technical procedures, which may tend to confuse rather than facilitate business. Figure 2-3 presents a set of fundamental procedures that can act as a starting point for a school board as it reviews and updates its procedures for conducting business.

[4] Ibid., pp. C–6 to C–7.

FIGURE 2-3 Procedure for Addressing the Chair and Making a Motion[5]

> Any member of the board who wishes to make a statement addresses the president and says, "Mr./Madam President." The president recognizes the board member (if no one else has the right to the floor) by saying, "Mr.___" (using the name of the board member he is recognizing). When this board member is thus recognized, he makes his statement. The only time a member need not address and receive recognition from the chair is when he is seconding a motion.
>
> **A Motion**
>
> 1. *Introducing the Motion.* Any member of the board may make a motion after being recognized by the president. The introductory statement of a motion is "Mr. President, I move that . . . "
> 2. *Seconding the Motion.* The main motion must then be seconded by another member of the board, who says, "I second the motion." If the motion is not seconded, it is lost.
> 3. *Withdrawing the Motion.* After a motion is made, the maker may change his mind about it or wish to prevent action upon the motion in order that more urgent business be acted upon. In case a member desires to withdraw a motion, he says, "Mr. President, I ask permission to withdraw my motion . . . " Ordinarily the request need not be seconded. The president then puts the request to a vote.
> 4. *Discussing the Motion.* After a motion is made and seconded, the president says, "You have heard the motion which has been seconded. Is there any discussion?" Discussion may follow. Each member who wishes to take part in the discussion must be recognized by the chair before he participates in the discussion.
> 5. *Amending the Motion.* When it is necessary to amend a motion, the amendment is presented and seconded in the same way as the original motion. The amendment of a motion may be made in any of the following four ways or forms:
>   a. Addition—When a member wishes to add to a motion he says, "Mr. President, I move the motion be amended by adding (or inserting) the words . . . "
>   b. Elimination—When a member wishes to eliminate some part of a motion, he says, "Mr. President, I move the motion be amended by striking out the words . . . "
>   c. Substitution—When a member wishes to substitute one or more words already in the motion, he says, "Mr. President, I move that the motion be amended by substituting the word . . . for the word . . . "

[5] Ibid., pp. C–9 to C–11.

    d. Division—When a member wishes to divide the original motion into two or more motions, he says, "Mr. President, I move that the motion be divided and that the board consider first . . . and second . . ."

6. *Tabling the Motion.* The purpose of this motion is to delay action on a question until some future time, either in the same meeting or some future meeting. When a member wishes to table a motion, he says, "Mr. President, I move to lay on the table a motion to . . . " To remove the motion from the table at some later time, a member says, "Mr. President, I move to take from the table the motion . . . "

7. *Voting on the Motion.* After the discussion on the motion seems to be finished, the president says, "Are you ready for the question?" If this question receives a general chorus of "Question" and no one rises to speak, the president concludes consideration of the motion by "putting the question." When he "puts the question" he repeats the motion (or asks the secretary to read it) by saying, "The question is whether the board wishes to adopt the motion that . . . " After the question has been stated, the president says, "You have heard the question. Those who favor the motion answer AYE, those against the motion NAY, as the roll is called." The secretary then calls the roll and records by name the individual votes on the motion for the minutes.

8. *Reconsidering the Motion.* It is sometimes necessary to reconsider an action taken at a former board meeting. If this is desirable, the form of the motion is "Mr. President, I move to reconsider the action of . . . taken at the meeting of . . . " (The minutes of the board may be amended during the time members are in office and before the rights of a third party are involved.)

Officers of the School Board

Various state statutes may provide for the organizational structure of the school board. However, a few generalizations can be made that will apply to all boards of education. First, a president or chairperson must be elected by the board members who will preside at board meetings. The elected person will act as the spokesperson for the entire board when it is necessary to make a public statement concerning an issue facing the board. The president also has the duty of signing official documents of the school district, such as contracts, and a facsimile of his signature should appear on all school district bank drafts. It is desirable to elect a vice president or vice chairperson who will assume the designated duties in the absence of the president/chairperson.

A treasurer of the school board should be elected who will be responsible for monitoring the financial affairs of the school district. This in no way should be understood to mean that the treasurer conducts the business operations of the district, which is an administrative responsibility. The budget operating summary presented at the monthly board meeting should be of particular concern and should be scrutinized by the treasurer. A facsimile of the treasurer's signature should appear on all school district bank drafts.

The secretary of the school board, who is also elected by the other board members, is responsible for the accurate recording of school board meetings, the safekeeping of official school district records, and attesting by signature to the accuracy of official school district reports. The secretary also attests to all contracts by signature. A recording secretary, who is an employee of the district and usually the superintendent's personal secretary, is responsible for handling the mechanics of the secretary's duty.

School Board Consultants and Advisory Committees

Our contemporary society is very complex and, therefore, so are the issues and problems facing boards of education. It has become common practice for school boards to hire consultants who have an expertise that can be used when dealing with such problems and issues. These consultants fall into two broad categories—those providing ongoing services and those providing occasional services for a specific problem or issue. Every school district will need the assistance of an attorney and a certified public accountant. It will be beneficial to the school district to have them employed on a continual basis so that they acquire an in-depth understanding of school district operations. It is important to annually review the quality of service rendered by the district's auditor and attorney as well as their fee schedule. But once an attorney and C.P.A. auditor are hired, it is unadvisable to change, unless the quality of performance diminishes and/or the fee structure becomes out of line with others in the profession.

When the school district is in need of occasional services from other professionals such as a property appraiser or an architect, the following procedure can be used for contracting with them: (1) the superintendent advertises that portfolios are being accepted by the district. Portfolios should include the credentials of the professional, his or her experience, references, and a fee schedule or structure; (2) the superintendent compares the credentials and experience of all the professionals; (3) the superintendent contacts the references; (4) the superintendent compares the fee structure in relation to the experience and skills of the professionals; (5) the superintendent presents a summary and recommendation to the school board on whom to hire; (6) the board of education contracts for the services. This procedure is also most appropriate when initially hiring an attorney and a C.P.A. auditor.

Valuable information and a great deal of good public relations can also be obtained by having the assistance of school district citizens and patrons when the board studies certain issues and problems. Citizens advisory committees, when given a specific charge to study and collect data for the board about such issues as student discipline, the criteria to be used in closing a school, and declining enrollment, can save the administration a large amount of time and energy in addition to providing the school board with a basis upon which to make a decision. The key to the successful use of a citizens advisory committee lies in following two principles: First, the school board should make the charge to the citizens advisory committee very specific and should establish guidelines that the committee can use to formulate the desired report. Second, the committee should work in cooperation with the superintendent of schools because he or she is the chief executive officer of the school board and should be continually informed about the committee's progress.

School Board Self-Evaluation

Accountability is demanded by boards of education from teachers, administrators, and staff members of their respective school districts. Performance evaluation procedures and instruments are commonly employed by school boards in demonstrating and implementing accountability principles. However, few school boards have a self-evaluation procedure to ascertain their own level of performance.

Developing an evaluation procedure could help a school board assess its successes and failures in addition to ensuring that the board is following ethical standards and avoiding abuses of power.

The evaluation process is basically the same as all personnel and program appraisals. The school board needs to set goals and objectives for itself, must decide on an assessment technique and instrument for measuring progress in attaining these goals, should carefully review the data generated by the assessment process, and finally, should formulate new goals for the next year.

The superintendent of schools is the individual who should research and present to the board those assessment instruments and techniques that the school board might adopt and/or modify to evaluate its performance.

While there is some controversy about whether the results of the evaluation should be made public, it is probably better for a school board to use the results for their own information and not to go public with them. Because school boards are political entities, making such an evaluation public could become a political liability to certain board members, possibly discouraging school boards from engaging in this needed activity.

BOARD-STAFF RELATIONS

Members of school boards are elected public officials and as such are subject to all the political pressures that partisan public officials find themselves confronted with. Teachers, administrators, staff members, classified employees as well as students, parents, and other categories of citizens are concerned about the potential decisions of school boards and how the board will handle issues that have an impact on them. Teacher unions and organizations have generally been the most politically active entities in school districts.

It should not be surprising that school board members, particularly those newly elected, will be personally contacted by employees from all levels of the school district, not only about policy level issues but also concerning problems that they are facing in their work for the school district. They will want board members to intervene on their behalf either directly or indirectly; in the latter perhaps with the administrative staff or individuals with whom they are experiencing difficulty. The most appropriate response is for the board member to initially refer the employee to his or her immediate supervisor in order to resolve the problem. If the results are not satisfactory to the employee, a board member can suggest appealing through the chain of command all the way to the board of education if necessary. Obviously, this requires the board of education to create a grievance policy, which the administration can develop into a procedure that will ensure fair and impartial treatment of all employees who are experiencing difficulty on the job.

A sympathetic response and just the fact that a board member listened to their concern may ease an employee's anxiety. The old cliché is true—"There are two sides to every story." It is not, however, the responsibility of a board member to listen to both sides but rather to refer the person to the proper staff member and to encourage the individual to use the grievance procedure. School board members must always remember that they enjoy no jurisdiction as individuals and can act only at a legally called board meeting.

SCHOOL BOARD POLICY DEVELOPMENT

In exercising their authority to govern schools, boards of education should carefully formulate and adopt policy statements. This very difficult task cannot be successfully accomplished without guidance from the professional educational staff and, at times, an attorney. There are many more influences in our contemporary society affecting board decisions today than there were just five years ago. Figure 2-4 illustrates these influences on policy formulation.

Some advantages of developing policies have been outlined in *The School and Community Relations* and may serve as a rationale for school boards:

FIGURE 2-4

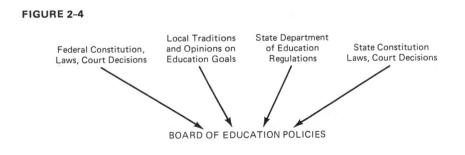

Federal Constitution, Laws, Court Decisions   Local Traditions and Opinions on Education Goals   State Department of Education Regulations   State Constitution Laws, Court Decisions

BOARD OF EDUCATION POLICIES

—Policy facilitates the orientation of new board members regarding relations between the school and community.

—Policy facilitates a similar orientation on the part of new employees in the school system, both professional and nonprofessional.

—Policy acquaints the public with the position of the school and encourages citizen involvement in educational affairs.

—Policy provides a reasonable guarantee that there will be consistency and continuity in the decisions that are made under it.

—Policy informs the superintendent what he or she may expect from the board and what the board may expect from him or her.

—Policy creates the need for developing a detailed program in order that it may be implemented.

—Policy provides a legal reason for the allocation of funds and facilities in order to make the policy work.

—Policy establishes an essential division between policy making and policy administration.[6]

School board policies should not be confused with administrative rules and regulations, which constitute the detailed manner whereby policies are implemented. Rules and regulations explain who does what, when, and where. In other words, they apply policy to practice. In fact, many rules and regulations may be required to implement one policy.

A properly conceived and phrased board of education policy has the following characteristics:

—It is stated in broad, general terms but is clear enough to allow executive direction and interpretation.

—It reveals the philosophy of the board of education as the members understand the desires of the community pertaining to educational matters.

—It provides purpose and rationale for the subject about which a policy is being made.

—It suggests how the matter is to be carried out; in a few instances, it may indicate who should execute the policy.

—It is never executive in substance or tone.

—It covers situations which are likely to occur repeatedly.

—It is usually brief but may be lengthy on a few concerns of the board.

—It is always subject to review by the board with the objective of improvement in accordance with changing conditions.

Likewise, the policy should:

—Provide support and authority for all school programs and activities.

—Be brief, clear, concise, and complete.

—Be stable even during personnel changes.

---

[6]Leslie W. Kindred, Dan Bagin, and Donald R. Gallagher, *The School and Community Relations* (Englewood Cliffs, N.J.: Prentice-Hall, 1976), p. 30.

—Contain minimal direct quotes from applicable state laws.

—Have adequate provisions for review and amendment.[7]

The policies of the school board must be incorporated into a manual format if they are to be effective in governing the school district. The following steps can be used in developing such a manual:

First, identify and code all existing policy decisions of the school board. These policies may be found in various publications, such as faculty and student handbooks, in addition to the minutes of school board meetings and formal, negotiated agreements. See Figure 2–5 for additional sources of existing school board policies.

Second, separate board of education policies from administrative rules and regulations. In the daily operations of a school district, policies and rules sometimes overlap in handbooks and manuals.

Third, identify and eliminate board of education policies that are obsolete or contrary to state and federal laws.

Fourth, identify and update board policies that contradict each other and are written in ambiguous language.

The administrative staff under the supervision of the superintendent may be charged with the responsibility of codifying and developing a policy manual. If a school district does not have a large administrative staff, it may be difficult to free up an administrator to handle the policy manual project. In such a case, the National School Boards Association and/or state school boards associations may be contracted with to provide this service.

Once a policy manual has been created, the immediate concern is keeping it updated. The superintendent should develop an administrative procedure by which newly created board policies are incorporated into the policy manual. Many districts update their policy manual once each year using the minutes of board of education meetings as a resource document.

Appendix B demonstrates the various formats a school board could use in formulating policies. The first format is the resolution style on which the school board takes action (Equal Employment Opportunity and Affirmative Action Policy). A second format sets forth the rationale for the policy and establishes broad goals, which are implemented through administrative rules and regulations (Personnel Goal Policy). The third style of policy is written in such a way that the responsibility for implementing policy is clearly set forth along certain parameters (Personnel Placement Policy). A fourth style not only designates the areas to be implemented by the policy but also sets forth the parameters of what the administrative rules and regulations will cover (Sex Equality in Education Policy). A fifth style is very detailed and is meant to eliminate any misunderstanding about how the policy is to be implemented (An Early Retirement Incentive Policy). The Risk

[7]Missouri School Boards Association, *A Manual for Missouri School Board Members* (Columbia, Mo.: The Association, 1981), p. H–3.

FIGURE 2-5 Sources of Existing Board Policies[8]

1. The present board policy manual and the state education code
2. The present book of administrative rules and procedures
3. The last several years' board minutes
4. The current compensation guide and contracts with professional and nonprofessional staffs
5. Currently active administrative memoranda
6. Current annual budget documents, particularly if they incorporate program goals and objectives, as in a program budget
7. Current teachers' and students' handbooks
8. Board approved staff committee reports
9. Board approved citizens' advisory and consultant reports
10. Board approved cooperative agreements with other districts, federal projects and foundations (these documents will have "guidelines" that have the force of policy)
11. Board approved building program and education specifications
12. Copies of the superintendent's and staff contract forms
13. Purchasing guides, requisition forms, purchase orders, etc.
14. Emergency operating procedures
15. School calendar
16. Use-of-school facilities forms
17. Organization charts
18. Job descriptions

Management Policy utilizes the third style format and has a set of administrative rules and regulations following it that demonstrate how a policy is translated into such rules and regulations.

SUMMARY

There is no typical school board member. People make decisions to run for the board of education for a variety of reasons, all of which are so personalized that they defy classification. Membership on a school board is the most important governmental position in our community, state, and nation. Our American society has always understood that freedom and the economic system of capitalism demand an educated citizenry.

[8] Missouri School Boards Association, *A Manual for Missouri School Board Members*, pp. H–7 to H–8.

Because all actions of a school board involve a potential change in school district policy, the dynamics of change must be understood and addressed by each member of the school board. Change is a phenomena which, in human experience, probably causes the most disruption to a school district. Timing is a legitimate variable in the process of change. It may dictate that a change, even a beneficial one, should be forestalled until the people most affected are prepared and ready for it.

A second variable at work when a school board meets to conduct business and make decisions is the hidden agendas of school board members. Each board member must be sensitive to their presence if the board is to be effective as an entity in providing for the educational needs of the children in the school district.

A final consideration in terms of school board dynamics is how decisions are reached. Problem solving methods involve two aspects: (1) logical steps in reaching a solution, and (2) organizational consideration in terms of who does what in the school district.

School boards are corporate entities and, as such, can function only at a legally constituted board meeting. Board members have no authority as individuals. The role and function of the school board in governing the school district centers around two major areas: (1) creating policies and (2) evaluating programs and those people charged with implementing the programs.

It is imperative to the effective governance of a school district that the board of education meet on a regular basis, probably once a month. Special meetings may be called from time to time for the purpose of handling problems and issues that cannot wait until the regular meeting or which would be better dealt with in a special meeting. Most state statutes have provisions that allow public bodies to meet in executive session on certain issues, which usually deal with personnel, property, law suits, and student discipline.

Board meetings will become disorderly and unproductive unless a formal agenda is prepared by the superintendent with board member input and mailed to members before the meeting. The agenda should be organized in the following manner: (1) call to order, (2) approval of the agenda, (3) scheduling visitor presentations, (4) approval of warrants, (5) unfinished business, (6) new business, (7) superintendent's report, and (8) adjournment.

All official actions of the school board must occur at a board meeting. The minutes of the board meeting are the formal and legal medium through which the board communicates and documents these actions. The minutes of board meetings are public documents and must be open to inspection by all interested citizens.

Because the board of education is a legislative body, it is essential to the orderly conducting of business that definite parliamentary procedures be adopted. Likewise, it is necessary to elect officers of the board charged with carrying out school board operations. The most typically designated offices are, of course, president, vice president, treasurer, and secretary.

From time to time, school boards will need the assistance of regular and occasional consultants. An attorney, C.P.A., auditor, property appraiser, or any other consultant should be hired according to a process ensuring the most qualified professional is employed. Valuable assistance can also be obtained through citizens advisory committees if the board is careful to give the committee a specific charge with guidelines and an understanding that it should work in cooperation with the superintendent.

The demands of the public for accountability should alert boards of education to investigate the desirability of conducting an annual self-evaluation on their successes and failures.

Members of the school board will be contacted from time to time by school district employees who will want the board member to intervene on their behalf because of a problem at work. It behooves board members to refer these individuals to their immediate supervisor and to encourage the person to appeal the grievance through the chain of command all the way to the board if the employee so wishes. Of course, this procedure is predicated on the existence of a school employee grievance policy.

In exercising their authority to govern schools, boards of education should carefully formulate and adopt policies. School board policies should not be confused with administrative rules and regulations, which are detailed procedures for implementing board policies. The policies of the school board must be incorporated into a manual format if they are to be effective in governing the school district.

IMPLICATIONS FOR SCHOOL BOARD MEMBERS

There are three implications for boards of education in this presentation on the dynamics of school board operations:

First, school board members should carefully guard against falling into the trap of becoming involved in the daily operations of the school district. School board members have no authority as individuals and can exercise their jurisdiction as a board member only at legally constituted board meetings. In fact, the actions of individual board members outside a board meeting in relation to school district operations could result in litigation that is not covered by school board liability insurance.

Second, school board members must become familiar and comfortable with the dynamics of conducting business at school board meetings because these meetings are the only vehicle available to effectively govern the school district. Placing items on the board meeting agenda, monitoring the minutes of previous meetings, and the proper use of parliamentary procedures are the tools a board member must use to create the desired education for children and young people.

Third, school board members must understand the importance of creating policies that will give the district's administration direction in managing daily operations of the school district. Too often boards of education become concerned with making decisions about current problems and neglect to address through policy making the broader, underlying issues creating the problems.

APPENDIX A
A CODE OF ETHICS FOR SCHOOL
BOARD MEMBERS[9]

I. As a member of my local board of education, representing all the citizens of my school district, I recognize

1. That my fellow citizens have entrusted me with the educational development of the children and the youth of this community.
2. That the public expects my first and greatest concern to be in the best interest of each and every one of these young people without distinction as to who they are or what their background may be.
3. That the future welfare of this community, of this state, and of the nation depends in the largest measure upon the quality of education we provide in the public schools to fit the needs of every learner.
4. That my fellow board members and I must take the initiative in helping all the people of this community to have all the facts all the time about their schools, to the end that they will readily provide the finest possible school program, school staff, and school facilities.
5. That legally the authority of the board is derived from the State, which ultimately controls the organization and operation of the school district and which determines the degree of discretionary power left with the board and the people of this community for the exercise of local autonomy.
6. That I must never neglect my personal obligation to the community and my legal obligation to the State, nor surrender these responsibilities to any other person, group, or organization; but that, beyond these, I have a moral and civic obligation to the Nation which can remain strong and free so long as public schools in the United States of America are kept free and strong.

II. In view of the foregoing consideration, it shall be my endeavor

1. To devote time, thought, and study to the duties and responsibilities of a school board member so that I may render effective and creditable service.
2. To work with my fellow board members in a spirit of harmony and cooperation in spite of differences of opinion that arise during vigorous debate of points at issue.
3. To base my personal decision upon all available facts in each situation; to vote my honest conviction in every case, unswayed by partisan bias of any kind; thereafter, to abide by and uphold the final majority decision of the board.
4. To remember at all times that as an individual I have no legal authority outside the meetings of the board, and to conduct my relationships with the school staff, the local citizenry, and all media of communication on the basis of this fact.

[9] National School Boards Association, *A Code of Ethics for School Board Members* (Washington, D.C.: The Association, 1961).

5. To resist every temptation and outside pressure to use my position as a school board member to benefit either myself or any other individual or agency apart from the total interest of the school district.

6. To recognize that it is as important for the board to understand and evaluate the educational program of the schools as it is to plan for the business of school operation.

7. To bear in mind under all circumstances that the primary function of the board is to establish the policies by which the schools are to be administered, but that the administration of the educational program and the conduct of school business shall be left to the employed superintendent of schools and his professional staff and nonprofessional staff.

8. To welcome and encourage active cooperation by citizens, organizations, and the media of communication in the district with respect to establishing policy and proposed future development.

9. To support my State and National School Boards association.

10. Finally, to strive step by step toward ideal conditions for most effective school board service to my community in a spirit of teamwork and devotion to the public education as the greatest instrument for the preservation of our representative democracy.

APPENDIX B
SAMPLE BOARD OF EDUCATION
POLICIES AND ADMINISTRATIVE
RULES AND REGULATIONS

EQUAL EMPLOYMENT OPPORTUNITY
AND AFFIRMATIVE ACTION POLICY

WHEREAS, the welfare of this school district, this state, and the United States of America rests upon the ability of their constituents to perpetuate and improve not only technological excellence but also sound egalitarian principles; and

WHEREAS, this school district both reflects and formulates the sociopolitical attitudes of the community; and

WHEREAS, appropriate human relations are taught by example instead of precept; and

WHEREAS, Article II, Section 4 of the State Constitution, and Public Law 88-352, otherwise known as Title VI of the Civil Rights Act of 1964, and Title VII of the Civil Rights Act of 1964, as amended by Public Law 92-261, effective April 1, 1972, and the applicable Department of Elementary and Secondary Education policy prohibits discrimination in employment; and

WHEREAS, the attitude of the constituents is important in implementing both the spirit and the letter of the law; and

WHEREAS, discriminatory practice affecting one person diminishes the dignity of all and reduces the quantity and quality of services rendered by public institutions;

NOW, THEREFORE, BE IT RESOLVED the board of education directs that its employment and personnel procedures guarantee equal opportunity for everyone and that all matters relating to the recruitment, selection, placement, compensation, benefits, educational opportunities, promotion, termination, and working conditions shall be free from discriminatory practices.

FURTHER, employment and personnel procedures shall insure proportional minority and female representation and participation in all employment opportunities.

PERSONNEL GOALS POLICY[10]

The personnel employed by the district constitute the most important resource for effectively conducting a quality learning program. Important contributions to a successful education program are made by all staff members. The district's program will function best when it employs highly qualified personnel, conducts appropriate staff development activities, and establishes policies and working conditions which are conducive to high morale and which enable each staff member to make the fullest contribution to district programs and services.

The goals of the district's personnel program shall include the following:

1. To develop and implement those strategies and procedures for personnel recruitment, screening, and selection which will result in employing the best available candidates, i.e., those with highest capabilities, strongest commitment to quality education, and greatest probability of effectively implementing the district's learning program.
2. To develop general deployment strategy for greatest contribution to the learning program, and to utilize it as the primary basis for determining staff assignments.
3. To develop a climate in which optimum staff performance, morale, and satisfaction are produced.
4. To provide positive programs of staff development designed to contribute both to improvement of the learning program and to each staff member's career development aspirations.
5. To provide for a genuine team approach to education, including staff involvement in planning, decision making, and evaluation.
6. To provide attractive compensation and benefits as well as other provisions for staff welfare.
7. To develop and utilize for personnel evaluation positive processes which contribute to the improvement of both staff capabilities and the learning program.

[10]Ronald W. Rebore, *Personnel Administration in Education: A Management Approach* (Englewood Cliffs, N.J.: Prentice-Hall, 1982), p. 334.

PERSONNEL PLACEMENT POLICY[11]

The placement of employees within the school system is the responsibility of the superintendent of schools. The superintendent may delegate the implementation to other appropriate administrators, but he or she retains ultimate jurisdiction over this task. In determining assignments, the wishes of the employee are taken into consideration if these do not conflict with the requirements of the district's programming, staff balancing, and the welfare of students. Other factors that will be taken into consideration in making assignments are educational preparation and training, certification, experience, working relationships, and seniority in the school system.

A staffing survey form will be secured from each employee annually in February to assist in making assignment plans for the forthcoming school year.

Professional staffing assignments will be announced by April 1. Administrators affected by an assignment change will be consulted and notified by the superintendent of schools. Teachers affected by a change in grade or subject assignments will be consulted and notified by their respective building principals. Teachers affected by a building transfer will be consulted and notified by an administrator from the personnel department.

Classified staffing assignments will be announced by May 1 and will become effective on July 1. Supervisors and managers affected by an assignment change will be consulted and notified by the superintendent of schools or his designated representative. Other employees affected by a change in assignment will be consulted and notified by their immediate supervisors.

SEX EQUALITY IN EDUCATION POLICY[12]

This policy applies to all aspects of the district's employment programs, including but not limited to, recruitment, advertising, process of application for employment, promotion, granting of tenure, termination, layoffs, wages, job assignments, leaves of absence of all types, fringe benefits, training programs, employer-sponsored programs, social or recreational programs, and any other term, condition or privilege of employment. Specifically, the following personnel employment practices are prohibited:

a. *Tests.*   Administration of any test or other criterion which has a disproportionately adverse effect on persons on the basis of sex unless it is a valid predictor of job success and alternative tests or criterion are unavailable;

b. *Recruitment.*   Recruitment of employees from entities which furnish as applicants only or predominately members of one sex, if such action has the effect of discriminating on the basis of sex;

[11] Ibid., p. 137.

[12] American Association of School Administrators, *Sample Policy For Sex Equality in Education* (Arlington, Va.: the Association, 1977).

   c. *Compensation.* Establishment of rates of pay on the basis of sex;

   d. *Job Classification.* Classification of jobs as being for males or females;

   e. *Fringe Benefits.* Provision of fringe benefits on basis of sex; all fringe benefit plans must treat males and females equally;

   f. *Marital and Parental Status.* Any action based on marital or parental status; pregnancies are considered temporary disabilities for all job-related purposes and shall be accorded the same treatment by the district as are all other temporary disabilities. No inquiry shall be made by the district in job applications as to the marriage status of an applicant, including whether such applicant is "Miss or Mrs." But, inquiry may be made as to the sex of a job applicant for employment if it is made of all applicants and is not a basis for discrimination.

   g. *Employment Advertising.* Any expression of preference, limitation, or specification based on sex, unless sex is a bona fide occupational qualification for the particular job in question.

   Policy enforcement. To ensure compliance with this policy, the superintendent shall:

1. Designate a member of the administrative staff:
   a. To coordinate efforts of the district to comply with this policy;
   b. To develop and ensure the maintenance of a filing system to keep all records required under this policy;
   c. To investigate any complaints of violations of this policy
   d. To administer the grievance procedure established in this policy; and
   e. To develop affirmative action programs, as appropriate; and
2. Provide for the publication of this policy on an ongoing basis to students, parents, employees, prospective employees, and district employee unions or organizations, such publication to include the name, office address, and telephone number of the compliance administrator designated pursuant to this policy.

   Grievance procedure. Any employee of this district who believes he or she has been discriminated against, denied a benefit, or excluded from participation in any district activity, on the basis of sex in violation of this policy, may file a written complaint with the compliance administrator designated in this policy, above. The compliance administrator shall cause a review of the written complaint to be conducted and a written response mailed to the complainant within ten working days after receipt of the written complaint. A copy of the written complaint and the compliance administrator's response shall be provided each member of the Board of Education. If the complainant is not satisfied with such response, he or she may submit a written appeal to the Board of Education indicating with particularity the nature of disagreement with the response and his or her reasons underlying such disagreement.

   The Board of Education shall consider the appeal at its next regularly scheduled board meeting following receipt of the response.

The Board of Education shall permit the complainant to address the board in public or closed session, as appropriate and lawful, concerning his or her complaint and shall provide the complainant with its written decision in the matter as expeditiously as possible following completion of the hearing.

Evaluation. The Superintendent shall present a report to the Board of Education in a public meeting each year, describing this district's compliance with this policy during the previous year, which report can be the basis of an evaluation of the effectiveness of this policy by the Board of Education and a determination as to whether or not additional affirmative action is necessary in light of all the facts.

AN EARLY RETIREMENT INCENTIVE POLICY[13]

To say that our district is facing serious financial challenges is not new. We are faced with reduced expenditures throughout the entire budget. The ever increasing spiral of inflation continues to erode the purchasing power of institutions such as school districts, as well as individuals. Declining enrollment places a financial burden upon school districts because of the relationship of state funding to enrollment and attendance.

Any serious attempts to minimize school costs must consider staff utilization, since employee salaries comprise such a large portion of the school budget. Maintaining staffing levels during declining enrollment results in more desirable class size. However, it is not economically possible when the local tax base is no longer increasing in assessed valuation as it did in the past. Frequently a result of declining enrollment and a stable assessed valuation is reduced revenues and increased operational costs necessitating staff and program reductions.

In staff reductions, the state Tenure Law requires districts to place probationary teachers on leave before tenured teachers. Probationary teachers receive smaller salaries than tenured teachers because of the differences in experience as recognized by our salary schedule. This practice increases the number of teachers who must be placed on leave to realize a saving on staff salaries. Another effect is an increasing percentage of staff members who are more experienced and better paid, a faculty where more and more teachers are near the top of the salary schedule.

The development of early retirement incentive programs is one way to reduce personnel costs and at the same time face the problem of how to reduce staff without resorting to wholesale reduction in force by unrequested leave of absence.

Early retirement programs have provided a vehicle for the reduction of staff with a direct reduction of costs that make these programs appealing to those who exhibit the concerns of both the humanist and the fiscal conservative.

---

[13] Lindbergh School District, *An Early Retirement Incentive Program* (St. Louis, Mo.: The School District, 1982).

Methods of providing incentives for early retirement have included: sharing the savings of turnover due to retirement with the person retiring; gradual withdrawal from full-time employment through part-time consulting services to the district; incentive pay. An examination of the different types of early retirement incentive programs indicates that most are based on financial rewards that lessen the loss of earnings for early retirees during the first several years, but still enable the school district to save a considerable amount of money through either not replacing retirees or replacing them with beginning teachers.

Early retirement programs are not always easily accepted by teachers. Some teachers feel that leisure is bad and they are not going to retire until forced to do so. Others are somewhat prone to believe that they are being forced out of employment. Any program of early retirement must be voluntary. It is up to each individual employee to determine whether early retirement is in their best interest and whether choosing that option will have a negative impact on the retirement program administered by the state.

An early retirement incentive program (ERIP) must be mutually beneficial to staff and district in order to be successful. While the primary purpose of an ERIP is voluntary staff reduction, it should be accomplished in such a manner that the district realizes a reduction in cost, while at the same time, retirement becomes an attractive choice for members of the staff. Other mutual benefits will occur with an effective ERIP: (1) saving tax dollars; (2) enabling the district to attract and retain quality teachers; (3) providing job security for younger staff members. Additionally, a successful program will allow the school district to regain a balance of experience on the staff.

This program offers a positive method of voluntary staff reduction which recognized the contributions of an experienced staff which has demonstrated a commitment to the youth of our community. It retains the essential features of successful early retirement plans which have been shown to be beneficial to the staff and to the districts.

The ERIP is being proposed at a particularly significant time in the district's history—a period of declining enrollment and the consolidation of district resources. The urgent need for prompt approval of this plan is evident and this committee hopes that the board can issue such approval so that the trauma of reduction in force through unrequested leave can be minimized, even this year.

The Early Retirement Incentive Program (ERIP) contains the following features:

1. "Age" shall be the age of the retiree as of June 30 of the final full year of teaching.

"Adviser or Consultant to the Board" shall mean a teacher who is participating in the Early Retirement Incentive Program who will be rendering professional advice in matters directed by the board through the superintendent. Such services may include, but not be limited to, curriculum work, in-service training, research or other service to the board as mutually agreed upon by the teachers and the board.

"Board" shall mean the Board of Education.

"Creditable service" shall mean prior service or membership service, or the sum of the two, if the teacher has both (as defined by the State Teacher Retirement System), in a public school system in the state.

"Early Retirement Incentive Benefit" shall mean the payment to a teacher participating in the ERIP as determined by the appropriate formula contained in "Calculation of Benefit." The benefit shall be paid to the teacher in three annual payments in January of each year for the three year period immediately following early retirement. All benefit payments shall be subject to applicable taxes and Social Security. This is a continuation of current practice.

"Final full year" shall mean the school year of teaching prior to retirement.

"Final salary" shall mean the total contractual compensation payable to a teacher for a school year less any amount paid under the extra duty salary schedule.

"School year" shall mean the year from July first of one year to June thirtieth of the next year, inclusive.

"Teacher" shall mean any teacher, counselor, librarian, supervisor, director or coordinator, administrative assistant, assistant principal, principal, assistant or associate superintendent, or superintendent who shall be employed by the school district, and who shall be duly certificated under the laws governing the certification of teachers.

2. *Eligibility:*

PLAN 1

A teacher who has thirty (30) years of creditable service, with no less than fifteen (15) years of experience in the school district, shall be eligible to participate in the Early Retirement Incentive Program (ERIP), according to the following formula:

Final Salary $\times$ Incentive = ERI Benefit

PLAN 2

A teacher who is fifty-five (55) years of age and who has twenty (20) years of creditable service with not less than fifteen (15) years of experience in the school district shall be eligible to participate in the ERIP according to the following formula:

Final Salary $\times$ Incentive = ERI Benefit

RATIONALE:

The primary purpose of an ERIP is voluntary staff reduction through early retirement. Teaching histories may be loosely divided into two large groups, teachers who began at a very young age and continued their careers without interruption, and teachers who began at a later age and/or whose career was interrupted. Both of these groups deserve equal consideration, thus the two-part plan. Initial eligibility would be the first time a teacher was eligible under either plan. Thereafter, the teacher would continue to use that plan in figuring the early retirement benefits.

3. *Calculation of Benefit:* The calculation of ERI Benefit for an eligible teacher shall be according to the formula stated in "Eligibility" above. The "Incentive" for initial eligibility shall be 100 percent. For the first year after initial eligibility the incentive shall be reduced by 20 percent, an additional 15 percent the second year, 10 percent the third through the seventh year, and 5 percent the last two years. At age 65 or 40 years of experience, all early retirement benefits shall cease.

Eligibility Requirement

CREDITABLE SERVICE	OR AGE X	FINAL SALARY X	INCENTIVE =	ERI BENEFIT
30	55	27,000	1.00	27,000
31	56	27,000	.80	21,600
32	57	27,000	.65	17,550
33	58	27,000	.55	14,850
34	59	27,000	.45	12,150
35	60	27,000	.35	9,450
36	61	27,000	.25	6,750
37	62	27,000	.15	4,050
38	63	27,000	.10	2,700
39	64	27,000	.05	1,350
40	65	27,000	.00	—0—

RATIONALE:

In order to promote early retirement, the greatest incentive should come when the teacher first meets the eligibility requirements of the ERIP. After that time, the incentive should be substantially reduced as the teachers are increasing their benefits under the state system as well as benefiting from full salary. To maintain the maximum benefit would encourage teachers to remain and would be counter to the purpose of an early retirement program. The above table illustrates the calculation of ERI Benefit for an eligible teacher whose final salary is $27,000. The ERI Benefit stops after 39 years of creditable service and at age 65.

4. *Insurance Benefits;* While serving as "Adviser" or "Consultant" to the board, the school district shall provide the same insurance coverage as is provided for other certificated personnel. If a teacher selects an insurance program greater than that which is provided by the district, the teacher may make his payment to the district monthly or may have his annual premium deducted from the annual payment.

RATIONALE:

Insurance coverage is the most important benefit paid to teachers. This practice is provided for teachers on early retirement at the present time and would be a continuation of this practice. After completing the three year commitment to the district as an "Adviser" or "Consultant," the retired teacher may remain a member of the district's group for insurance purposes. If the retired teacher so chooses, he or she shall submit to the board monthly an amount equal to the sum of that paid by the board and by the individual under full employment contract for the coverage selected by the individual.

5. *Notification of Intent:* A teacher who wishes to participate in the ERIP shall notify the district in writing before April 1 of the final full year of teaching and shall include his or her resignation to be effective the last day of that school year.

RATIONALE:

It is particularly important that the trauma of unrequested leave be avoided whenever possible. It is also beneficial to the district to be aware of the plans of the staff so that adequate staffing plans can be prepared prior to giving tentative staff assignments on April 1.

6. *Survivorship:* In the event of the death of the teacher during the period covered by the ERIP, any payments due shall be paid to the designated beneficiary or to the estate of the deceased on a prorated basis.

7. *Implementation:* The ERIP shall be implemented for the 1982–83 school year. For the initial implementation of the ERIP for the 1982–83 school year, no teacher who chooses to retire under this plan shall suffer any loss of benefit. Thereafter, the ERI Benefit shall be calculated as specified in "Calculation of Benefit."

RATIONALE:

The first year of this program is critical. A sizable reduction of staff is indicated. Teachers who exceed the minimum standards of this program should not have their benefit reduced as the first year of this program is truly the first time they are eligible for participation in the program. To reduce their benefit at this time without affording them the opportunity to elect early retirement would seem to be punitive.

RISK MANAGEMENT POLICY[14]

The governing board shall provide for a program of risk management for this school district consistent with all the legal requirements pertaining thereto and consistent with the financial ability of the district to finance. The board shall purchase

[14] Association of School Business Officials, *Risk Management and School Insurance Policy Guide* (Park Ridge, Ill.: The Association, 1974), pp. 3–4.

with district funds the type and amount of insurance necessary or shall set aside adequate reserves to self insure in order to protect itself as a corporate body, its individual members, its appointed officers, and its employees from financial loss arising out of any claim, demand, suit, or judgment by reason of alleged negligence or other act resulting in accidental injury to any person or in property damage within or without the school buildings while the above named insured are acting in the discharge of their duties within the scope of their employment and/or under the direction of the board.

Furthermore, within its program of risk management the governing board shall purchase from district funds the type and amount of insurance coverage to insure and/or self-insure all real and personal property of the district, to insure and/or self-insure the district from losses due to employee dishonesty, injury or death, and to provide a program of health and welfare benefits for employees to the limits established from time to time by the governing board.

Within the scope of this policy, the superintendent is directed to develop and maintain rules and regulations necessary for carrying out all aspects of this policy including the designation of the district employee responsible for administration and supervision of the risk management program.

RISK MANAGEMENT ADMINISTRATIVE RULES AND REGULATIONS

1.0 *Management and Control of District's Risk Management Program.*

1.1 The management and control of the district's risk management and any and all insurance authorized by the governing board shall be a function of the Business Division through such staff allocation of responsibilities as the assistant superintendent/business services (business manager) shall designate.

1.2 The assistant superintendent for business services (business manager) or his designated assistant, shall be the risk manager for the district.

1.3 The risk manager shall have authority to establish rules and procedures, consistent with board policy, to insure the safety and well being of pupils, employees and the public while on or in school district property that will aid in keeping the district's liability to a minimum and the premiums for insurance as low as possible consistent with the insurance requirements and the exposures insured.

2.0 *Placement of Insurance.*

2.1 The assistant superintendent for business services (business manager), through the superintendent, shall recommend to the governing board, and the governing board shall appoint a broker-of-record to assist and advise the district in the placement of insurance in each major line of insurance including fire, liability, fidelity, casualty and employee health and welfare benefits. Such appointment shall be effective until withdrawn or superseded by action of the board.

2.2   The broker-of-record shall have the following qualifications:

    2.2.1   Licensed general insurance broker.

    2.2.2   Principally engaged in the business of general insurance for a period of at least five years.

    2.2.3   Maintains an office within or near the general area of the school district with a staff of at least one other principal and necessary clerical service.

2.3   The risk manager shall report the need for insurance, together with all relevant information including statements of costs obtained by the broker-of-record from insurance companies, and his or her recommendations for the placing of such insurance to the superintendent who shall present his or her recommendations to the governing board.

2.4   Upon authorization by the governing board, the risk manager, in cooperation with the broker-of-record shall place such insurance in accordance with said authorization and the relevant provisions of these rules and regulations.

2.5   In an emergency, the risk manager shall place insurance and the superintendent shall immediately report such placement for ratification by the governing board.

2.6   Insurance carried by the governing board shall be obtained through negotiation, and when deemed necessary and to the best interests of the district, by competitive bids and shall be awarded to those insurance companies who agree to furnish the coverage required at the lowest and best price consistent with good service and security.

3.0   *Kinds of Insurance Authorized.*

The following insurance shall be carried in accordance with applicable rules and regulations:

3.1   Fire and extended coverage insurance covering all buildings owned or occupied by the district, in such amounts as are authorized by the governing board.

3.2   Comprehensive liability covering members of the governing board, the school district's officers and employees while acting in the discharge of their duties within the scope of their employment and/or under the direction of the governing board. Such insurance, if permitted under the laws governing the operation of the district, shall extend maximum coverage in such amounts as are authorized by the governing board.

3.3   Fidelity bonds protecting the members of the governing board against loss occasioned by fraud or dishonesty of officers and employees of the district.

3.4   Workmen's compensation insurance covering all employees of the district, in accordance with the laws of the state governing workmen's compensation, sufficient to provide the benefits as prescribed by such laws.

3.5   Casualty, fire and theft insurance covering all vehicles owned or operated by the governing board to the limits as specified by board action.

3.6   Burglary and robbery insurance covering such property as specified by board action.

3.7   Boiler and pressure vessel property damage insurance covering steel boilers and such other pressure vessels and property to the limits deemed sufficient by the risk manager and as authorized by the governing board.

3.8 All risk insurance covering any property specified by the risk manager and authorized by the governing board.

3.9 Sprinkler leakage insurance on property where designated by the risk manager and authorized by the governing board.

3.10 Programs of insurance in the area of employee fringe benefits such as hospital and medical insurance, dental insurance, life insurance, long-term disability insurance but only in the kinds and to the limits authorized by the governing board.

3.11 Such other insurance coverage as the governing board may authorize.

4.0 *Insurable Value—Buildings and Contents.*

4.1 The insurable value of a building shall be defined as the replacement cost of such building less the noninsurable items set forth in the district's fire insurance forms.

4.2 The term "contents," as used in connection with insurance, shall be defined to include all personal property not specifically excluded by the terms of the standard form for fire insurance policies. The valuation of contents, for insurance purposes, shall be depreciated on the basis of an average total depreciation of 25 percent.

5.0 *Settlement of Losses.*

5.1 When any property covered by insurance is lost, damaged, or destroyed, a notice concerning the loss shall be sent immediately to all affected carriers or their representatives. The risk manager shall act as adjuster for the governing board in the settlement of losses and he shall sign the Proof of Loss as authorized. The superintendent shall recommend to the governing board, as soon as practicable, a basis for settlement and, upon adoption by the governing board, the agreed amounts shall be collected from the insurance company(ies) and deposited to the credit of the district in accordance with the laws governing such collection.

6.0 *Liability Claims Procedure.*

6.1 A written notice of rejection shall be sent to the claimant in all cases where a written claim has been filed in accordance with the laws of the state governing the filing of such claims and the school district's liability insurance carrier has advised the district in writing that the claim has been rejected. Such rejections shall be reported to the governing board by the superintendent for board approval.

SELECTED BIBLIOGRAPHY

EDUCATIONAL RESEARCH SERVICE, "Local Boards of Education: Status and Structure," Circular No. 5, 1972.

KOWALSKI, THEODORE J., "Why Your Board Needs Self-Evaluation," *The American School Board Journal,* Vol. 168, No. 7 (July, 1981), pp. 21-23.

MISSOURI SCHOOL BOARDS ASSOCIATION, *A Manual for Missouri School Board Members* (revised edition). Columbia, Missouri: The Association, 1981.

UNDERWOOD, KENNETH E., WAYNE P. THOMAS, TONY COOKE, SHIRLEY UNDERWOOD, "Portrait of the American School Board Member," *The American School Board Journal,* Vol. 167, No. 1 (January, 1980), pp. 23–25.

ZIEGLER, L. HARMON, M. KENT JENNINGS, G. WAYNE PEAK, *Governing American Schools: Political Interaction in Local School Districts.* North Scituate, Mass.: Duxbury Press, 1974.

CHAPTER THREE
THE RELATIONSHIP
OF THE SCHOOL BOARD
TO THE SUPERINTENDENT
OF SCHOOLS

The single most important task of a school board is the selection of a superintendent of schools.

No position within the educational profession has received more attention in the news media over the past decade than the superintendency. "The job is much more political than ever before," appears to be the reason why the tremendous turnover rate among superintendents rivals that of losing baseball managers.[1] Declining enrollment, teacher layoffs, dwindling financial resources, labor union strikes, and low pupil achievement test scores constitute some of the major problems facing contemporary public schools. The individual who is often singled out as exacerbating these problems rather than helping to solve them is the superintendent of schools. He or she becomes the tangible target for hurled criticism when the real culprits are too elusive to be found.

The quality of the relationship that exists between a board of education and the superintendent will directly affect the quality of education received by the children and youth in the district's schools. A good board of education will demand a good superintendent of schools. This may also be reciprocal. The school community will, over time, be able to perceive the school board's attitude towards the superintendent and the superintendent may influence the community's perception about individual board members. Thus it is critical for the board of education to

---

[1] National School Public Relations Association, *Education USA*, Vol. 22, No. 47 (July 21, 1980), p. 347.

establish a good working relationship with the superintendent that will enhance rather than detract from the school district's mission, which is to educate children.

This chapter addresses three responsibilities of the school board in relation to the superintendency that constitute the basis upon which a working relationship can be established. First, the board of education will occasionally be required to hire a superintendent of schools, and if this process is not handled properly, an individual who does not meet the needs of a specific school system could inadvertently be selected. Second, the school board must create a compensation plan for the superintendent that will reward performance reasonably and become an incentive for a good superintendent to remain with the district. Third, the board of education must establish an evaluation process that will continuously monitor the superintendent's performance and ensure that the school community has the kind of leadership necessary to meet the challenges facing the school district.

SELECTING AND HIRING A SUPERINTENDENT OF SCHOOLS

There are nine steps which, if followed by a board of education, should result in the selection of a superintendent who has a reasonable probability of being successful in a given school district. This is, of course, the major purpose of all personnel selection processes: to minimize the possibility of hiring the wrong person and to maximize the district's potential to attract highly qualified applicants. Some school boards have in many cases used haphazard and ineffective methods of choosing the educational leader for their district. The following steps will hopefully provide a school board with a model that can be adapted to their particular school district and will increase both the tenure and effectiveness of superintendents.

Step One—Appoint a Selection Committee

The school board should begin the process of selecting a superintendent by appointing a committee that will be charged with monitoring the entire process, which includes recruiting and screening candidates, and recommending several individuals to the board of education for final selection.

The committee should consist of several board members, teacher representatives, parents, secondary school students, central office and building level administrators, various community representatives, and classified employees. It is important to have a committee that is not so large as to be cumbersome, but it must be large enough to be truly representative of the entire school community. Each segment of the school community should recommend representatives to the school board for appointment to the committee. For example, the various teacher organizations and unions should recommend their representatives, the PTA should recommend the parent representatives, and the high school student council should recommend the student representatives to the school board.

A common practice is for the school board to hire outside consultants to assist in recruiting and screening applicants. A superintendent from another school district, a professor from a school of education, or a professional consultant constitute the major categories of consultants. Sometimes school boards use consultants in lieu of a committee. These consultants are charged with seeking input from various segments of the school community before making recommendations to the school board.

Myron Lieberman warns that, "No shortage of ways exists to manipulate a list of finalists to make sure one of the consultant's favored candidates gets the job."[2] In order to ensure against this and other abuse, he makes the following suggestions:

1. Make sure you don't pay for busy work. Have a clear idea of what the board wants, and get right to the point with the consultant. Debate the candidate's qualifications on your time, not the consultant's.
2. Try to employ consultants whose chief or only business is personnel selection, or whose other activities suggest few or no conflict-of-interest problems.
3. If the consultant's billing is on a per diem basis, define what a day's work is, and have the consultant list the number of days worked. Also make sure the consultant is willing to sign a statement affirming that he or she is not billing the board for time or work allocated to any other employee.
4. Have the consultant state any financial or professional relationship with any of the candidates submitted to the school board for selection. If you are asked to hire the consultant's brother-in-law, you ought to know about the relationship.[3]

Outside consultants can be very helpful, and the possibility of abuse will be minimized if the consultant works with and supports a selection committee. The primary responsibility of a consultant should be educating and advising the selection committee on how to perform their responsibilities as outlined in the following steps.

Step Two—Establish a Budget for the Selection Process

The board of education must recognize that selecting and hiring a superintendent can be a very expensive process. The school board should decide on a reasonable dollar amount that will get the job done but one that will not become an embarrassment.

The cost of printing a recruitment brochure and application forms along with postage to mail these items to applicants is a minor expense, as is the cost of advertising the position in professional journals and local newspapers. All these expenses combined might approach one to two thousand dollars.

[2] Myron Lieberman, "The Case Against Letting a Moonlighting Professor Pick Your Next Superintendent," *The American School Board Journal,* 165, No. 4 (April, 1978), p. 36.
[3] *Ibid.,* 46.

Transportation and housing costs for bringing finalists to the school district to be interviewed by the selection committee and school board constitute the major expenses in the selection process. Some school boards will also want all or a few of their members to travel to the finalists' home school districts for the purpose of interviewing colleagues, parents, and students who have first-hand knowledge about a particular finalist.

A rule of thumb that should guide a school board as it establishes a budget for the selection process is that the total cost should not exceed one-third of the anticipated first year's salary for the newly hired superintendent. If the school board expects to offer the chosen finalist between fifty and sixty thousand dollars, the total cost of the selection process should not exceed twenty thousand dollars.

Step Three—Establish a Calendar
for the Selection Process

A detailed calendar should be established by the board of education so that the selection committee will understand the time contraints under which they will function. Such a calendar can also include designated responsibilities, which should ensure the timely selection of a superintendent. Figure 3-1 presents a model calendar of events and activities addressing the major considerations in the selection process. This model calls for the selection to be completed within a six-month period of time. Because of the importance of the superintendency, it is necessary for the school board to establish a time period which will not hinder but rather enhance the process. It is questionable that a time period of less than six months can be long enough to adequately carry out an effective selection.

Step Four—Identify Qualifications
for the Superintendency
and a Selection Criteria

There are several reasons for identifying desired qualifications and establishing selection criteria: This information (1) should be included in the recruitment brochure; (2) will facilitate the work of the selection committee and consultant in screening applicants; and (3) will ensure the objectivity of the selection process.

The following qualities should be of value to a selection committee and consultants as they proceed with the difficult task of identifying appropriate qualifications for the contemporary superintendency.

—*Leadership.* He (or she, in all references) inspires teamwork, maintains high morale, directs the school system toward given objectives, and helps others grow on the job. The community sees the superintendent as an educational leader, and the superintendent raises community expectations of its schools.

—*Scholarship.* He is scholarly and analytical but not pedantic; he is widely read and understands the need for empirical support for recommendations; he keeps abreast of current educational trends.

FIGURE 3-1 Calendar of Events and Activities

MONTHS	ACTIVITY	RESPONSIBILITY
1st	Appointment of a selection committee	Board of Education
	Advertise, accept, and evaluate proposals from potential consultants	Board of Education
2nd	Hire a consultant or consultant firm	Board of Education
	Initial discussions concerning the philosophy, process, and procedures for selecting a superintendent	Board of Education Selection committee Consultant
	Begin to identify qualifications for the superintendency and selection criteria	Selection committee Consultant
	Begin to develop a recruitment brochure and application form	Selection committee
3rd	Have recruitment brochures and application forms printed	Consultant
	Approval of qualifications and selection criteria	Board of Education
	Establish a deadline for receiving applications	Selection committee Consultant
	Advertise position vacancy in professional journals, association bulletins, and newspapers	Consultant
4th	Initial screening of applicants against qualifications	Selection committee Consultant
5th	Final screening of applicants, planning for interviews of top 5–10 candidates	Board of Education Selection committee Consultant
	Investigating credentials and references of top 5–10 candidates	Board of Education Consultant
6th	Interviewing top 5–10 candidates	Board of Education Selection committee
	Recommendation of top 3 candidates to the school board	Selection committee
	Visiting the home school districts of the top 3 candidates by a committee of the school board	Board of Education
	Notify selected candidate, negotiate contract and establish transition period activities	Board of Education Candidate
	Notify unsuccessful candidates and school committees identifying the successful candidate	Board of Education Consultant

—*Judgment.* The superintendent's actions and decisions reflect knowledge and use of common sense.

—*Alertness.* The superintendent is intellectually and intuitively able to interpret and respond effectively to new conditions, situations, problems and opportunities as they arise.

—*Initiative.* He can originate and/or develop ideas and "sell" them to board and staff. In the language of the early sixties, he's a self-starter.

—*Cooperation.* He has the ability and desire to work with others in a team situation; authority, role and power are not his paramount considerations.

—*Drive.* The superintendent's continuing urge is to improve the educational program without frightening others.

—*Self-confidence.* He's self-reliant and tactful.

—*Communications.* The superintendent expresses himself clearly and coccisely as a writer and speaker.

—*Flexibility.* He adapts to new situations and does not regard his own opinion as inviolable.

—*Stability.* The superintendent remains calm and poised under pressure; he appreciates but is not bound by tradition and custom.

—*Reliability.* He performs according to promise on matters within his control.[4]

These abstract qualities can then be translated into specific qualifications as outlined in Appendix A, *Model Recruitment Brochures for the Position of Superintendent of Schools.* Successful experience and expertise in financial management, human relations, curriculum development, program planning, personnel management, and in public relations are a few of the necessary qualifications for the superintendency. Each of the identified qualifications can then be weighted or ranked by the selection committee and consultant from the most important to the least important qualification. This in essence then becomes the selection criteria which will be compared against the credentials submitted by interested candidates.

It is the responsibility of the board of education to give final approval to the qualifications and selection criteria recommended by the consultant and the selection committee.

Step Five—Develop a Recruitment Brochure and Application Form

The recruitment brochure exhibited in Appendix A can serve as a model to a selection committee and consultant(s) as they proceed with the very important task of constructing a brochure. The recruitment brochure provides potential candidates with extensive information, enabling them to better ascertain if they wish to apply for the position and if they possess the minimal requirements.

---

[4]Charles W. Fowler, "Twelve Earmarks of a SUPERintendent," *The American School Board Journal,* 162, No. 9 (September, 1975), p. 20.

The format for such a brochure will vary, but certain information is usually provided. The most important information to communicate includes the announcement of the vacancy, the procedure for applying, a description of the qualifications that the successful candidate must possess, information about the community served by the school district, and data about the district, which normally includes financial, personnel, and curricular information. The recruitment brochure and application form should be mailed to individuals inquiring about the position.

Applications for positions are generally of two types. The first type emphasizes detailed and extensive factual information about the individual, with little or no attention given to the person's attitudes, opinions, and values. Conversely, the second style emphasizes the applicant's attitudes, opinions, and values and asks for little factual information.

It is more appropriate to utilize the application form for the purpose of ascertaining the objective qualifications of potential candidates and to use the interview experience to obtain an understanding of the candidates' attitudes, opinions, and values. Body language and the applicant's manner of addressing questions dealing with subjective matters can be used to better assess intangibles, whereas the written word can be manipulated in a calculating way. Thus application forms requesting detailed factual information, such as the one exhibited in Appendix B, are more helpful to a selection committee and consultant. The model application in Appendix B also incorporates those features which will ensure that the application forms meet affirmative action and equal employment opportunity requirements consistent with current legislation and court decisions.

The basic principle in constructing application forms is, "Only ask for information you need to know." Most information requested on applications falls under one of the following headings: personal data, education and professional information, work experience, and references. Such information should be sufficient to screen out those applicants who do not meet minimal qualifications. It is the responsibility of the selection committee and consultant to construct the application form or to choose one that has proven to be an effective screening instrument.

Step Six—Advertise the Position Vacancy

The search for a new superintendent should not be limited to just the local community or state in which the school district is located. Rather, advertising nationally will give talented individuals across the country an opportunity to become candidates, which will in turn definitely increase the school board's chances of hiring a proven educational executive. Many professional administrator associations have job bulletins which will prove to be a valuable source of applicants. In addition, the vacancy announcement should be listed in all major professional journals, in national and local newspapers, and at the placement offices of major universities with nationally renowned schools of education. The consultant is usually charged with writing and placing the position vacancy announcement.

Step Seven—Screening Applicants

The selection committee and consultant should carefully screen all of the applications that have been received by the deadline stated in the position vacancy announcement. The screening process involves comparing the information on the application forms against the selection criteria to sift out the top five to ten candidates who are most qualified.

The selection committee and consultant should then meet with the school board and report on the screening process, indicating the number of applications received and outlining how the screening was conducted along with any additional information requested by the board. The consultant can then plan and initiate an interview schedule for the school board and selection committee with the top candidates.

Step Eight—Interview Candidates

The school board and selection committee should separately interview the top five to ten candidates. There are four areas that should be addressed in the interviews: (1) the applicant's opinions on the relationship between the school board and the superintendent, particularly in regards to policy and administrative matters; (2) the applicant's views on current issues in public education; (3) the applicant's opinions on managing the curriculum, personnel, community and pupil relations; and (4) the applicant's understanding of public school finance.

Some school boards and selection committees tape record the interviews so that they may be studied and compared in greater depth at a later time. The selection committee should then recommend three candidates to the school board. Of course, the board is in no way obliged to accept this recommendation and may find none of the candidates recommended by the committee to be satisfactory. This is most unlikely, but it is the reason why both the school board and selection committee should interview the top candidates.

Step Nine—Hiring the Best Candidate

It is a common practice for the school board or a committee of board members to visit the home school districts of the finalists. The colleagues, students, parents, and other individuals in the school districts can be questioned by the board members about the abilities and performance of each finalist.

The consultant, under the direction of the school board, can at this time begin to verify the credentials of the finalists and to contact the individuals designated on the applications as references.

Once a decision is reached, the successful candidate should meet with the entire board to negotiate a contract and to establish those transition activities which will ensure the appropriate communication to the school community concerning the newly-hired superintendent.

The board of education or consultant is responsible at this point for notifying all applicants that the position has been filled and by whom.

COMPENSATING THE
SUPERINTENDENT OF SCHOOLS

Compensation constitutes more than salary and includes such fringe benefits as multiple forms of insurance and, in some districts, an expense account and the use of a district-owned automobile. The particular compensation package developed by a given board of education should be defensible. In other words, the superintendent of schools should be compensated in a manner suitable to the school district and community.

Gathering data from neighboring school districts, from municipal governments, and from private service institutions such as hospitals will help a school board assess the appropriateness of its compensation plan for the district's superintendent. It is obvious that the financial condition of the school district will also have a significant effect upon the ability of the district to compensate the superintendent in a manner comparable to other school districts and private institutions with similar positions of responsibility. It is most unlikely that a school district will attract and be able to retain a qualified superintendent if the compensation package is not comparable at least to other school districts in the region where the district is located.

The major component of the compensation package is, of course, the wage paid the superintendent. It is also common practice to offer the superintendent the following types of insurance: major medical and hospitalization insurance, dental insurance, term life insurance, errors and omissions liability insurance, accidental death and disability insurance, and annuity programs. Some states have mandatory retirement programs that must be paid into by the superintendent and the school district. Offering some of this insurance coverage to the family of the superintendent is also a common practice, especially in regards to major medical, hospitalization, and dental insurance.

It has become more common within the last five years to help pay the moving expenses for a newly-hired superintendent living outside the immediate region where the district is located. The use of a district-owned automobile and an expense account along with paying the superintendent's membership dues in professional associations are typical fringe benefits for medium and large size school districts. Attendance at state and national conferences, workshops, and conventions is important in keeping the superintendent informed about current trends in addressing educational problems and issues. The expenses, therefore, incurred in attending these meetings are also usually paid by the school district.

It is important for the board of education to reduce the components of the superintendent's compensation package to writing in the form of a contract. Many school boards only include the wages and neglect to include the fringe benefits in the superintendent's contract.

The contract should also serve as a communication tool between the superintendent and school board, addressing such items as (1) the authority and responsibilities of the superintendent; (2) an evaluation procedure along with a due process clause; and (3) a procedure to renegotiate the contract.

It is most appropriate to offer the superintendent a multiple-year contract usually for a three to five year period, depending upon state statutes and local practices. The ability of a newly-hired superintendent to make significant changes in school district operations will require a minimum of three years.

EVALUATING THE PERFORMANCE
OF THE SUPERINTENDENT
OF SCHOOLS

More than any other time in the history of public education, the superintendent of schools has come under attack on multiple fronts covering a variety of problems and issues. Pressures that squeeze superintendents and ultimately cause many good individuals to rethink their careers in education are summarized below.

1. Too many school board members want to run the show. They overlook the specialized training and competencies that superintendents have for handling administrative tasks effectively and efficiently.
2. Budget cuts, accompanied by shrinking tax revenues, are increasing with alarming frequency. This places the superintendent in a pincer. On the one hand he or she tries to be imaginative in searching for ways to find more money; on the other a sympathetic ear must be turned toward staff who complain chronically about the skimpiness of their work environment.
3. It's becoming more hectic to coordinate information in order to complete reports on time.
4. Dissent among school board members gobbles time and causes serious, sometimes lasting rifts. (Superintendents have recently noted, however, that the number of these schisms is on the wane.)
5. Declining enrollments are matched inversely with increasing expenditures, mainly because operating costs are rising fast—as are installations of new programs mandated by law or public fancy.
6. Taxpayers are starting to sour on teachers; it's those strike patterns and salary demands that annoy.
7. Union tactics are growing stronger and more refined.
8. Special interest groups make more noise these days, and they're gaining substantial headway in their appeals.
9. Students have changed—admittedly, an understatement. Their altered philosophies and actions place particular strains on families and schools; this trend is reflected by the upsurge in the number of school vandalism and discipline cases.
10. The news media want headlines. Their banners—whether oral or written—often convey an erroneous impression of what actually is happening in schools.
11. The processing of local, state, and federal regulations creates carloads of paperwork and weekends of overtime.[5]

[5] Edward P. Travers, "Eleven Pressures That Squeeze Superintendents," *The American School Board Journal,* 165, No. 2 (February, 1978), p. 43.

However, the demise of many superintendents stems from a lack of sophisticated communication and organizational skills, which leaves them ill-prepared to work effectively with school boards, the staff, and the community. David Fultz lists some of the major reasons why superintendents lose their jobs, with emphasis on these professional and personal deficiencies.

1. *Weak rapport with the board poses the biggest threat.* This is a reiteration of the central point mentioned earlier, but it bears repeating because of its importance. So: A school board is irked most by refusal of an administrator to seek and accept criticism; by his lack of demonstrated effort to work in harmony with the board; by his failure to support board policy and follow the board's instructions.

2. *Lack of staff respect bodes ill for the superintendent.* Statistics gathered in this section of the Michigan study indicated that the school administrator needs firm backing from his staff. Without such respect and support his or her days are numbered, because there is no cohesion within the chain of command to get work accomplished on time and in good order.

3. *Poor communications up and down the line present problems.* Failure to be understood readily and clearly puts an administrator at a serious disadvantage. It places him or her in a particularly precarious position with school personnel, board members, and the community. In addition, efforts must be made to excel at public speaking, since this counts as an art of communication and figures prominently in survival, according to findings that were included in the study.[6]

Some superintendents fail to recognize the imminence of their demise, which in many cases stems from the fact that they are not formally evaluated by their respective boards of education. The decline in effective performance often occurs at an accelerated rate and may catch the superintendent off guard. As alluded to earlier, an evaluation process with due process considerations should be written into the superintendent's contract. The purpose of the selection process for hiring a superintendent and the reason for developing an attractive compensation plan is to hire and retain the best possible educational executive for the school district. Consequently, the evaluation process should encourage the professional growth of the superintendent and should provide the superintendent with the opportunity to stay with the school district as long as he or she is an effective administrator. With all the turmoil in public education, stability in leadership will help the school board effectively address the many problems and issues that have become modus operandi in many districts.

The superintendent is responsible for developing the evaluation process, which includes the following steps:

First, the superintendent annually prepares a list of objectives to be accomplished during the school year. Such a list might include improving his or her understanding of the community or might center on improving communications with the school board. These objectives along with all aspects of the evaluation pro-

[6] David A. Fultz, "Eight Ways Superintendents Lose Their Jobs," *The American School Board Journal,* 163, No. 9 (September, 1976), p. 42.

cedure should be submitted to the board for consideration at an executive session. A list of five to ten objectives would be reasonable each year.

Second, the superintendent develops a plan of action on how he or she will carry out these objectives. Such a plan to improve communications with the school board might include sending the board members a weekly newsletter outlining current issues and problems facing the district. This would help board members answer the questions of parents, students, employees, and other citizens as they are encountered without first contacting the superintendent, a procedure which would help board members to demonstrate to their constituents that they are "on top" of problems. This plan of action is normally presented to the school board along with the objectives.

Third, the superintendent prepares an interim report to the board, which is usually made approximately half way through the school year, on progress in meeting the approved objectives. At this time revisions and/or new objectives and action plans can be developed.

Finally, the superintendent prepares a self-evaluation report on how effectively he or she has met objectives, and submits supportive documentation to the school board. The board is responsible for assessing the results and will begin to prepare a written evaluation of the superintendent's performance in meeting the objectives along with suggestions on how to improve performance. The type of objectives that should be developed by the superintendent for the next year will also be prepared by the board.

If the superintendent's performance is unacceptable, the school board should include in the evaluation report a specific list of deficiencies, a time limit on when improvement is to be expected, and suggestions on how to improve performance. The board of education, of course, always has the option of not renewing the superintendent's contract, but the above due process procedure is a humane way of handling deficiencies in performance. This due process is also mandatory if the superintendent's lack of performance is such that the board may need to eventually terminate employment.

SUMMARY

No position within the educational profession has received more attention in the news media over the past decade than the superintendency. Declining enrollments, teacher layoffs, dwindling financial resources, labor strikes, and failing pupil achievement test scores constitute some of the major problems facing contemporary public schools. The superintendent of schools is often the tangible target for criticism as a school district deals with these problems.

The quality of relationship that exists between a board of education and the superintendent will directly affect the quality of education received by the children and youth in the district's schools. The school board has three responsibilities to the superintendency that form the basis of an effective working relationship between them: selecting and hiring a superintendent, creating a compensation package for the superintendent, and establishing an evaluation process for measuring the superintendent's performance.

There are nine steps which, if followed by a school board, should result in the selection of a superintendent who has a reasonable probability of being successful in a given school district:

1. Appoint a selection committee
2. Establish a budget for the selection process
3. Establish a calendar for the selection process
4. Identify qualifications for the superintendency and a selection criteria
5. Develop a recruitment brochure and application form
6. Advertise the position vacancy
7. Screen applicants
8. Interview candidates
9. Hire the best candidate

Compensation constitutes more than salary and includes multiple types of fringe benefits. The compensation package created by the school board for the superintendent should be suitable to the school district and community. One method of ensuring suitability is for the school board to gather data on the compensation packages offered by neighboring school boards to their respective superintendents. In addition, the compensation packages offered to local hospital administrators and the chief executives of municipal governments are also useful comparative data.

It is a common practice in many districts to offer the superintendent multiple types of insurance in addition to the use of a district-owned automobile and an expense account in certain medium to large size school districts. Many districts also pay the moving expenses for a newly-hired superintendent living outside the immediate region where the district is located. Paying the membership dues to professional associations for the superintendent and paying the expenses of the superintendent as he attends conferences, conventions, and workshops are also common fringe benefits.

It is important for the board of education to state the components of the superintendent's compensation package in the form of a written contract. Multiple year contracts are appropriate and should also include provisions setting forth the scope of the superintendent's authority and responsibility, a performance evaluation procedure, due process procedure, and a procedure to renegotiate the contract.

The demise of many superintendents stems from a lack of sophisticated communication and organizational skills, which leaves them unable to work effectively with school boards, the staff, and the community. Many superintendents fail to recognize the imminence of their demise. A formal evaluation of the superintendent's performance by his or her respective school board would provide the superintendent with the opportunity to grow professionally which, in turn, would help the progress of the school system.

There are four steps in the evaluation process: (1) The superintendent prepares a list of objectives; (2) The superintendent develops a plan of action on how he or she will carry out the objectives; (3) the superintendent prepares an interim report on progress in meeting the objectives; and (4) the superintendent prepares a self-evaluation report on how effectively objectives have been met.

If the superintendent's performance is unacceptable, the school board should include in their written assessment of the superintendent's performance a specific list of deficiencies, a time limit on when improvement is expected, and suggestions on how to improve performance.

IMPLICATIONS FOR SCHOOL
BOARD MEMBERS

There are three implications for school board members that emerge from this presentation concerning the relationship of the school board to the superintendent of schools.

First, school board members must recognize the importance of establishing an evaluation procedure for assessing the performance of the superintendent. Such a procedure could become an opportunity for the superintendent to grow professionally and, if this helps the superintendent to become successful, it will ultimately help the school district to progress. School board members should communicate with board members from other districts about the evaluation process and attempt to create a procedure which incorporates the best features of each plan.

Second, school board members must be careful not to overcompensate or undercompensate the superintendent of schools. The former situation will create dissatisfaction among other district employees and the community; the latter situation may result in the departure of a successful superintendent and will make that district's superintendency unattractive to quality professionals.

Third, when necessary, school board members must create a selection process to hire a superintendent that ensures participation by representatives of the school community. In addition, the process must ensure that the best possible individuals are made aware of the vacancy and have an opportunity to become a candidate.

APPENDIX A
MODEL RECRUITMENT BROCHURES
FOR THE POSITION OF
SUPERINTENDENT OF SCHOOLS

POSITION AVAILABLE
SUPERINTENDENT OF SCHOOLS
GOODVILLE SCHOOL DISTRICT

An Equal Opportunity and
Affirmative Action Employer

ANNOUNCEMENT OF VACANCY

The Board of Education of Goodville School District is seeking a superintendent of schools.

The salary of the superintendent selected will be determined by his or her professional preparation and by his or her successful experience in educational administration, as well as by other qualifications.

Professional assistance for the initial screening of applicants has been acquired. It is a special consultant committee consisting of:

—A superintendent from a neighboring school district
—Dean, School of Education, Goodville University

All letters of application, nominations, inquiries, credentials, and copies of legal proof of administrative qualifications should be mailed to the President of the Goodville School Board.

To receive consideration, applicants must do the following by January 1:

1. Submit a formal letter of application indicating a desire to be a candidate for the position.
2. Send up-to-date confidential credentials from your University, up-to-date resumé, and a listing of your educational accomplishments by title.
3. Legal proof or other evidence showing qualification to be a superintendent.

THE PERSON SOUGHT

The Board of Education of the Goodville School District and the community it serves are committed to the continuing development of quality schools. They are seeking a person who has had successful administrative experience as a superintendent, or in a central office position with comparable responsibilities. The superintendent they are seeking should have a thorough understanding of public school education; a concern for the welfare and motivation of students is of prime importance. By experience, knowledge, and stature, the successful candidate must reflect credit upon him- or herself and the district he or she serves.

The superintendent selected must be skilled in providing educational leadership, and must be a goals-oriented educator with proven success in the continuing development of teamwork among the administrative/teaching staff, board of education, and community.

Although no candidate can be expected to meet all qualifications fully, preference will be given to candidates with capabilities and/or potential as follows:

> —Successful experience in financial management, budgeting, and fiscal responsibility, with the ability to evaluate the financial status of the district and establish a management plan based on projected future revenues and curriculum programs.
>
> —In the area of human relations, the ability to work with the public, students, and staff, thus leading to good school personnel management. This process should also include evaluation of and in-service training for staff.
>
> —An "educational manager" who delegates responsibility, yet maintains accountability through the management-team concept.
>
> —Ability to exercise leadership and decision making in selection and implementation of educational priorities—a person with a realistic and responsible educational philosophy.
>
> —The ability to objectively select, evaluate, and assign staff.
>
> —Willingness to help formulate, review, and effectively carry out board policies; and to communicate and relate openly and honestly with the board of education, keeping members informed on issues, proposals, and developments within the district.
>
> —Ability to maintain desired student behavioral patterns.
>
> —Successful administrative experience in a comparable district.
>
> —A strong academic background in and a constant evaluator and planner of proper curriculum and programs who constantly keeps in view the present and future financial status of the district.
>
> —Skillful educational leadership in the development of long- and short-range district goals and objectives.

THE COMMUNITY

The Goodville School District is currently serving the educational needs of nearly 22,000 residents in a geographic area of great growth potential. It covers 90 square miles—one of the largest school districts in the state.

The district is highly diverse and is rich in cultural background and lifestyles. Approximately 25 percent of our residents live in a rural setting, with the remaining 75 percent located in suburban communities. Our district is enriched by a broad range of ethnic and racial compositions.

Located just 15 miles south of a major metropolitan area, many of our residents can conveniently commute to and from the city to work.

Local employment continues to be enhanced with the growth of many industrial parks.

As a microcosm of lifestyles and cultures, the school district encourages unique opportunities in community living and education.

It is a district of parks, churches, schools, shopping centers, and excellent recreational facilities. We are served by two local newspapers, in addition to a large daily newspaper and a local radio station. Goodville State University is located in our district, and many other colleges and universities are within driving distance.

THE SCHOOLS

The Goodville School District enrolls approximately 5,000 pupils in K-12. Additionally, the district offers services for preschool, special education, and adult education programs. Currently there are four K-5 elementary schools; one middle school, 6-8; and one high school fully accredited and recognized. The school system is supported by approximately 275 Certified Staff and 100 support personnel.

Concern and support for the teaching of basic skills has been equally recognized by the school board and administrative staff. In addition to basic skills, however, many innovative services and programs are provided to teachers, parents, and students. An alternative education program for secondary students is recognized as the finest in the county. Additionally, great steps have been made toward identification of pupils' educative styles and the proper mode of instruction to enhance these styles.

Extracurricular activities have always been a vital part of the school curriculum. The district prides itself on its athletic programs and its band and orchestra activities for both boys and girls.

PHILOSOPHY OF THE BOARD OF EDUCATION

Policy-making Body

The Board of Education is primarily a policy-making body and shall maintain an organization to operate the schools efficiently with the funds available; shall constantly strive to improve all phases of the school system; and shall keep the public well informed of its problems.

Education of the Child

The Board believes that the education of each child in the district is the heart of the entire school operation and that administration, business management, building construction, and all other services should be appraised in terms of their contributions to the progress of instruction. It shall be the goal of the Board to offer each child the opportunity to develop his or her potentialities to the maximum. It shall be the intention of the Board of Education to provide for equality of educational opportunity for all children regardless of race, color, creed, or national origin.

THE STAFF

Administration:	1	Superintendent
	2	Assistant Superintendents
	6	Principals
	3	Assistant Principals
	1	Business Manager/Treasurer
Staff:	243	Classroom Teachers
	7	Counselors
	6	Library/AV
	5	Special Education Classrooms
	4	Nurses
	5	Learning Disabilities' Classrooms
	5	Speech Correctionists
	20	Paraprofessionals
	35	Secretarial/Clerical Positions
	45	Custodial/Maintenance Positions
Student Composition:	500	Black, Non-Hispanic
	120	Hispanic
	30	Asian or Pacific Islander
	2	American Indian or Alaskan Native
	4,348	White, Non-Hispanic
	5,000	Total Enrollment

FINANCIAL DATA

Assessed Value	$235,000,000.00
TAX RATE	$4.50
Bonded Indebtedness	$4,000,000.00
BUDGET EXPENDITURES	$15,000,000.00

APPENDIX B

APPLICATION FOR THE POSITION OF SUPERINTENDENT OF SCHOOLS
GOODVILLE SCHOOL DISTRICT

Date _____

I. Personal Information:

Name _____
          Last   First   Middle

Date of birth _____ Age _____

Social Security Number _____

Present address _____ Phone _____
          Street   City   State   Zip

General condition of health _____

Are you willing to take a physical exam? _____

Community Activities and Honors _____

_____

II. Professional Information:

List Administrator Certificates held: _____

_____

Membership in professional organizations _____

_____

List your professional achievements, awards, and honors _____

_____

_____

III. Teaching and/or administrative experience:

List experience in chronological order (starting with first position held), and account for each school year since you began your professional career.

No. Yrs. Exp.	Inclusive Dates From	To	Name of School District	Number of Pupils in District	Location City or County	State	Position	Annual Salary

In your present position list the number of people responsible to you:

_____

Indicate the annual budget for the school district in which you are currently employed: _____

List the major accomplishments you have achieved in your present position:

_____

_____

_____

IV. Educational Information:
Total Number of Hours to Date: _____ Undergraduate _____ Graduate _____
Major _____ Number of Major Hrs. _____ Minor _____
Number of Minor Hrs. _____

	Name of Instit. Attended	State	Dates Attended From To	Time in Yrs. and Fractions of Yrs.	Graduation Date	Degree	Subjects Major	Minor
A. College or Univ.								
B. Graduate Work								
C. Additional Education								

V. Professional References:
Location of confidential placement file _____

It is the responsibility of the applicant to have his/her placement file and college/university transcripts sent to the school district.

Please list three people who have first-hand knowledge of your work performance. Have these individuals send a letter of reference to the President of the School Board. One of the three reference letters must be from your current or last immediate supervisor.

Name	Official Position	Present Address

Use the back of the application to provide additional information to the school board about your qualifications for the superintendency.

Signature: _____

SELECTED BIBLIOGRAPHY

AMERICAN ASSOCIATION OF SCHOOL ADMINISTRATORS and NATIONAL SCHOOL BOARDS ASSOCIATION, *Compensating the Superintendent.* Arlington, Virginia: The Association, 1980.

EISENBERGER, KATHERINE E., "How Much Should You Involve Your Community in Picking Your Next Superintendent?" *The American School Board Journal,* 162, No. 11 (November, 1975), pp. 33–34, 64.

FOWLER, CHARLES W., "How to Let (and Help) Your Superintendent be a SUPERINTENDENT." *The American School Board Journal,* 162, No. 9 (September, 1975), pp. 19–22.

FOWLER, CHARLES W., "Twelve Earmarks of a SUPERintendent." *The American School Board Journal,* 162, No. 9 (September, 1975), pp. 19–22.

FULTZ, DAVID A., "Eight Ways Superintendents Lose Their Jobs." *The American School Board Journal,* 163, No. 9 (September, 1976), pp. 42, 51.

HELLER, MEL, "Subjectivity Beats Objectivity Every Time in Picking a Superintendent." *The American School Board Journal,* 162, No. 10 (November, 1975), pp. 32–33.

JOHNSON, CARROLL F., "How to Select a Superintendent." *The American School Board Journal,* 162, No. 11 (November, 1975), pp. 27–33.

LIEBERMAN, MYRON, "The Case Against Letting a Moonlighting Professor Pick Your Next Superintendent." *The American School Board Journal,* 165, No. 4 (April, 1978), pp. 35–36, 46.

ROELLE, ROBERT J., and ROBERT L. MONKS, "A Six-Point Plan for Evaluating Your Superintendent." *The American School Board Journal,* 165, No. 9 (September, 1978), pp. 36–37.

CHAPTER FOUR
LEGAL CONSIDERATIONS
FOR SCHOOL
BOARD MEMBERS

Those who govern our public schools are held accountable to their responsibilities through the American judicial system.

School boards have experienced an increased involvement in tort litigation over the last decade due to the fact that soverign immunity has been abrogated by many legislatures. Soverign immunity is a common law principle that evolved from the philosophical concept that "the King can do no wrong." Translated to our contemporary society, this means that the officers and employees of governmental entities cannot be held liable for tortious acts. Because school districts are governmental subdivisions of the state operating on the local level, soverign immunity is functioning in those states where the doctrine is honored. However, over twenty-eight states have taken away this cloak of immunity and the 1980's may see most of the remaining states take a similar position.

In addition, school boards are far more vulnerable today to judicial review of their decisions and policies than boards of a decade ago. Even if school board members act in good faith and with reasonable deliberation, they may find themselves defending their decisions in court. Boards of education function under the law and may safely assume that state and federal courts and agencies will hold them accountable within the limits of their respective jurisdiction.

It is therefore imperative that school board members have a rudimentary understanding of the American judicial system and are capable of formulating policies that are legally defensible and that protect board members and school district employees from those damages which may arise out of tort litigation. In order to more fully understand this responsibility, a detailed explanation of the American judicial system follows along with a discussion of tort liability.

THE AMERICAN JUDICIAL SYSTEM

According to anthropological research every society known to have existed had some system of laws governing its members. Law in this context is a set of principles that have evolved because of the problems resulting from people living together. In fact, the very concept of society carries with it the notion of law and order because people would be incapable of interaction without guidelines governing their actions.

Much of the law in the United States can be traced back to Ecclesiastical Law established in the English courts of the fifteenth century. Although law existed in England for many centuries prior to this date, it was the time when systematic records of court decisions became available.

There are two systems of law that need to be mentioned here for the sake of clarification. The civil law system is descended from Roman law and attempts to establish all laws in the form of statutes enacted by a legislative body. These laws are usually referred to as a codex. Perhaps the most famous example of a civil law system was the French Napoleonic Code. Under Napoleon's direction, a group of legal scholars organized all the laws of France incorporating the avant-garde ideal of the French Revolution that "all men were equal before the law." Most of the continental European and South American countries along with Spain, Mexico, and in the U.S., Louisiana, have adopted this civil law approach.

The common law system was and still is the basic approach used in England. It was adopted in theory by most of the states in our country. Under this system the decisions rendered by a court become a guide or precedent to be followed by the court in dealing with future cases.

A strict civil law system will result in numerous statutes because all human situations have a potential for exceptionality. Courts, therefore, find themselves interpreting not only numerous but also technically construed statutes. However, the principles established as precedents through a common law approach are easily adapted to many factual situations.

As was previously mentioned, most states follow a common law approach while federal law is basically derived from statutes enacted by the United States Congress.

However, when problems arise in society that cannot be resolved through common law principles, legislatures create statutes to deal with these situations. Laws that delineate and define crimes and their respective punishment are called criminal statutes and are found in all of our states.

Consequently, the system of law in the United States is a mixed system using both civil and common law principles.

Sources of Law

There are three primary sources of law that form the foundation of the American Judicial System: constitutions, statutes, and case law.

Constitutions are bodies of precepts that provide the framework within which government carries out its duties. The federal and state constitutions contain provisions which secure the personal, property, and political rights of the individual citizen.

School boards are continually confronted with constitutional issues, many of which have resulted in judicial review. Some of these major issues have dealt with compulsory education, student vaccinations, academic freedom, the rights of students, censorship of library books, student newspapers, praying in school, public aid to parochial schools, teacher certification, teacher tenure, confidentiality of student records, corporal punishment, student and faculty dress codes, equal employment opportunities for women and minorities, desegregation, and methods of financing education. It behooves school board members, therefore, to require the superintendent of schools and their school attorney to continually provide them with information about court decisions which affect school board policy construction. Ignorance of the law has never been accepted as an excuse for violating constitutional rights.

Principles safeguarding the constitutional rights of students, parents, teachers, administrators, and staff members have been incorporated into the preceding and following chapters as they treat the various aspects of school district governance.

Statutes are the enactments of legislative bodies more commonly called laws. The word statute is derived from the Latin term "statutum," which is translated, "It is decided." Thus, either Congress or a state legislature decides that our country or state needs clarification about an issue by enacting a new law or by changing an old one.

Statutes may be reviewed by the courts to determine if they are in violation of the precepts of state and federal constitutions. The presumption is that the enactments of legislative bodies are constitutional and the burden of proof is on the plaintiff. Thus, if a state legislature passes a law requiring boards of education to provide free textbooks to parochial school children from the general revenue of the school district generated through the property tax, a citizen may ask the state supreme court to consider the constitutionality of this law because of a provision in the state constitution calling for the separation of church and state. The burden of proof is on the individual citizen or group of citizens to provide a legal argument through their attorney setting forth the reasons why such a law is unconstitutional.

It is important to keep in mind that the enactments of a state legislature may not be in violation of state constitutional provisions nor the provisions of the Federal Constitution, in which case the review would be made by the United States Court of Appeals or Supreme Court. Laws enacted by the United States Congress, on the other hand, supersede the provisions of state constitutions and, therefore, are only subject to review in federal courts with respect to the Federal Constitution.

The public schools in the United States are governed by state statutes. School operations, therefore, must be in compliance with state statutes, and it is the responsibility of the school board to establish written policies that ensure this compliance. In this context the policies of the board of education must not be in conflict with state statutes and, of course, boards may not create a policy that conflicts with the acts of Congress or the provisions of either the federal or state constitutions. Thus, if a school board created a policy prohibiting handicapped children in their school district from attending school with other children, this policy would be in violation of the Federal Public Law 94-142, probably the due process guaranteed by the Fourteenth Amendment to the Federal Constitution, and maybe a state constitution stipulating that a free education must be provided for all children.

The final source of law is common law, more properly called case law because it eminates from the courts rather than from legislative bodies. Common law originated in England and the term "common" designated a custom from one part of the country that became common practice throughout England.

In the American judicial system past court decisions are considered to be binding on subsequent cases if they have similar factual situations. This is the doctrine of precedent referred to in legal terminology as the rule of "stave decisis," which comes from the Latin language and means, "Let the decision stand." Lower courts usually adhere to the precedent (rule of law) established by higher courts in the same jurisdiction. The United States Supreme Court and state supreme courts can reverse their own previous decisions and thereby change the rule of law. Thus, a state circuit court may apply a rule of law established by a state supreme court as to what constitutes proper teacher supervision of children at recess in a case alleging negligence which resulted in injury to a child. In a later case the supreme court may redefine proper supervision and thus change the rule of law.

Major Divisions of Law

Law may be divided into two major categories, civil law and criminal law. This distinction arises out of the rights that are protected under law. Civil law attempts to protect those rights that exist between individuals, between corporations, or between an individual and a corporation. It is concerned with resolving disputes between these entities. The state is usually not a party to the dispute but, through the court system and the judge, acts as an impartial arbitrator.

There are many subdivisions of civil law that are familiar to most people and include the following fields: contracts, real estate, divorce, wills and estates, corporations, and torts. Some civil cases are normally tried before a jury such as those involving contracts and torts; others, such as a suit in equity, are tried only before the court. Of course, a jury trial may always be waived by the defendant.

In this regard, a dispute may arise between the superintendent of schools and the board of education over the terms of the superintendent's contract. A superintendent may allege that a due process clause in his or her contract was not followed in his or her dismissal by the board of education. Because the school district is a state agency and because the dispute involves contract law, the lawsuit would be filed by the superintendent's attorney in the state circuit court. The plaintiff is the superintendent of schools and the defendant is the corporate entity, the school board. This is, of course, a civil law case and the board of education may waive a jury trial and have the case heard just before the judge, who will render a decision and award damages if the due process clause was violated. If the case was tried in equity, the court would order the board of education to go back and follow the provisions of the due process clause in the superintendent's contract.

Criminal law attempts to protect the rights of society against the individual. The act of violating one of these societal rights is called a crime. The rights of society are formally protected through statutes enacted by Congress and state legislatures that prohibit the doing of an act and which, in many instances, impose a certain penalty for committing the prohibited act. The victim in a crime may be an individual person or a corporate entity such as a school district.

Therefore, an elementary school building may be broken into at night by a person who steals a typewriter from the principal's office and a video tape recorder used for classroom instruction. In this case a felony was committed against a corporate entity, the school district, because expensive equipment was stolen through illegal entry into the school building. A minor offense is, of course, called a misdemeanor. Minor vandalism to a school building, such as deliberately breaking a window, is an example of a misdemeanor and is usually punishable by the court imposing a fine against the individual. A felony, on the other hand, is usually punishable by imprisonment in a penitentiary.

It is also important to understand that certain offenses may or may not be serious, depending upon the circumstances under which they are committed. This is commonly referred to as a graded felony. A school bus driver who is intoxicated may be guilty of a serious offense if he is involved in an accident when the bus is filled with children and in which a number of children are injured.

When a person is arrested and charged with committing a crime, it is the federal or state government, depending on the offense, that prosecutes the individual. All costs are borne by the government. This is, of course, in direct contrast to civil law cases in which the cost is borne by the individuals or corporations involved in the dispute. It is typical in civil law cases, however, for the party against whom a judgement is made to also pay court costs.

It is worth emphasizing this fundamental difference between civil and criminal law. In criminal cases, it is the obligation of the government to bring the alleged criminal to trial. In civil law, a case will come to court only if the potential plaintiff decides to initiate the suit. The civil rights of individuals and corporations are protected only when someone is willing to bear the cost and inconvenience of initiating a lawsuit. At times this will be extremely expensive, as in the Bakke case, which eventuated in the United States Supreme Court. A civil law case may run into the hundreds of thousands of dollars before the dispute is set to rest.

In this discussion of civil and criminal law, a final point must be made to complete the treatment. A civil and criminal wrong can exist at the same time. In the above-mentioned case of the school bus driver who caused an accident because of being intoxicated, the state may prosecute for drunken driving and the parents of the injured children may sue the school district for damages, because the bus driver was not properly supervised and an accident resulted.

The Role of the Judiciary in American Government

The judiciary is, of course, one of the three separate but equal branches of our American governmental system. Because laws must be made, interpreted, and enforced, our local, state, and federal governments are each divided into the following three branches of jurisdiction:

The *Legislative Branch*—composed of Congress on the federal level, General Assemblies on the state level, and City Councils on the municipal level. These legislative bodies make the laws.

The *Judicial Branch*—composed of federal, state, and municipal courts. These judicial bodies interpret the laws.

The *Executive Branch*—composed of the President, governors, and mayors, along with their respective law enforcement agencies (F.B.I., Highway Patrol, local police). These executives enforce the laws.

Each of these three branches acts as a check and balance against the other branches. Examples of this monitoring system are numerous. Among the most obvious are:

1. If the legislature enacts laws beyond the limits permitted by the constitution, the courts have the power to declare the law unconstitutional.
2. The President, governors, and mayors usually have the right to veto enactments of Congress and their respective legislatures.
3. The President, governors, and judges may be impeached by the legislative branch.

Function and Powers of the Judiciary

The courts in the United States perform two essential functions. First, the court is required to settle disputes placed before it in a suit by applying laws or principles of law to the material facts set forth in the case. The court is obliged to initially apply statutory or constitutional provisions. In the absence of such statutes and/or constitutional provisions, the court will rely for direction on the common law principles of precedent.

When the court is applying statutes to the facts in a case, the court is actually interpreting the statutes. In the process of applying statutes, it is the duty of the court to determine legislative intent by assuming that the words of the statute are conveying this intent through their ordinary and well understood meaning. It is also assumed, therefore, that the legislature incorporated each word of a statute by design. This is of great significance to boards of education, because they may use this assumption as a guideline when consulting state statutes concerning such issues as teacher tenure, reduction in force, and collective bargaining.

The second essential function performed by courts is determining the constitutionality of legislation. In performing this function, the courts must presume that the acts of a legislative body are constitutional and the burden of proof must rest upon the person, group of people, or corporation maintaining the contrary.

In determining constitutionality, the intent of the legislature in enacting the statute is of primary consideration. Thus, the courts will review the history and conditions under which the legislation was enacted. In contrast to the first function of the court in applying statutes to the facts in a case mentioned above, the literal meaning of the words used in a statute does not necessarily convey its legislative intent, and the court is in no way restricted in its deliberations to the mere consideration of a statute's wording.

The Court Structure

The federal and state constitutions provided the framework for the establishment of our court systems. These systems operate on three levels in accordance with their respective jurisdiction. On the local level, municipal courts deal with the enforcement of city ordinances and handle such problems as traffic and housing code violations.

At the state level, the primary court is generally prescribed by the various constitutions, which also grant to the state legislatures the power to provide for the specific operation of these primary courts. In addition, the state constitutions grant the legislatures the authority to create new and additional courts. Most states have four categories of courts: courts of special jurisdiction, circuit courts, courts of appeal, and supreme courts.[1]

Courts of special jurisdiction are limited in the subject matter or business which may be conducted before them. Examples of these special courts include magistrate courts, juvenile courts, probate courts, domestic relations courts, and small claims courts.

Circuit courts are ordinarily considered to be the general court of original jurisdiction. All major criminal and civil cases are tried before this court. It is also commonly referred to as the general trial court, because the majority of jury trials are held in the circuit court. This court is of particular significance to boards of education because disputes involving contracts, tenure, and tort liability will be tried in the state circuit court. In like manner, because education is a state function, the state court system rather than the federal system has jurisdiction over the resolution of most issues. A notable exception involves racially segregated school systems. Lawsuits alleging segregation will be tried in the federal court system because of previous court decisions stating that segregation violates tenets of the Fourteenth Amendment to the Federal Constitution.

---

[1] Kern Alexander, Ray Corns, and Walter McCann, *Public School Law: Cases and Materials* (St. Paul: West Publishing Co., 1969) p. 9.

Appellate courts are found in all fifty states and are commonly referred to as "supreme courts." In some states, including Missouri, New York, and California, there are intermediate courts of appeal that have jurisdiction to hear and terminate certain types of cases on appeal from the circuit court, while other cases may be further appealed to the state's supreme court. In all appellate courts there is no trial. Rather, briefs are prepared and submitted to the court and both sides are given the opportunity to orally argue in favor of their respective position. The appellant is, of course, the appealing party who sets forth what he or she believes the trial court did or failed to do which prejudiced his or her rights in the circuit court trial. The other party is the respondent, who attempts to uphold the decisions and actions of the trial court. The decision of the appellate court is usually referred to as an opinion, which is also published. The opinion states whether or not the trial court erred and sets forth the law which supports the appellate court decision.

At the federal level, the United States Constitution provides for the establishment of a supreme court and gives Congress the authority to create inferior courts.[2] This power has been exercised by Congress with the resulting network of special jurisdiction courts, district courts, and the United States Court of Appeals. The federal courts of special jurisdiction, like the state courts of special jurisdiction, are limited by the subject matter or business which may be conducted before them. A few of these courts with high recognition include: Tax Court, Court of Claims, Bankruptcy Court, Court of Custom and Patent Appeals.

The Federal District Courts, like the State Circuit Courts, are general courts of original jurisdiction. It is also the trial court that hears litigation between citizens from two or more states and litigation involving federal civil or criminal statutes and/or the Federal Constitution. This court is presided over by one judge but in cases involving an injunction against the enforcement of a state or federal statute, a three-judge court is convened.

The decisions of a Federal District Court may be appealed to the United States Court of Appeals or, in certain cases, directly to the United States Supreme Court. There are eleven federal judicial circuits, each one containing a Court of Appeals. The Eighth Circuit United States Court of Appeals, for example, will hear appeals from United States District Court decisions in the states of North Dakota, South Dakota, Arkansas, Minnesota, Iowa, Nebraska, and Missouri.

The United States Supreme Court is the highest court in the country, beyond which there is no appeal. The Supreme Court hears cases brought before it by appeal, by writ of certiorari, or by original jurisdiction. The Supreme Court exercises its original jurisdiction by interpreting the constitutionality of federal legislation; this court exercises its appeals jurisdiction by reviewing the decisions of a United States District or United States Appeals Court. However, most cases that involve issues incumbent upon education are taken to the Supreme Court by writ of certiorari. This means that the Supreme Court is asked to take jurisdiction over a case because the federal constitutionality of a state or federal statute is questioned,

[2] Alexander, Corns, and McCann, *Public School Law,* p. 10.

or when any title, right, privilege, or immunity is alleged under the Federal Constitution. Thus, cases involving a charge of racial segregation or racial bias in hiring are litigation which may eventuate before the United States Supreme Court.

Courts of Equity

Courts of Equity have their origins in English medieval history. The Lord Chancellor of England traditionally sat as a judge when dealing with certain kinds of problems which were not ordinarily handled by the English courts. The concept was that the Lord Chancellor safeguarded the King's conscience and provided the people with relief on an equitable basis.

In our American judicial system, this distinction is still preserved, and certain types of problems that were decided in equity by the Lord Chancellor are decided in equity by the American courts. The major difference lies in the fact that the same courts handle both law and equity issues.

Certain issues are traditionally tried in equity. The most familiar to boards of education are injunctions. Because teachers are state employees, a school board may go to a state circuit court to ask for an injunction directing a group of teachers to leave the picket lines and return to the classroom. Similarly, a Federal District Court may issue an injunction against the school board of a particular school district to begin a busing program for the purpose of ending segregation. Obviously, if the parties named in an injunction fail to obey the court order, they are in contempt of court and may be punished by a fine or by being jailed.

There are other issues, however, which can be tried in equity or in law depending on the remedy sought by the plaintiff. If a board of education entered into a contract with a construction company to remodel an existing school building and if this firm failed to carry out the project, the school board may sue the construction company in law for specific performance whereby the circuit court would levy damages to be paid to the school district by the contractor.

Trial by Jury

The practice of having a trial to settle disputes has a colorful history dating back three to four hundred years, when trial by ordeal and trial by battle were common occurrences in England. Trial by jury gradually developed in the English courts but has always been a constitutional right in the United States.

Unless the right to a jury trial is waived, every citizen is entitled to have a jury in all criminal or civil cases. Because most lawsuits involve questions of fact, a board of education must be sensitive to preserving a record of their deliberations, which may serve as evidence in a lawsuit. This is of particular significance in tort liability cases, which will be discussed later. It is sufficient to state that lawsuits against a school district will usually be heard by a jury.

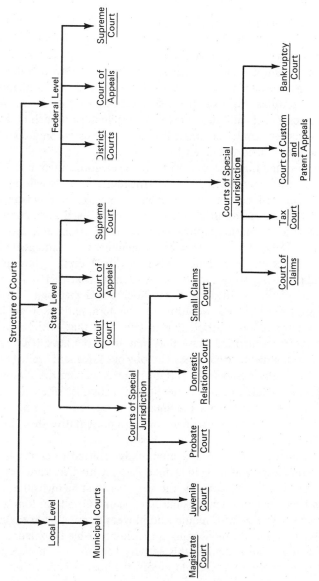

FIGURE 4-1

TORT LIABILITY AND BOARDS
OF EDUCATION

The term tort is a French derivation and literally means "twisted." As used in law, it refers to a civil wrong, other than a breach of contract, committed against a person or a person's property as distinguished from a crime that is a wrong committed against the state.[3] Common law constitutes the substantive law of a tort. However, state legislatures have broadened or narrowed these common law principles through the enactment of statutes. For example, many states have passed a wrongful death statute which imposes civil liabilities in favor of certain persons including the surviving spouse and children. Under common law, an individual wrongfully causing the death of another person incurred no civil liability.

Torts are so varied that it is very difficult to categorize them but, for the sake of clarification in this treatment, three classifications of torts will be elucidated. Intentional torts are actions that interfere with a person or a person's property. Even though it does not necessarily follow, most intentional torts are also crimes. Assault, battery, and defamation are the most common forms associated with personal interference. Defamation occurs when something is communicated either by word of mouth (slander) or in writing that is false (libel), bringing hatred or ridicule on a person and producing some type of harm to the person. Defamation of character is an area of potential litigation for school board members, particularly in relation to personnel decisions resulting in the termination of an individual's employment with the school district. It is not the fact that a school board terminates an employee for a justified cause that may lead to a lawsuit but rather how that decision is communicated to others. The obvious safeguard against any form of defamation is for board members to refrain from discussing the reasons for their personnel decisions outside of a board meeting with anyone. When an official statement is appropriate or when such a statement is requested by the news media in a highly publicized case, the superintendent or his representative should be responsible for the communication.

A second classification of torts is commonly referred to as absolute liability. An individual who keeps a wild animal in a cage in his backyard is liable if the animal escapes and injures someone by the very fact that he owns the wild animal. A more relevant example for school boards concerns ultrahazardous activities. A school district administrator who requires employees to mix highly toxic chemicals that are used for pest control or cleaning is absolutely liable if someone sustains an injury. If that administrator requires this activity because it is an accepted school district practice, the injured party could enjoin the board of education in a lawsuit because the board members neglected to formulate a policy on the use of toxic chemicals by employees.

This example overlaps with the third category of torts, negligence. This type

---

[3]Edward C. Bolmeier, *The School in the Legal Structure* (Cincinnati: The W. H. Anderson Company, 1968), p. 110.

of tort involves conduct falling below an established standard that results in an injury to another person or persons. The board of education has a duty and responsibility to govern the school district in such a manner that members of minority groups have an equal opportunity to become candidates for position vacancies. Their responsibility is fulfilled if the school board creates an affirmative action program so that the rights of protected groups are not violated. Even though a charge of discrimination would probably be filed with the Equal Employment Opportunity Commission, there is also the possibility of a civil lawsuit being filed against board members by a minority applicant who was denied an interview which, in turn, meant the loss of a job opportunity.

A more common situation involves bodily injury cases. If a student is injured as a consequence of playing on gymnastic equipment, the physical education teacher might be sued for being negligent in properly supervising and instructing the student on how to use the equipment. The principal might be sued for neglecting to properly evaluate and remove a teacher who does a poor job of supervising children. The superintendent might be brought into the lawsuit because he or she neglected to remove a principal who inadequately supervises teachers. The board of education might be sued because the members neglected as a corporate body to monitor the superintendent in his or her responsibility to evaluate the performance of principals. This path then follows the chain-of-command in a school district and ensures that the responsible party or parties will be identified by the court. There is a tendency to take this shotgun approach in some types of civil lawsuits, particularly in torts, when identifying defendants in a litigation.

In a civil lawsuit resulting in a judgement favoring the plaintiff, the defendant will usually be required to pay actual damages, which is the amount of money that the injury cost. A broken arm will result in physician, hospital, and allied expenses that could total thousands of dollars. The loss of a job opportunity, on the other hand, has a potential for costing the school district hundreds of thousands of dollars.

If it can be demonstrated in court that a defendant or group of defendants deliberately caused an injury, punitive damages may also be levied. This dollar amount is a punishment for intentionally bringing about the civil wrong. In some cases, punitive damages may equal or supersede the actual damages accessed by the court. Board members who publicly disagree with the concept of affirmative action and who tell ethnic jokes might be laying the groundwork for an allegation that the board of education deliberately neglected to establish an effective affirmative action program.

Errors and Omissions
Liability Insurance

It should be clear from this presentation that each and every member of a board of education should be protected by errors and omissions liability insurance. Sources for obtaining such coverage include school board associations and the

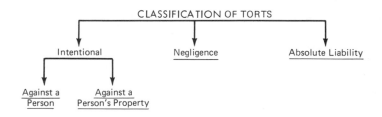

CLASSIFICATION OF TORTS

Intentional   Negligence   Absolute Liability

Against a   Against a
Person   Person's Property

FIGURE 4-2

school district's insurance carrier. Many large insurance companies provide such protection under a group policy for school board members that may be extended to cover central office administrators, principals, teachers, and any other category of employees. Finally, it should be remembered that most errors and omissions liability insurance policies do not cover punitive damages because this would amount to condoning an act that was deliberately precipitated.

THE ROLE OF THE SCHOOL BOARD ATTORNEY

Historically, the school attorney has been involved in lawsuits filed against a school district and against board members and/or school employees when such litigation arose out of their performance or alleged lack of performance in educational matters. An attorney is also usually consulted when the school district is entering into business contracts or when the school board authorizes a tax levy or bond issue election. Condemnation of property for the purpose of constructing a school building is a very complex legal process that always requires the assistance of an attorney.

The Role of an Attorney in Litigation

A common misconception about the role of the attorney in a lawsuit is that he or she will handle the litigation entirely without the involvement of board members or other school district employees. Even in litigation initiated to challenge a law, input from school board members and school administrators is necessary when a legal brief is prepared.

An attorney basically performs three functions when litigation is involved. First, an analysis will be made of the issue to determine the facts and real questions involved. Secondly, the attorney will research court cases and statutes for the purpose of deciding what is the *law.* Finally, he or she will put together a workable solution to the issue in relation to the material facts and the *law,* and this solution could involve a number of alternatives.

The Emerging Role of the School
Board Attorney

Technical competence as a lawyer is, of course, an absolute necessity for an attorney representing the school district, board members, or school employees in a lawsuit. The last ten to fifteen years, however, have ushered in a set of circumstances that require new competencies for attorneys employed by boards of education. These competencies reflect the emerging role of the school attorney as counselor on school district governance and administration.

In this new role the attorney must be an expert on government, with an understanding not only of the nuances and functions of the legislative, judicial, and executive branches of local, state, and federal government but also how these three branches impinge upon the governing of the local school district. Because school districts are state agencies operating on the local level, the policies enacted by boards of education have a legal character, and the effect of these policies on students and employees is subject to review by state courts and, in certain instances, the federal court system. A considerable amount of time, energy, and money may be conserved by school boards if they consult their attorney in the creation of school district policies.

In like manner, administrative procedures initiated by the superintendent and other school administrators in implementing the policies of the school board will be more legally defensible if they are reviewed by the school attorney. In this manner, potential areas of litigation can be minimized and administrators may be spared the unpleasant experience of being sued, which usually takes considerable time and energy away from their regular duties.

A final consideration about the school board attorney centers on the avenue of communication with the board of education. Difficulties have arisen in some school districts where the school attorney reported directly to school board members. Because the superintendent of schools is the chief executive officer of the school board, the school board attorney must operate with and through the superintendent's office. This, of course, is not an issue in those school districts that are large enough to employ an attorney as a full-time member of the central office staff. The only exception to this reporting procedure is when the board of education needs the advice and counsel of an attorney in the selection or termination of the superintendent.

ANATOMY OF A LAWSUIT[4]

Although lawsuits do not follow a set pattern, there is enough commonality in civil litigation to make a few general observations.

[4]Ronald W. Rebore, *Personnel Administration in Education: A Management Approach* (Englewood Cliffs, N.J.: Prentice-Hall, 1982), p. 324.

The plaintiff files a petition with the appropriate court of jurisdiction, setting forth the cause of action, which is the allegation. A summons is then delivered by the court to the defendant, who is required to appear in court her- or himself or through an attorney on a given date for the purpose of answering or pleading the petition.

The next step involves clarifying the allegation and material facts that support it. This may be accomplished by the taking of depositions, a formal procedure in which the parties to the lawsuit answer questions posed by the respective attorneys. Written queries may also be required by the attorneys in lieu of or in addition to the taking of depositions.

A motion may then be filed to dismiss the petition if the material facts do not appear to support the allegation. If the judge does not dismiss the petition, a trial date will be placed on the court's docket. In civil cases involving such issues as tenure, a business contract, or a tort, the defendant usually has the option of a jury trial or of having the judge render the decision.

If the decision is rendered in favor of the plaintiff, a remedy is assessed against the defendant that may involve a number of options, depending on the nature of the case. In a tenure case, the plaintiff may be reinstated to his or her teaching position with the school district. In a tort liability case, the remedy will usually be the paying of damages.

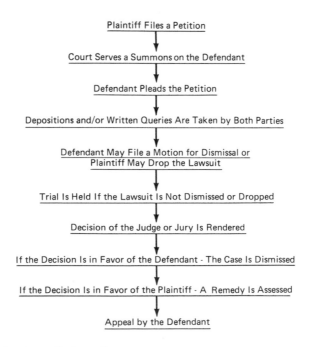

FIGURE 4-3 Anatomy of a Lawsuit

There are certain circumstances under which the decision in a trial may be appealed to a higher court for review. The two generalized circumstances involve either a question of law or the impartiality of the trial proceedings.

The defendant in a civil lawsuit is determined by the nature of the petition and the material facts. In a tenure or teacher contract dispute, the board of education as a corporate body is usually the defendant because the school board approves all personnel contracts. In a tort liability case, an individual (superintendent of schools) or a group of individuals (teacher, principal, and superintendent) may be named as defendants.

SUMMARY

Boards of education have experienced an increased involvement in tort litigation over the last decade due to the fact that sovereign immunity has been abrogated by many state legislatures. In addition, school boards are far more vulnerable today to judicial review of their decisions than boards of a decade ago. It is imperative, therefore, that school board members have a rudimentary understanding of the American judicial system and are capable of formulating policies which are legally defensible.

Anthropological research has shown that every society known to have existed has had some system of laws governing its members. Much of the law in the United States can be traced back to Ecclesiastical Law established in the English courts of the fifteenth century.

There are two systems of law. The first is called a civil law system, which attempts to establish all laws in the form of statutes enacted by a legislative body. Most of the continental European countries and South American countries along with the state of Louisiana have adopted a civil law approach.

The second is referred to as a common law system, which is the basic approach used in England, and was adopted in theory by most of the states in our country. Under this system, the decisions rendered by a court become a precedent to be followed by the court in dealing with future cases. The system of law in the United States is a mixture between civil and common law principles.

There are three primary sources of law that form the foundation of the American judicial system: constitutions, statutes, and case law. Constitutions are bodies of precepts that provide the framework within which government carries out its duties. Statutes are the enactments of legislative bodies and are more commonly called laws. As stated above, common law emanates from the decisions of courts rather than from legislative bodies.

Law may also be categorized according to particular rights being protected. Civil law attempts to protect those rights that exist between individuals, corporations, or between an individual and a corporation. Criminal law protects the rights of society against the individual.

The judiciary is, of course, one of the three separate but equal branches of our American governmental system. The courts perform two essential functions:

first, settling disputes placed before them in a lawsuit; second, determining the constitutionality of legislation.

The judicial system is composed of municipal, state, and federal courts. Most states have four categories of courts: courts of special jurisdiction, circuit courts, courts of appeal, and supreme courts. In like manner, there are four categories of federal courts: special jurisdiction courts, district courts, the United States Court of Appeals, and the United States Supreme Court.

Our American judicial system also preserves the concept of equity. The state circuit and United States district courts may handle both law and equity issues. Not only are certain cases traditionally tried in equity but also the type of remedy sought determines the posture of the court. The most familiar equity cases handled by the courts involve the issuing of injunctions.

Tort liability has become a serious consideration for boards of education over the last decade. A tort is a civil wrong committed against a person or a person's property. There are three categories of torts: intentional, absolute liability, and negligence. Negligence involves conduct falling below an established standard that results in an injury to another person or persons. That is, perhaps, the most vulnerable tort for board members, because they are responsible for governing the school district in such a manner that the rights of students and employees are safeguarded.

The last ten to fifteen years have ushered in a set of circumstances that require school board attorneys to have competencies above the technical skills necessary to handle litigation. Today, the school board attorney must also be a counselor to boards of education on school district governance and administration.

Litigation eludes a set pattern. However, there is enough commonality in civil lawsuits to allow board members to make general observations that should be helpful as they create policies to govern their school districts.

IMPLICATIONS FOR SCHOOL
BOARD MEMBERS

There are five implications for boards of education that emerge from this treatment of the American judicial system and allied issues.

First, ignorance of state and federal legislation and court decisions is no excuse for creating school district policies that are in conflict with such legislation and case law.

Second, school board members should attend workshops, seminars, and convention programs dealing with legal issues. State school board associations and the National School Boards Association have convention programs and offer other services to school boards which address the legal character of school governance.

Third, school boards should require the superintendent of schools and his or her staff to keep board members informed about relevant state and federal legislation and court decisions. The school board attorney should be of valuable assistance to the superintendent as he or she fulfills this responsibility.

Fourth, school board members must be active in promoting state and federal legislation that supports the educational goals of school districts. This is best accomplished through participation in state school board associations and through membership in the National School Boards Association.

Fifth, it is imperative that school board members be protected through errors and omissions liability insurance.

SELECTED BIBLIOGRAPHY

ALEXANDER, KERN, RAY CORNS, and WALTER McCANN, *Public School Law: Cases and Materials.* St. Paul, Minn.: West Publishing Co., 1969.

ALEXANDER, KERN, RAY CORNS, and WALTER McCANN, *1975 Supplement to Public School Law: Cases and Materials.* St. Paul, Minn.: West Publishing Co., 1975.

BOLMEIER, EDWARD C., *The School in the Legal Structure,* American School Law Series. Cincinnati: The W. H. Anderson Co., 1968.

HAZARD, WILLIAM R., *Education and the Law* (2nd ed.). New York: The Free Press, 1978.

MORRIS, ARVAL A., *The Constitution and American Education.* St. Paul, Minn.: West Publishing Co., 1974.

REZNY, ARTHUR A., *A Schoolman in the Law Library* (2nd ed.). Danville, Illinois: The Interstate Printers and Publishers, Inc., 1968.

CHAPTER FIVE
THE ROLE
OF THE SCHOOL BOARD
IN THE
DISTRICT'S COMMUNITY
RELATIONS PROGRAM

The legal structure of public education attests that the authority to govern schools is derived from the people and, therefore, ongoing communications should occur between the school board and the public.

All public and private institutions and organizations have relations with their various constituencies. Thus, a board of education has no alternative but to develop an approach on "how" the various publics that make up the school district will be addressed. The options are few but the impact of these various options can have a significant effect on how well the school district is able to reach its primary objective, educating students. Basically, the school board can choose to let its relationship with the community develop by chance or it can choose to develop a systematic, organized, and continual program.

The basic principle upon which an effective community relations program must rest is the public character of the schools. The schools are brought into existence, financed, and governed by the people. The state legislature, which is composed of the elected representatives of the people, creates school districts by and through the laws of the state; school districts receive their revenue through taxation; and school boards members are elected by the people.

Because of this basic principle, a community relations program in the public sector is viewed much differently than a public relations program in the business community. A community relations program is not a "sell job" or a "publicity program" aimed at developing an image of the district which will bring a favorable response from the community. Rather, a community relations program is an ongoing, two-way communication program between the school district and the various publics which make up the school community. This community must not be limited to just students and parents but must also include senior citizens, parochial school parents, public officials, and tax payers without children. In effect, all those who reside within the boundaries of the school district are the constituents of the school board and must be part of community relations activities.

Even from a pragmatic perspective, the effects of a good school district are invaluable to all citizens. It is sometimes stated, for example, that people without children in school have no need of the services provided by the public schools and, therefore, often vote against tax levy and/or bond issue elections. A common yet true response to such a statement is the fact that our future physicians, architects, artists, entrepreneurs, political officials, and all those others who will be providing us with vital services in the near future will be educated in our public schools. In a much more immediate way, a good school district will increase real estate values by ten percent. Ask any real estate agent for verification of this fact! From a philosophical point of view, the public schools are the vehicle by which our American culture and heritage are transmitted from generation to generation. In fact, our free republican form of government and capitalistic economy are dependent upon the quality of education received by our citizens.

Therefore, two-way communication is the foundation of an effective community relations program. All publics must be included; the various segments of the community must understand the importance of the public school; and the input of all publics must be sought by the board of education.

STEPS IN DEVELOPING A COMMUNITY RELATIONS PROGRAM

Creating a Community Relations Policy

The effective development of all programs in a school district is dependent upon the support of the school board. In fact, because it is the governing body in the district, no program has official status until it is authorized by the board of education. The traditional method by which the board mandates and sanctions programs is through the creation of policies setting the direction and scope of the programs.

There are many formats available to a school board in the development of policies, as has been addressed in chapter two. It is critical, however, that board of education policies be put in written form and made known to the public. Having appropriate written policies is not a major problem. There are many model community relations policies available from state school boards associations and from the National School Boards Association that can be used in developing individual district policies. Figure 5-1 represents a sample policy developed by the Missouri School Boards Association, which would meet the needs of most school districts.

FIGURE 5-1[1] Sample Board of Education School-Community Relations Policy

The Board recognizes that intelligent, informed public support of the school district is dependent upon full knowledge, understanding, and participation in the efforts, goals, problems, and programs of the district. The Board is also aware of its responsibility to provide the public with information and opportunities leading to participation in the establishment of programs and policies.

Therefore, the Board and the school district will strive:

—To develop intelligent citizen understanding of the school system in all aspects of its operation.

—To determine how the public feels about the school system and what it wishes the school system to accomplish.

—To develop citizen understanding of the need for adequate financial support for a quality educational program.

—To foster public understanding of the need for constructive change and solicit public advice on how to achieve educational goals.

—To earn the good will, respect, and confidence of the public with regard to school staff and services.

—To promote a genuine spirit of cooperation between the Board and community in sharing leadership for the improvement of the community.

The achievement of these goals requires that the Board and the staff, individually and collectively express positive attitudes toward the district in their daily contacts with students, parents, patrons, and one another. They must also make a systematic, honest, and continuing effort to discover what the public thinks, what patrons want to know, and to interpret the district's programs, problems, and accomplishments for the public. Finally, they must take an active interest in the community, in working toward the improvement of both the educational programs and making the community a better place in which to live.

The major problem is making the public aware of the community relations posture of the school board. This is generally accomplished not by distributing the policy statement but rather through the activities of a community relations program.

Establishing a Community Relations Administrative Position

The second step in the process of developing a community relations program is establishing an administrative central office position, usually titled Director for Community Relations. This should be a staff position reporting directly to the

[1] Missouri School Boards Association, *A Manual for Missouri School Board Members* (Columbia, Mo.: The Association, 1981), pp. F-10, F-11.

superintendent of schools. Because the superintendent is the chief executive office of the school board, it is important for the board as a group and as individuals to channel all official communications through the superintendent's office. At that point, the superintendent can inform the director for community relations about the issue to be communicated, and the director, in turn, can select the appropriate media for delivering the message to the public.

The job description of the director for community relations, therefore, should center around planning and directing the internal and external communications program for the school district. The director is the chief advisor to the superintendent on community relations matters.

The duties and responsibilities of the director for community relations include:

Making all contacts with members of the press and with television and radio stations;

Writing press releases;

Directing tax levy and bond issue election campaigns;

Creating staff development programs for district employees concerning community relations techniques;

Assessing the attitudes of the various publics about school-related issues and programs;

Coordinating the school district's photographic needs;

Writing, editing, and producing staff and community newsletters and publications;

Representing the superintendent with service and civic groups.

Qualifications for the position of director for community relations will vary with the needs of individual districts. However, many experts in the field of community relations indicate that a degree in journalism and experience in community relations with a public institution, experience in public relations in private business, or experience in journalism constitute the ideal qualifications for this position.

Most school districts with enrollments of three thousand and more students should employ a full-time director. If a district has more than ten thousand students, it will be necessary to establish a community relations department and to employ a number of assistant directors.

Very small school districts and districts faced with severe financial problems will have the same needs as other school districts for the services of someone to direct their community relations program. However, these districts will be forced to search for alternatives to the full-time director described above. These alternatives include (1) assigning community relations duties to an administrator with a communications background; (2) decreasing the teaching load of a teacher with a background in journalism, English, or communications in order to assume some community relations duties; (3) looking for someone in the community with public relations skills or a newspaper reporter to volunteer some time or be hired part time to work on community relations tasks; (4) hiring a consulting firm to handle a limited number of community relations duties.[2]

Learning about the School District Publics

A third step in developing a community relations program is collecting data about the various groups that comprise a school district. Data about the community pertinent to a community relations program include:

1. The needs and expectations of citizens in relation to the school district,
2. The formal and informal power structures in the community,
3. Immediate and long-term problems,
4. Identifying the most appropriate channels of communicating with the public,
5. Identifying groups and individuals who are friendly and unfriendly towards the school district,
6. Identifying the type and number of service and civic organizations in the community.[3]

A sociological survey of the community is the most appropriate vehicle for gathering the data suggested above. The survey should concentrate on customs and traditions, population characteristics, economic conditions, leadership in the community, political structures, social issues, and communication channels.[4]

Conducting research into these areas may involve a number of different techniques. No one technique will provide all the answers. Therefore, it is most advantageous to choose complementary approaches, which will eventuate in providing the school board with a total view of the community. Some of the most common opinion research methods are: (1) forums and conferences, (2) advisory committees, (3) telephone surveys, (4) written questionnaires, and (5) direct interviews.[5]

A final word about the indirect power structure in a community should be made here. The influence of the individuals who make up this group must not be underestimated by the board of education and school district administration. Unless these individuals are identified and dealt with, the best efforts of the board and administration are doomed to failure. Members of the indirect power structure in a community can influence political and economic decisions by reason of their financial, family, political, or labor connections. These individuals are usually intelligent people who possess genuine leadership abilities and who are members of powerful clubs and organizations. They usually develop a system of reward and punishment

[2] Don Bagin, Frank Grazian, Charles Harrison, "PR for School Board Members," *AASA Executive Handbook Series* (Arlington, Va.: American Association of School Administrators, 1976), Vol. VIII, pp. 13–14.

[3] Leslie W. Kindred, Don Bagin, Donald R. Gallagher, *The School and Community Relations* (Englewood Cliffs, N.J.: Prentice-Hall, 1976), p. 35.

[4] Ibid., p. 36.

[5] Ibid., p. 48.

as the primary vehicle for wielding their influence. For example, those who make large financial contributions to political candidates generally have an opportunity to provide input that these politicians consider before making political decisions.

Developing Techniques
for Communicating

The fourth step in developing a community relations program is identifying and initiating appropriate techniques for communicating with various publics. Each school district will find that certain techniques are more effective than others for their respective communities.

Printed materials. The central advantage of using publications is the detailed data and concepts that become available to a large number of people at a minimum cost. Like all other methods of communicating, it is essential to identify the audience to be addressed by the various publications. A publication prepared for parents might have as an objective increasing parents' knowledge of education programs or educating parents about selected school problems and issues. On the other hand, the objective of a publication aimed at the general public might be to inform citizens about the policies and practices of the school district or to thank individuals and groups for supporting the cause of public education.

A commonly used publication aimed at the general public is the district "Newsletter," which is mailed to all citizens generally on a monthly basis. Another publication which has across-the-board appeal to all publics is the "Superintendent's Annual Report," which highlights the accomplishments of the school district along with the financial condition of the district and objectives for the future. Figure 5-2 presents a listing of internal, external, and joint purpose publications commonly employed by school districts. No one district, of course, will use all of these publications.

The Press. Newspapers play a significant role in the school district's community relations program. They are widely read and provide the entire community with an ongoing account of those issues and problems facing not only public education but also specific school districts. It is imperative that the director of community relations develop the newspapers as a primary avenue through which the school district can communicate with various publics.

The key to successful news coverage is the relationship developed by the director for community relations with reporters who are assigned to your school district. Reporters have a job to perform, and they will do it with or without your help. It is obviously more productive to be of assistance to reporters, because you gain the opportunity to provide accurate information and an interpretation of the data.

Almost every school activity or event will have some newsworthy aspects. The director for community relations must keep the press informed about upcoming events, organize information about the events, and be willing to answer ques-

FIGURE 5-2[6]

INTERNAL PUBLICATIONS

—Employee Manual: To acquaint all employees with rules and regulations, district policies, etc.

—Specialized Employee Manual: To familiarize special employee groups— secretaries, bus drivers, etc.—with the requirements of their job.

—New Employee Bulletin: To help new employees adjust to their first weeks on the job.

—Handbook for Substitutes: To inform substitute teachers of the required procedures.

—Telephone Communications Bulletin: To assist secretaries and other employees in dealing with the public on the phone.

—Student Handbook: To acquaint students with school rules and regulations.

—Parent-Teacher Conference Booklet: To show teachers how to conduct a successful conference.

—Resource Center Brochure: To let faculty and staff know what materials are available for their assistance.

—Field Trip Booklet: To provide help to teachers and helping mothers on field trips.

—Board Briefs: To inform faculty and staff of actions taken by the board at its meetings.

—Pay Envelope Stuffer: To provide various informational items to employees when they receive their pay checks.

—Curriculum Idea Exchange Bulletin: To familiarize teachers with successful teaching practices used by other district teachers.

—Communications Guidebook: To inform staff members of the district's communications program and suggest how they might help.

—Article Reprints: To keep employees informed of recent news and feature articles in local news media.

EXTERNAL PUBLICATIONS

—Rumor Control Bulletin: To help quell rumors with facts. Sent to opinion leaders and key communicators.

—Welcome Leaflet: To welcome new residents into the district with school facts and registration procedures.

—Report Card Stuffer: To provide parents with information and special announcements.

---

[6]Don Bagin, Frank Grazian, Charles Harrison, "PR for School Board Members," pp. 31–33.

—Wallet-Size Calendar: To familiarize residents with important dates and vital school information.

—Recruitment Brochure: To attract high quality faculty and administrators to the district.

—Parent Handbook: To acquaint parents with important school information.

—Guidance Booklet: To suggest to parents how to help children adjust to important educational periods in their lives.

—Curriculum and Special Service Brochure: To explain to residents the various programs offered.

—Work-Study Report: To familiarize prospective employers with the vocational and career oriented programs in the high school or vocational school.

—Special Purpose Publications: To solve specific problems as they arise. This category might include a drug abuse booklet, a brochure on busing, etc.

INTERNAL AND EXTERNAL
PUBLICATIONS

—Annual Report: To acquaint the board, staff, and public with the district's efforts for the year.

—Budget and Bond Issue Publications: To gain public and staff acceptance for budgets and building programs.

—Facts and Figures Booklet: To provide in pocket-size format vital facts about the district.

tions to clarify information. News conferences are another vehicle providing reporters with an opportunity to clarify issues and problems of interest to the community.

The cardinal principle in working with the press is *honesty*. Never try to mislead or interfere with the press. Be open and available to reporters and the school district will have a better chance of receiving good and accurate news coverage.

From time to time a school district may receive radio and even television coverage. This is especially true when controversial issues are facing the school board, such as the prospect of closing schools due to decreases in pupil enrollment or when teachers are on strike. It goes without saying that those same concepts and principles pertaining to relationships with the press are applicable to all members of the news media. The director for community relations must not neglect newscasters and interviewers when establishing those relationships that will open up channels of communicating through radio and television.

In addition, the Federal Communications Commission, in licensing radio and television stations, usually requires all stations to devote some air time to public service broadcasting. If a school district does not have a well-defined process of requesting coverage of school events and requesting appearances by board members, administrators, teachers, and staff members on public service programs, then the radio and television stations may overlook your district.

Special activities. Community relations is sometimes viewed narrowly, including only utilization of printed material and news media. There are, however, many different activities which have significant benefits to a community relations program. This discussion will center on four publics and the kinds of activities that can be used with them for a community relations purpose.

First, the most important public to a school district is the student body. The education of pupils enrolled in our schools constitutes the primary reason for a school district's existence. Many programs and activities geared for student participation will enhance the instructional program and, at the same time, will act as a community relations vehicle. Student advisory committees, suggestion boxes, and student council activities are a case in point. Further, public performances by the music, drama, and forensic departments in addition to interscholastic sport activities demonstrate how well the school district has been able to develop the talents and skills of the students. Student newspapers and other student-generated publications will be avenues available to spread the word about the quality of the educational programs. Finally, alumni associations are a method of continuing student interest and support for the school district.

Second, parents are a vital source of support for a school district. Visits to the school and to classrooms, parent conferences with teachers, PTA and/or PTO organizations, room mothers, club booster organizations, and parent volunteer programs are all examples of how parents can be brought into the schools. Such participation is certain to have the beneficial effect of gaining the support of parents when a school board is faced with such issues as the financial support of public education and other problems dealing with pupil discipline.

Third, school district employees have a definite community relations role to play in terms of how they interact not only with students but also with parents, citizens, and those who have a business relationship with the district. The school district, on the other hand, must demonstrate to employees that they are key people to the district and are respected members of the staff. Internal advisory committees, recognition of accomplishments, functions, and internal publications help to get this message across to not only teachers and administrators but also to classified personnel such as cooks, custodians, and secretaries.

Fourth, community groups can provide the board of education with necessary input to help evaluate the effectiveness of a community relations program in addition to providing the district with invaluable expertise. The citizens advisory committee can be successfully employed by a school board to study such issues as school closings and attendance-area consolidation, the financial condition of the school district, and the need to upgrade the facilities. The adage that the more involved, the greater the support has been proven by experience.

Almost every activity has a community relations effect. How the administration handles a parental complaint, the appearance of the buildings, and even how the board meetings are conducted (see Appendix B) can generate negative or positive feelings about the school district.

Tax levy and bond issue campaigns. Economic conditions have caused many school districts to seek additional revenue through an increase in property taxes. Inflation and decreased federal and state revenues are the major factors that have created the need to cut back school district staff members and programs. When this retrenchment seriously affects the quality of education, often the only answer is to ask the taxpayers for more money. Tax levy election campaigns have, therefore, become commonplace, but the success rate of such efforts has been negligible.

Some school districts are also in need of building new school buildings, renovating existing facilities, and/or making other buildings energy efficient. Capital improvements are traditionally financed through issuing bonds for sale through taxpayer approval.

The director for community relations is the administrator who has the primary responsibility for coordinating tax levy and bond issue election campaigns. Major aspects of this effort that need to be addressed include: determining the proposal, establishing a campaign strategy, timing the campaign, financing the campaign, adopting a theme and slogan, establishing a speakers' bureau, absentee ballots, canvassing the school district, and election day plans.

Appendix B presents a step by step model program centered on the community relations aspects of a bond issue election. Most of the activities outlined are applicable not only to bond issue elections but to tax levy elections as well.

Evaluating the Community
Relations Program

The final step in developing a community relations program is evaluating its effectiveness. As with all school programs, there are two aspects to the evaluation process. First, an evaluation must be made, especially in the initial stages of development, concerning the organization and implementation of the program. This will provide feedback about the weaknesses and strengths of the program, which can be used by the superintendent and director for community relations in modifying or changing the program structure to more effectively accomplish its goals and objectives. The most common method of evaluating this aspect of the community relations program is through checklists and rating scales similar to the one developed by Thomas Colgate, reproduced in Figure 5-3. This instrument contains thirty-three items, each followed by a maximum point value. Various members of the staff and board members will have the broad-based understanding about the program necessary to use this type of instrument. If an individual believes that the program does not meet the item completely, a lesser value than the maximum is awarded. The total points are then applied to the graph provided with the rating scale and a judgement can then be rendered about the community relations program.

FIGURE 5-3[7]   Community Relations Evaluation Survey

Directions: Appraise your district's efforts in each of the listed criteria. Each statement is followed by a maximum point value that may be awarded if your school district meets the statement completely. A value less than maximum may be awarded according to the extent that the statement is met. Place the appraisal points in the *points credited* column at far right.

APPRAISAL STATEMENT	MAXIMUM POINT VALUES	POINTS CREDITED
1. There *is* a definite planned program of public relations.	5.5	_____
2. Purposes of our public relations program have been discussed and approved by all members of the school board, administration, and faculty.	5	_____
3. School district advisory committee is used to plan public relations program for our district.	5.5	_____
4. Public relations program is evaluated regularly.	6	_____
5. Public relations program is conducted with dignity and aggressiveness.	6	_____
6. Public relations program involves as many people as possible.	5.5	_____
7. All school board members, top level administrators, department heads, faculty, and nonacademic staff contribute to our public relations program.	6	_____
8. Superintendent or an appointed specialist is responsible for our public relations program.	5.5	_____
9. Board and superintendent provide leadership and gear district or school policy toward good public relations.	6	_____
10. Board and superintendent provide clear lines of authority and responsibility for public relations procedures	5.5	_____

11. Duties related to public relations are delegated in terms of functions and jobs to be done.   6   _____

12. Boardmen and superintendent understand clearly the purposes and organization of public relations program for the district.   6   _____

13. Board and superintendent utilize guidance and assistance of central public relations office.   5.5   _____

14. Board and superintendent cooperate with the central public relations director.   6   _____

15. Central public relations department determines administrative channels for public relations release.   5.5   _____

16. A written statement of public relations policies is given to each departmental faculty and non-academic staff.   5   _____

17. Faculty and nonacademic staff understand their roles in the public relations program of the school district.   5.5   _____

18. Each departmental faculty member shares responsibility for public relations program of the school district.   6   _____

19. Faculty promotes good public relations.   5.5   _____

20. Faculty members are active in professional organizations.   5.5   _____

21. There are good faculty-pupil relationships.   6   _____

22. All available media are used.   5.5   _____

23. Topics are treated honestly and fairly; exaggeration is avoided.   6   _____

24. The publics served by the school district are identified.   6   _____

25. Specific information is directed toward each public.   5.5   _____

26. Surveys are conducted regularly to accumulate information for public relations releases.   4.5   _____

27. Topics of human interest value are used for public relations releases.   4.5   _____

28. All information gathered is utilized.   5   _____

29. Superintendent makes full use of his annual report as a public relations instrument.   6   _____

30. There is a close working relationship between departmental faculty and overall district faculty.   6   _____

31. Value of a sound educational program as a foundation for public relations program is understood.   6   _____

32. There are regular attempts to improve the educational program.   6   _____

33. Students in the educational program exhibit favorable attitudes toward their respective programs.   5.5   _____

                                                                          Your

          Perfect Total: 185.5   Total: _____

Sum up the points credited to obtain the total. Apply this total score to the empirical graph below to rate your school district's public relations program.

POINTS CREDITED	RATING
0.0 – 26.5	NONEXISTENT—No actual program of effort.
27.0 – 53.0	VERY POOR—Bare minimum, insufficient program.
53.5 – 79.5	POOR—A weak, loose program.
80.0 – 106.0	FAIR—A moderate, admissible program.
106.5 – 132.5	GOOD—A sufficient, satisfactory program.
133.0 – 159.0	VERY GOOD—A truly beneficial program.
159.5 – 185.5	EXCELLENT—The best or superior type of program.

A second aspect to program evaluation concerns the outcome of the program. In other words, does the school district have better relations with its respective publics as a result of the community relations program? Determining this is best accomplished by asking community members about their knowledge, understanding, and feelings concerning the school district. Some of the most common methods of gathering such data include: telephone surveys, questionnaires, and panel discussions, in addition to analyzing complaints and asking key members of the staff to elucidate their personal observations about the effectiveness of the program.

SUMMARY

Public school districts, by reason of their mission and very existence, have relations with various publics. Therefore, a board of education can either choose to develop a systematic community relations program or let its relationship with the community develop by chance. The consequences of this latter position can have a devastating effect upon the success of a district in fulfilling its mandate to educate children.

The basic principle upon which an effective community relations program must rest is that the schools are brought into existence by the people, governed by the people, and financed by the people. Therefore, two-way communication between the school district and its various publics is the foundation of a community relations program.

Community relations is quite different from a public relations program in private business and industry. Community relations is not a "sell job" or "publicity" program but rather a method of communicating.

There are five steps in developing a community relations program. First, the board of education should create a policy which will give the administration direction in managing a community relations program and which will establish the scope of the program. Second, the board of education should establish a central office administrative position, usually titled Director for Community Relations. This should be a staff position under the superintendent, and it should be the director's job to plan and direct the school district's internal and external communications program. Third, the director for community relations should initiate a process with procedures for collecting data about the various publics that make up the school district. A sociological survey is the most appropriate vehicle for gathering this data. Fourth, from this data the director for community relations can identify and initiate techniques for communicating with the various publics. Printed materials and working with and through the news media are significant methods of communicating. The final step is evaluating the effectiveness of the program, not only in terms of program organization but also in terms of program outcomes.

IMPLICATIONS FOR SCHOOL
BOARD MEMBERS

There are three implications for boards of education that emerge from this treatment of community relations.

First, boards of education must become aware of the impact that good community relations has on carrying out its mission of educating children and young people.

Second, after creating a community relations policy, the school board should establish a central office staff position titled Director for Community Relations. This individual should be responsible for planning and implementing an ongoing, two-way communications program with the various publics in the school district. It is important for the school board to channel all official communications through the community relations office.

Third, school board members should make themselves available to participate in community relations activities, such as speakers' bureaus and community forums.

APPENDIX A
40 WAYS TO USE YOUR BOARD
MEETING AS A VEHICLE
FOR PUBLIC RELATIONS
AND COMMUNICATIONS[8]

1. Make the board room environment as physically attractive and inviting as possible (comfortable chairs, room temperature, ash trays, coffee, carpeting).

2. Plan ways to exhibit student work at each meeting.

3. Have students participate in each meeting (musical presentations, reports, introductions, etc.).

4. Have adequate parking close to board room.

5. Distribute agendas to key people in the community as well as the press and staff members.

6. Schedule meetings for convenience of the public (afternoon and evening).

7. Allow the public opportunities to speak to the board on agenda items—but set ground rules.

8. Involve staff members in the presentation of as many items as possible in each board meeting—with introductory remarks by the superintendent or assistant superintendent.

9. Have a special bulletin containing highlights of each board meeting out and in the hands of all staff members, key citizens, and media people the next day.

10. Invite special groups to have representatives attend board meetings—taxpayers' associations, PTA, LWV, etc. Be sure they are introduced when they first attend—and spoken to at each meeting. Tell them you're glad they've come.

11. Hold budget meetings in the evenings—and publicize them well. Budget guides are helpful, too . . . even shopping lists.

12. Recognize outstanding programs and practices in the schools. Have the staff members responsible at the meetings and introduce them publicly.

13. Recognize the community contributions of citizens, especially those who have been involved in the schools. Send official letters of congratulations to each.

14. Be positive in approach.

15. Invite visitors to give their opinions at meetings—at a special time on the agenda.

16. Invite local ministers to your meetings to give the invocation.

17. Invite students and/or local Boy and Girl Scout Troops to give the Pledge of Allegiance.

18. Have WELCOME TO OUR MEETING flyers available to first time visitors.

19. Have an Administrator in the audience to answer community questions on how to address the Board.

20. Put aside a special segment of your meeting for YOU to ask the community members present questions about their schools.

---

[8]Ann H. Barkelew APR, Vice President for Corporate Communications, Dayton-Hudson Corporation, President of the National School Public Relations Association (1979–1980).

21. Whenever speaking to citizen groups or private individuals addressing the Board, make sure they know you are interested in what they have to say.

22. Send a follow-up letter to every community patron who addresses the Board. Thank them for their interest and, if possible, give them further information about their topic.

23. Have coffee available to the public.

24. Establish a curfew time for public comments.

25. Have outstanding students presented to your Board for a special commendation.

26. Have a fifteen minute positive presentation on a program in your District at one Board meeting every month.

27. Don't talk in EDUCATIONALEZE. Remember you have an audience who may not know ECE from ADA

28. If you are explaining intricate budget formulas, use a chalkboard or overhead.

29. Do not be afraid to admit you don't know the answer. Always offer to find out and DO.

30. When you have a break in the meeting, go into the audience and speak to the public.

31. Have a special section set aside for the Press. If possible, have a Public Information Officer available to answer their questions.

32. When asked for an interview by a reporter, answer as sincerely as possible. If you do not know the reporter, he may take everything you say seriously.

33. If you are presenting an important item to the Board, prepare a statement in advance to hand out. You will more likely be quoted correctly.

34. Learn the names of the reporters covering your meetings.

35. If you are taking a position that is contrary to that of your administration, be prepared to answer their questions. HAVE BACK-UP MATERIALS SO THAT YOU CAN SUBSTANTIATE YOUR DECISION.

36. If no news media representative attends your meeting, call the city editor following your meeting and offer to report highlights.

37. WHEN TRUSTEES GET ALONG, THERE IS NOT MUCH NEWSWORTHY ABOUT THEIR MEETINGS. GRANDSTANDING FOR PURE PUBLICITY CAN LOWER PUBLIC OPINION ABOUT YOUR PERFORMANCE AS A BOARD MEMBER. EVALUATE CAREFULLY YOUR PLAN OF ATTACK.

38. When you speak in your community, invite your audience to attend Board meetings.

39. If you refer to paragraph 2 on page 3, be sure everyone has (or can see) that same page or paragraph.

40. Move your meetings around to school sites occasionally and invite parents to attend.

APPENDIX B
A POSITIVE VOTER BEHAVIOR
PROGRAM FOR A PUBLIC
SCHOOL DISTRICT OR HOW TO
GET A BOND ISSUE PASSED IN
13 WEEKS[9]

Even though the historical trends, over the past 15 years, have indicated the increasing number of defeated bond issues, research findings have also indicated that a number of positive things can be done prior to an election to affect voter behavior. Certainly, the Board of Education should come out unanimously in favor of the need for the bond issue. Other factors which can affect positive voter response include the following.

School boards should be honest and keep the public informed.

The facts should be reported clearly, completely, and to all available media.

Voters of the district should be shown the planning of a long range capital program and what it will cost.

Finally, research also indicates that approximately 75 percent of the voters tend to make up their minds about a bond issue the very first time they hear about the issue. For this reason, the first announcement should be well planned and effectively demonstrated.

ACTION PLANS AND DATES	TARGET GROUP
13 Weeks Prior to the Election	
The Board of Education formally approves the placement of a $1,432,119 bond referendum, to build a new elementary school building, on the general election ballot.	District-wide registered voters
The district administrative team issues a phone invitation to local newspapers, radio and television stations to be present for an important news briefing at the Board of Education office at 3 p.m. that day. The purpose is to give first-hand information to the news media and increase the effectiveness of the first public announcements regarding the bond issue.	News media personnel and news media publics
An architectural firm is commissioned to build a scale model of proposed building indicating site, construction, etc. This model is to be completed eight weeks prior to the election day for the placement in a local shopping center until election day.	Consumer public in district

[9] Russell E. McCampbell, Graduate Assistant of the Missouri School Boards Association (Columbia, Mo., 1982).

The administrative team of the district and selected teachers are appointed to create a slide presentation showing the total educational program, especially the elementary program and buildings. The slide presentation is to be completed in three weeks so school officials and a citizens' task force can use it in making presentations before religious, social, civic and political groups.

The organizational-oriented public

12 Weeks Prior

Selection and confirmation of appointment of local citizens to a citizens' task force should be made. It should be headed by local patron in favor of the bond issue. Concentrated effort should be made to include representatives from all areas of the district, with equal representation of male and female, senior citizen, parents and members of the ethnic groups and minorities.

A wide-based patrons group to spearhead the bond election drive

11 Weeks Prior

There should be at least two meetings of the local citizens' task force to organize plans and procedures for a bond election drive. The plans and procedures include a speakers' bureau which will contact all religious, social, civic and political groups in the district to see if they would like to have a guest speaker, slide presentation and/or question and answer session regarding the election. The creation of telephone and mailing committees to be utilized later in campaign efforts will also be discussed in this meeting.

A wide-based patrons group to spearhead the bond election drive

An announcement is made to the news media of the Golden Age Senior Citizens Pass good for free admission to all school performance functions, i.e., athletics, musical, dramatic, etc.

Senior citizens

Effort is made by the adult education coordinator to expand the adult education program to include GED classes and many craft and personal development courses. Many of these may be located in the elementary school in question.

Educationally oriented public

The school public information specialist is assigned the task of incorporating all facts, information and financial figures in the monthly school bulletin which is mailed to all patrons in the district. The same information will be included in the proposed staff bulletin to be published "in-house" for weekly distribution to all school staff members.

District patrons and all staff members of the school

10 Weeks Prior

An in-service workshop for our staff members will be scheduled for this week. The workshop program will include a full presentation of facts about the election and the critical need for the elementary building. This will enable all faculty members of the district to understand the significance of the election. Special efforts will be made to include the noncertificated staff members in a similar orientation session.

All school staff employees, certificated and non-certificated

9 Weeks Prior

The local Future Farmers and Young Farmers organizations will begin a concentrated program of introducing their organizational concepts to the community farmers, The Farm Bureau, National Farmers Organization, other groups with the intent of eventually providing information sessions concerning the general operation of the school, including the elementary program and the building needs.

Farmers and the agriculturally oriented public

The high school journalism class begins a weekly serial on the local FM and AM radio station giving general school news and special interviews regarding the bond election.

General public in district

8 Weeks Prior

Invitations are extended from all levels of the school to invite grandparents to the grandparents school week to be held in possible conjunction with National Grandparents Day. Grandparents are invited to come to school with their grandchildren, observe classes, eat lunch and participate in educational programs. Members of the senior high student council and other organizations will adopt grandparents from the local retired housing community and invite them to school.

Senior citizens

8 Weeks Prior–7 Weeks Prior

The building level parent-teachers' organization meetings are held with a presentation of bond election information by the citizens' task force and building administrators. This includes the slide presentation and question and answer session.

Parents of children in school

8 Weeks Prior–4 Weeks Prior

Two staff awareness meetings are held. This brings the professional and support staff members

All school staff employees

up-to-date on the status of the election and
election plans.

Small groups of religious leaders, priests, ministers and presidents of all social, civic, and political
organizations are invited to awareness meetings in
the board office. Information will be presented
about the election and availability of the speakers
bureau for various meetings.

Leaders in the com-
munity

High school drama and choral groups will tour
nursing homes for small group presentations in the
next four weeks. Remember nursing home
patients may vote by absentee ballot.

Senior citizens

Announcement is made that the local Chamber
of Commerce and Community Betterment Organization is sponsoring a poster contest for all elementary children with prize winning posters
pictured in business windows in three weeks. The
theme is: "We are proud of our city . . . Come join
our pride." This gives exposure of the elementary
program to the community.

General public, busi-
nesses and parents of
school children

Voter registration drive—a special lesson plan
for the senior contemporary issues or other social
studies course allows senior class members 18
years of age or older to register to vote. Also,
there will be distribution of voter registration
material to parents of students newly transferred
to the district.

Educationally oriented
public

7 Weeks Prior

The high school booster club initiates a
campaign to give "spirit packs" to all businesses
in town. Door stickers saying "Pulling for City
Pirates" and "Pushing for City Pirates" will be
given away to develop loyalty to the local senior
high school teams. This will have a subliminal carry-
over affect. Most people answer the name of their
high school when asked where they went to school.
Therefore, there will be a carry-over affect to
promote voting for the elementary bond issue.

Local businesses and
general public

All parents of transfer students into the district
are invited to the local school buildings for
receptions and get-acquainted meetings. This
will allow them to become familiar with the school,
its buildings, the educational programs and
references made about the election.

Parents new to the dis-
trict

6 Weeks Prior

The citizens' task force distributes bumper
stickers supporting the election.

General public

5 Weeks Prior

The citizens' task force commissions ten bill-board advertisements regarding the bond election. All billboards are spaced throughout the community, using already established spaces.

General public

4 Weeks Prior

The local newspapers publish the column "From the desk of the superintendent," in which there is a complete outline of the district needs for the elementary school and what the completed new building will be.

General public

The citizens' task force compiles two lists. One includes the parents of children in school. The second is a complete voter list from the last election. These lists are used for the concentrated mailings to parents and a telephone campaign shortly before the election.

Educationally oriented public and district registered voters

Paid political advertisements are placed in the local newspapers featuring important questions and answers taken directly from the various meetings conducted by the citizens' task force speakers bureau.

General public

3 Weeks Prior

Homecoming week for the local high school includes big splashy events such as parade, floats, bon fire, spirit building week, spirit breakfast, and open house of all schools on homecoming day. The citizens' group makes a concentrated effort to contact former students of the school for the past four years as they come back for homecoming and give them information relative to the bond election and forms for absentee voting. Remember many of these kids will be in college on election day and will want to vote by absentee ballot.

General and educationally oriented public

2 Weeks Prior

An international week is planned at all schools in the district. The central theme is planned around United Nations Day or another appropriate day. Ethnic minority groups in the community will be invited to the schools for participation and/or presentation of materials.

Minority and ethnic groups

1 Week Prior

Principals of the elementary schools visit the individual classrooms and talk to students about the election and answer questions. They also display the model of the proposed building.	Educationally oriented public
Members of the citizens' task force, the board president, and superintendent visit local radio and television talk shows.	General public
The Chamber of Commerce and local business merchants in the city sponsor a holiday window painting contest to be done by the local elementary and junior high students.	General public businessmen, parents
The citizens' task force letter to all members on the voter list is mailed. Also, the special school bulletin is mailed to each parent of children in school.	District voters and parents
Concentrated 15 and 30 second television spots are aired on the local station emphasizing the need for the bond issue.	General public
Members of the local citizens' task force go house-to-house in the city and much of the county with a knock-on-the-door campaign. They ask such questions as "Have you heard about the bond issue? Are there any questions we could answer for you?" They will utilize local people in each area, not strangers.	District-wide voters
Paid advertisements are placed in newspapers and on radio and television stations indicating that transportation to the polls will be provided and giving the telephone number to call.	District-wide voters

1 Day Prior

All school marquees have information announcing the date of the election.	Educationally oriented public
The concentrated telephone campaign to only those persons identified as being favorable to the election conducted by the citizens' task force, PTA members, and concerned parents.	Voters favorable to bond issue

Election Day

The transportation system to the polls is implemented with members of the PTA, citizens' task force, and concerned parents manning the cars, telephones, etc.	District-wide voters
A special note will be sent to all school staff employees that "Today is election day. Exercise your right to vote."	Educationally oriented public

Members of the citizens' task force, administrative staff and board of education members are
invited to the board office to await results of the
election. The assistant elementary principal will be
assigned to the court house to record the tabulation
of votes and phone results to the board office.

Election Day Victory

One Day–Four Weeks after the Election

The board begins preparation for the sale of bonds for
revenue and implements bidding procedures for the approved elementary building.
A letter of thanks is sent to significant campaign
leaders from the superintendent, board of education, and
citizens' task force.

SELECTED BIBLIOGRAPHY

BAGIN, DON, FRANK GRAZIAN, CHARLES H. HARRISON, *School Communi-
cations: Ideas That Work.* Chicago: McGraw-Hill Book Company, 1974.
——— , "PR for School Board Members," *AASA Executive Handbook Series, Vol.
VIII.* Arlington, Virginia: American Association of School Administrators,
1976.
CARITHERS, POLLY, *How to Conduct Low Cost Surveys: A Profile of School
Survey and Polling Procedures.* Arlington, Virginia: National School Public
Relations Association, 1973.
KINDRED, LESLIE W., DON BAGIN, DONALD R. GALLAGHER, *The School
and Community Relations.* Englewood Cliffs, N.J.: Prentice-Hall, Inc., 1976.
SUMPTION, MERLE R., YVONNE ENGSTROM, *School-Community Relations:
A New Approach.* New York: McGraw-Hill Book Company, 1966.

CHAPTER SIX
THE ROLE
OF THE SCHOOL BOARD
IN DISTRICT
BUSINESS OPERATIONS

School districts perform many business functions common to private corporations; thus school districts should incorporate into their operations those business practices which have proven effective in the private sector.

It sounds almost trite to say that everything has a price tag, but the truth of this statement is evident as school boards go through the painful process of cutting programs, activities, and personnel in this time of rising costs and shrinking balances and revenues. Thus the importance of business operations and activities in school districts has been dramatically heightened over the last decade. Operational practices common to the business and industrial community have been adopted by school districts as they attempt to become more accountable to tax payers. Such practices can help to demonstrate that the school board and the administration are providing educational programs that meet the needs of children and are still cost effective.

The educational program is supported by two other programs that are usually managed from the business office—the pupil transportation and food service programs. In addition, all the programs of the school district are made more efficient by using data processing programs. This chapter, therefore, deals with the operations of the business office as it administers the financial and auxiliary programs of the school system.

SCHOOL DISTRICT FINANCIAL MANAGEMENT

The financial management of school districts includes many interrelated functions, which ultimately demonstrate that the revenue and expenditures of the district support the best educational program possible given the fiscal resources available.

The major components of financial management include: (1) budgeting procedures; (2) financial accounting procedures; (3) purchasing, warehousing, and distribution procedures; (4) investing procedures; and (5) auditing procedures.

Constructing the School District Budget

The school district's budget is a plan for delivering the educational program and for projecting the district's revenues and expenditures that will support this program. The last twenty years have seen many management innovations that addressed the budget construction process, including: Program Planning Budgeting System (PPBS), Zero Based Budgeting, and Performance Budgeting. The thrust behind these and many other approaches to budgeting is the quest for a process that can serve as a useful management tool while providing the school board with a method of prioritizing needs. No system of budgeting will satisfy all the needs of a school district. Modifications will, therefore, be introduced that address the particular character of the school district.

There are four basic steps to an effective budgeting process. First, the budget is not an entity unto itself but rather a vehicle for accomplishing a purpose. The purpose of a school district is to educate children. This purpose is more refined through establishing goals and objectives. The board of education is responsible for setting these goals after having received input from teachers, administrators, parents, students, and other school district patrons.

Second, these goals and objectives can then be translated into a curriculum and finally set forth in terms of educational requirements. The professional staff under the direction of the superintendent of schools can begin the process of attaching dollar amounts to educational requirements. For example, a school board may believe that a secondary school remedial reading program is needed. The superintendent along with the building principals, teachers, and other central office administrators will be required to perform a needs assessment for the purpose of identifying the number of secondary school children who require remedial reading. The superintendent and his staff should then proceed to calculate the personnel, supplies, and material costs that will be needed to effectively introduce this program.

Third, the administration will be required to make a revenue projection, which will be combined into a budget document that also sets forth the proposed expenditures operationalizing the goals and objectives of the school district.

Finally, the board of education must approve the budget. The school board can certainly challenge the budget submitted by the superintendent before approving the document. In fact, the school board may wish to make changes in the expenditures based upon the board's perception of the needs of the district.

Budgeting is a continual process usually beginning in January each year for the next fiscal year and terminating with budget revisions approved by the school board the following December. The fiscal year in most states begins July 1 and ends on June 30.

The actual budget document may take various forms but should include the following: (1) a budget message by the superintendent describing the important features of the budget and major changes from the previous year's budget; (2) projected revenue from all local, state, and federal sources with a comparison of revenue for the last two years by fund and source; (3) proposed expenditures for each program with a comparison of expenditures from the last two years by fund, object, and function; (4) the amount needed to pay the principal and interest for the redemption of the school district's bonds maturing during the fiscal year; and (5) a budget summary.

Figure 6-1 exemplifies program goals established by a school board that could be used by the administration in constructing the budget. Figure 6-2 sets forth how programs are broken down in order to identify total costs.

Financial Accounting

Financial record keeping is an absolute necessity for the effective functioning of every school district. Such records set forth the financial transactions of the school district that form the basis upon which sound financial decisions can be made by the board of education.

The systematic keeping of financial transactions also allows for the tracing back of individual items transacted and will identify what was expended, for what purpose, by whom, in addition to information about the source of the money used for the expenditure. Such data may be needed when unanticipated requests are made by the school board, the public, the superintendent, or another government agency.

While financial record keeping is usually referred to as bookkeeping, this is only one phase of a complete system that involves the recording, classifying, summarizing, interpreting, and reporting of results about the school district's financial activities. This system is commonly known as *accounting*.

Because education is *big business*, it involves numerous financial transactions occurring on a daily basis. Therefore, a sound accounting system must provide the school board and the administration with the following services: (1) an accurate record of the details involved in business transactions; (2) safeguards that the fiscal resources of the school district are used for their designated purpose; (3) data that can be used by the school board and administration in planning; (4) information to

FIGURE 6-1 Statement of Goals for a School District Budget[1]

FOREIGN LANGUAGE PROGRAM
FOR ELEMENTARY AND MIDDLE
SCHOOL STUDENTS:

—To work with each child to help him or her learn the basic intellectual skills of linguistic flexibility in thought and tongue through a foreign language.

—To develop fluency in a foreign language to such a degree that an eighth grade student could visit a foreign country and understand and converse with a native speaker on an elementary level, comprehend partially a publication in that language, and make him- or herself understood in writing and language.

OBJECTIVE STATEMENT
AND EVALUATIVE CRITERIA

AT THE END OF THE EIGHTH GRADE:

—That 75% of the students be able to communicate in the language of instruction at an elementary level with a native speaker of that language as evaluated by the teacher.

—That 50% of the students should be able to read a magazine or newspaper article in the language of instruction and state briefly in that language a brief summary of the article as measured by the teacher.

—That 80% of the students will be able to write with ease a dictation exercise in Spanish based on previously studied material from the text based on a teacher prepared dictation test.

—That 75% of the students will give a five minute oral report in the language of instruction on a topic of the student's choice to the teacher's satisfaction.

—That 70% of the students will pass the vocabulary test provided in the text with 85% accuracy.

PROGRAM DESCRIPTION

The foreign language program covers the four years of fifth, sixth, seventh, and eighth grades in the subjects of Spanish and French. There are six teachers in the program, three in each subject. The fifth and sixth grade students receive 150 minutes of instruction weekly, the seventh grade students 135 minutes of instruction weekly, and the eighth grade students 110 minutes of

[1]National School Public Relations Association, *PPBS and the School: New System Promotes Efficiency, Accountability* (Arlington, Va.: The Association, 1972), p. 21.

instruction weekly. Instruction is provided in a classroom environment using textbooks, and includes both written and oral work. Teachers may use other instructional materials such as songs, plays, magazines, newspapers, flashcards, etc. A language laboratory is available containing records, tape recorders, and filmstrips.

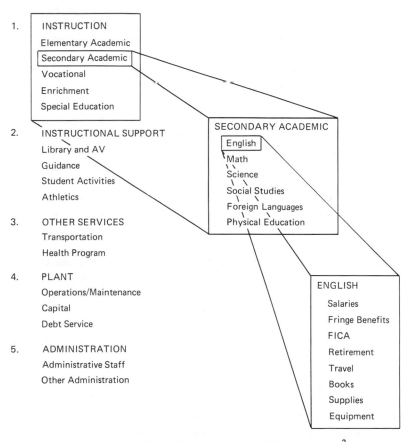

FIGURE 6-2 Categories of Expenditures for a School District Budget[2]

local, state, and national government agencies about the financial operations of the school district; (5) facilitate an analysis of how the administration expended the school district's monies in relation to the educational goals implicit in the approved budget.

[2]Ibid., p. 18.

In addition, an adequate accounting system must meet certain minimal criteria common to the accounting profession. First, the system must have a reasonable degree of internal controls that will continuously ensure accuracy of recording transactions. Second, the accounting system should be consistent with generally accepted governmental accounting principles, incorporating uniformity of procedures and the use of standard terminology and definitions. Third, the accounting system should be simple and flexible, not only to accommodate new programs with minimal disruption but also to be a help rather than a hindrance to the schools' administration. Fourth, the accounting system designed should be a double-entry, accrual, and encumbrance system.[3] Fifth, as a governmental accounting system, transactions should be recorded in the following dimensions in order to answer certain critical questions: What was purchased? (object); from what financial source? (fund); for what purpose? (function); for which school? (operational unit); to provide what specific service? (program).

An accrual and encumbrance accounting system provides a school district with a much more realistic appraisal of its fiscal position. When the financial books are opened, the appropriated budget approved by the school board is recorded. When purchase orders are signed and contracts approved, the dollar amount is entered in an encumbrance column. When payments are made, the dollar amount is charged to a payment column and the original amount encumbered is credited to encumbrances. This procedure gives a continual analysis of the progress in expending the budget, because the budget balance is appropriations minus expenditures and encumbrances.[4]

The accounting system can thus provide the administration and the school board with a summary of revenues and budget balances not only on a continual basis but such data can also be formalized into a *budget operating summary* and presented to the board at its regular monthly business meeting.

Purchasing, Warehousing, and Distribution of Supplies and Materials

School districts are important buyers and consumers because the amount of supplies, materials, and services needed to conduct the educational enterprise reaches into the millions of dollars. Such large expenditures demand the creation of board policies and administrative procedures that will ensure the proper purchase and use of these goods.

Central Office Purchasing Department.   In a medium to large size school district, purchasing will probably be accomplished by a central office department instead of individual schools. The building principals should be charged with filling

[3] Department of Health, Education and Welfare, *Principles of Public School Accounting* (Washington, D.C.: U.S. Government Printing Office, 1967), pp. 1–4.

[4] Roe L. Johns and Egar L. Morphet, *The Economics and Financing of Education: A Systems Approach* (Englewood Cliffs, N.J.: Prentice-Hall, 1975, 3rd ed.), p. 442.

out purchase requisitions or supply lists. A board of education policy should designate how items will be purchased. For example, items costing up to five hundred dollars may be purchased through catalogue pricing; items costing up to two thousand dollars by taking quotations from vendors; and items costing over two thousand dollars by formal bidding from specifications. A cooperative purchasing program is a method by which a number of school districts pool their supply, equipment, furniture, and other material needs for the purpose of getting cheaper prices because of volume purchases. Copies of the purchase orders should be sent to the accounts payable and warehouse departments.

Warehouse and Distribution Department. This department in a centralized system receives items from vendors. Smaller school districts may have items delivered directly to the schools. The employees in the warehouse and distribution department are usually charged with checking the shipping manifest against the items; with affixing identification tags to the items; with preparing an asset inventory card; with sending a copy of the purchase order marked "received" to the accounts payable department; and with delivering the items to the schools or with warehousing the items for future distribution by memo requisition.

Accounts Payable Department. When this department receives a copy of the purchase order from the warehouse and distribution department, it is coded per the chart of accounts. The purchase order is checked against the invoice and entries are posted in the accounting books. Finally, disbursement checks are prepared and after approval by the board of education at the next board meeting, they are mailed to the vendor.

This process will ensure that items are purchased in the most cost-effective manner and will further ensure that such items are inventoried and used for their designated purpose.

Investing School District Funds

Most school districts can significantly increase their nontaxable revenue by developing an investment plan that places idle cash in interest-bearing money instruments. The budgeting process and accounting system can provide the superintendent with data concerning the cash flow requirements of the school district. Comparing revenue receipts and expenditures on a monthly basis with previous years is especially helpful in projecting cash needs.

The following strategies can be used to increase the amount of cash available for investments: (1) depositing cash receipts on the day they are received; (2) deferring the payment of bills as late as possible under established terms; (3) deferring the payment of payroll withholdings as long as possible under the law; (4) using warrants instead of checks because funds are not needed until the warrant is presented back to the issuer for payment; (5) using bank floats, which is the difference between cash balances shown on the books and cash actually in the bank; (6) developing a program deferring purchases throughout the entire year rather than in large amounts one or two times a year.

Each investment transaction has three actions: purchasing the instrument, cashing in or selling the instrument, and receiving the interest. There are also three considerations when investing idle cash: the risk, yield, and liquidity of the instrument. Yield, of course, refers to the rate of return on the investment and liquidity refers to when the instrument can be sold or cashed in without a penalty. Most states have statutes limiting the type of investments that can be made with public funds. Speculation types of investments in the stock market are usually prohibited, and most investments are limited to money instruments such as treasury bills, repurchase agreements, and certificates of deposit.

Balancing the risk, yield, and liquidity of investments is a judgment call requiring a great deal of expertise on the part of the administrator charged with this responsibility. The banking and other financial institutions in our country have experienced considerable regulation changes over the past five years and may experience additional changes in the future, making the task of investing even more difficult.

Figures 6-3 and 6-4 exhibit the relationship between risk and liquidity, which should help to clarify these two concepts. The board of education must be informed on a regular basis and probably at their regular monthly business meeting with details concerning the school district's investments.

Auditing School District Accounts and Programs

Auditing accounts and programs is a standard operating practice in private business and industry as well as in government agencies. Most large corporations and large school districts have *internal* auditing procedures carried out by employees for the purpose of identifying ineffective and improper practices that could result in legal and/or financial problems. However, the emphasis in this treatment is on the *external* audit, which is usually conducted by an outside certified public accounting firm at the end of a fiscal year. This external audit covers the scope of the school district's operations and attempts not only to analyze the accuracy of recording financial transactions along with verifying the financial books but also the practices and procedures utilized in conducting the business activities of the school district.

In performing an audit, the certified public accountants must have access to certain records that will provide necessary data. The following is a list of those records usually examined: the minutes of school board meetings, the budget, accounting books such as ledgers and journals, revenue and nonrevenue receipt records, bank accounts, investment records, insurance policies, surety bonds, deeds to property, inventory lists, and original documents relating to the authorization of expenditures and the making of payments.

While audit reports vary somewhat, they generally include the following: (1) a letter of transmittal; (2) a description of the scope and the limitations of the audit; (3) a summary of the examination findings; (4) financial statements and

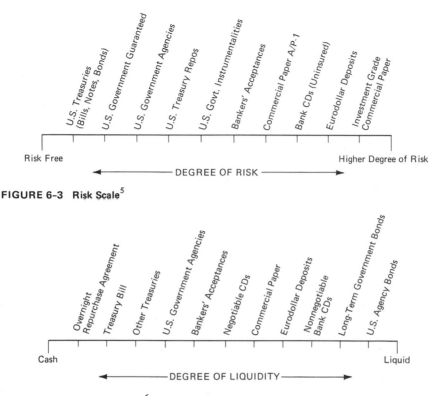

FIGURE 6-3 Risk Scale[5]

FIGURE 6-4 Liquidity Scale[6]

schedules; (5) recommendations for improving the accounting procedures and/or the business operations of the school district.

From time to time, the board of education will find it defensible to take bids from auditing firms to ascertain if the fee being paid to their auditors is competitive with other firms. It is important for the school board to employ a firm based not only on the fee but also on the experience and qualifications of the accountants working for the firm. School boards are usually required to take the *lowest and best* bid and not merely the lowest. A multiple year contract with an auditing firm will give the auditors sufficient time to accurately assess in detail the business operations of the school district.

The audit report is usually presented directly to the board of education with copies going to the superintendent and his or her staff. A good auditing program provides the school board and the public with the assurance that the administration

[5] Municipal Finance Officers Association, *A Public Investor's Guide to Money Market Instruments* (Chicago, Ill.: the Association, 1982), p. 78.

[6] Ibid., p. 79.

is conducting the business activities of the district in an honest and appropriate manner. Thus the audit also becomes a method of protecting those charged with managing the fiscal resources of the district.

THE DATA PROCESSING
PROGRAM

It is an understatement to say that we live in a computerized society. In fact, the instruction program must incorporate three separate components dealing with computers if the students of a school district are going to meet the challenges facing them when they graduate from high school. Computer literacy is the first component and is usually part of an elementary school program. The use of computers must become an integral part of a middle or junior high school curriculum, with computer programming being the final component taught in high school.

This section, however, deals with the administrative use of data processing as a vehicle supporting the instructional program. In most school districts, data processing can be applied to the following areas: budgetary accounting, payroll, personnel, scheduling, grade reporting, pupil accounting, attendance accounting, inventory, and enumeration census.

Data processing services can operate from an in-house installation or computer time can be purchased from a private service bureau. An alternative to these two approaches is for a number of school districts to form a cooperative by which one district either purchases or merely houses the equipment, and the cost is shared by the member school districts, or they buy time on the computer if the equipment is owned by a single district. Figure 6-5 is a checklist that can be used by the administration of a school district first to determine if there is a need for data processing and second to determine the adequacy of a district's existing data processing program. This figure also lists those components of a program that must be addressed if such a program is to be effective. These major areas are: goals and objectives, proper staffing, procedures for safeguarding the privacy and confidentiality of data, efficient operational procedures, and creative administration of the program.

The board of education should be briefed from time to time on the effectiveness of the data processing program by the superintendent and his or her staff. This is particularly important because the operation of this program interfaces with a great many other school district activities.

THE PUPIL TRANSPORTATION
PROGRAM

The board of education has an obligation not only to provide students with the opportunity to be taught by competent professionals at school but also to help parents get their children to school by establishing and maintaining a safe and ef-

FIGURE 6-5 Checklist to Determine the Need for and the Adequacy of a School District's Data Processing Program[7]

Indicate the degree to which the district conforms to the standards as follows: na = not applicable; 1 = unsatisfactory; 2 = fair; 3 = satisfactory; 4 = exceptional.

PART I—NEED FOR D.P. SERVICES
FOR DISTRICTS CURRENTLY WITHOUT D.P. SERVICES

1. The district has sufficient and timely accounting information.	na	1	2	3	4
2. The district has sufficient and timely payroll/personnel information.	na	1	2	3	4
3. Scheduling of students is accomplished using efficient and effective procedures.	na	1	2	3	4
4. Progress reporting of students is accomplished using efficient and effective procedures.	na	1	2	3	4
5. The district has sufficient and timely pupil information.	na	1	2	3	4
6. The district has adequate procedures available for meeting other informational needs.	na	1	2	3	4
7. The district has given consideration for the utilization of data processing services.	na	1	2	3	4

PART II—DESCRIPTORS FOR DISTRICTS
CURRENTLY UTILIZING D.P. SERVICES

Indicate the Source(s) of D.P. Services:

(Check One)   In-House Installation _____
               Service Bureau/Cooperative Approach _____

Data Processing Goals and Objectives

8. Goals and objectives are formulated by the total administrative staff.	na	1	2	3	4
9. Objectives are prioritized by the administrative staff.	na	1	2	3	4

Staff

10. The district has a written organizational chart for data processing.	na	1	2	3	4

[7]Department of Elementary and Secondary Education, *Checklist to Determine the Need for and the Adequacy of a School District's Data Processing Program* (Jefferson City, Mo.: the Department, 1980).

11. The district has a written job description for   na   1   2   3   4
    each D.P. employee based on written perform-
    ance standards.
12. The district has a formal education program that   na   1   2   3   4
    meets the needs of the D.P. staff.

Administration of D.P. Facilities

13. The district has a written multiyear D.P. plan   na   1   2   3   4
    consistent with both short- and long-range
    objectives.
14. The D.P. plan is evaluated and revised annually   na   1   2   3   4
    or more frequently.

Privacy, Security, and Confidentiality

15. The district has written procedures governing the   na   1   2   3   4
    privacy and confidentiality of data.
16. The district has written procedures providing for   na   1   2   3   4
    the security of software and data files.
17. The district has written procedures providing for   na   1   2   3   4
    the security of the computer facility.

Systems and Programming

18. The district has developed written procedures for   na   1   2   3   4
    requesting and developing D.P. services.
19. The district has developed procedures for   na   1   2   3   4
    monitoring applications during the develop-
    mental process.
20. The district has written systems and program-   na   1   2   3   4
    ming standards that are followed in all cases.
21. User manuals and/or instructions are provided   na   1   2   3   4
    for each application.
22. The district has developed written procedures   na   1   2   3   4
    for monitoring the effectiveness of existing
    applications.

Computer Operations

23. The district maintains a daily and weekly   na   1   2   3   4
    machine processing schedule.
24. The district has job accounting procedures   na   1   2   3   4
    relative to computer usage.
25. The district maintains operator manuals ade-   na   1   2   3   4
    quate to schedule and process applications.
26. The district has a written procedure to monitor   na   1   2   3   4
    D.P. supplies.

Data Input/Output

27. The district has procedures which control and secure the processing of all incoming data.	na	1	2	3	4
28. The district maintains a daily and weekly data preparation schedule.	na	1	2	3	4
29. The data entry section has complete instructions for preparing all input data.	na	1	2	3	4
30. The district has procedures whereby new and revised forms are reviewed and developed jointly by the users and the D.P. department.	na	1	2	3	4
31. The district has procedures for proper distribution of all output.	na	1	2	3	4
32. The district has procedures for proper disposition of test runs or other exceptional output.	na	1	2	3	4
33. The district has procedures for the verification and accuracy of all output.	na	1	2	3	4

fective pupil transportation program. The significant increase in automobile traffic and the lack of sidewalks in suburban areas, along with inadequate public transportation in urban areas have increased the importance of pupil transportation programs.

The pupil transportation service can also be considered as an extension of the curricular and extracurricular programs. Buses are needed not only to transport children from their homes to school and back again, but also for field trips, which certainly extend the educational horizons of the children beyond the classroom. In addition, it would be very difficult for children to participate in an interscholastic athletic program if the school district did not provide a means of getting to athletic events.

Most if not all states have statutes governing the pupil transportation program. It is common for school districts to be required by law to provide pupil transportation, within limitations, for the regular instructional program at no direct cost to parents. However, school districts are usually permitted to charge parents for transporting their children to athletic events and for field trips.

Figure 6-6 provides a checklist that can be used by boards of education as they evaluate the adequacy of their school districts' transportation program. Not only the quality of service but also the cost effectiveness of the program is directly related to the policies created by the school board in governing the pupil transportation program. These policies will give direction to the administration as they establish management procedures for administering the program.

FIGURE 6-6 **Checklist to Determine the Adequacy of the School District's Pupil Transportation Program**[8]

Indicate the degree to which the district conforms to the standards as follows: na = not applicable; 1 = unsatisfactory; 2 = fair; 3 = satisfactory; 4 = exceptional.

1. The board of education has adopted specific written policies and rules regarding the pupil transportation program for district-owned and contracted vehicles.   na 1 2 3 4

2. The board of educational policies include a definition of what is considered a safe and reasonable walking distance for children.   na 1 2 3 4

3. Transportation is furnished to physically handicapped children regardless of the distance involved.   na 1 2 3 4

4. The board of education has adopted a specific and detailed policy regarding the use of buses for instructional or other nonroute trips. (Nonroute trip: any trip made by a school bus for a purpose other than transporting children over a regularly scheduled route.)   na 1 2 3 4

5. The school has a definite program for teaching children to become safe bus passengers.   na 1 2 3 4

6. When pupil transportation is provided through contractual services, all the terms of the contract are in written form and signed by the contractor and the board of education.   na 1 2 3 4

7. Transportation contractors are required to give a bond for the faithful fulfillment of the terms of the contract.   na 1 2 3 4

8. The board of education prescribes the minimum amount of insurance to be carried by the contractor as a condition of the contract.   na 1 2 3 4

9. Contracted equipment is inspected at regular intervals by competent inspectors.   na 1 2 3 4

10. Reports of the inspections of contracted equipment are required by the board of education as a condition of the contract.   na 1 2 3 4

11. A cost analysis for the operation of each individual bus is made periodically. Records show the following information for each bus in the fleet:

[8]Department of Elementary and Secondary Education, *Checklist to Determine the Adequacy of the School District's Pupil Transportation Program* (Jefferson City, Mo.: the Department, 1980).

(a) Original cost and date of purchase	na	1	2	3	4
(b) Total miles operated to date	na	1	2	3	4
(c) Miles operated per day on assigned route	na	1	2	3	4
(d) Number of pupils transported on assigned route	na	1	2	3	4
(e) Cost of gasoline, oil, and grease	na	1	2	3	4
(f) Cost of repairs	na	1	2	3	4
(g) Specific information on accidents	na	1	2	3	4
12. District maintains records involving property damage, traffic violations, and road failures.	na	1	2	3	4
13. School bus accident reports to the Department of Education are submitted promptly.	na	1	2	3	4
14. Records are kept for the use of buses for route trips and separate records kept for non-route trips.	na	1	2	3	4
15. Repair parts and supplies are carried on an inventory account and charged off to each individual bus only as used.	na	1	2	3	4
16. An up-to-date map of the transportation area in a scale large enough to be functional is kept.	na	1	2	3	4
17. A locator system showing the following information is maintained:					
(a) Location of all roads.	na	1	2	3	4
(b) Type of all roads (hard surfaced, gravel, etc.).	na	1	2	3	4
(c) Distances between major intersections.	na	1	2	3	4
(d) Location of all school buildings in which classes are held.	na	1	2	3	4
(e) Location of pupils to be transported.	na	1	2	3	4
(f) Location of these pupils in a manner which clearly indicates which are kindergarten, elementary school, and secondary school pupils.	na	1	2	3	4
(g) Exact route of each bus.	na	1	2	3	4
(h) Weight capacity of all bridges.	na	1	2	3	4
(i) Location and nature of major route hazards.	na	1	2	3	4
18. Drivers are familiar with routes before transporting pupils.	na	1	2	3	4
19. Bus stops are designated so that they are not on steep grades, blind curves, or near the crest of a hill.	na	1	2	3	4
20. Children are picked up and discharged only at designated stops.	na	1	2	3	4
21. A time schedule showing the approximate time the bus can be expected is established for each trip.	na	1	2	3	4
22. Transportation is provided for pupils living more than one mile from school.	na	1	2	3	4

23. Reasonable walking distances, waiting times,   na 1 2 3 4
    and riding times are established for pupils.
24. The size of the bus assigned to each route is in   na 1 2 3 4
    every instance appropriate (in terms of capacity)
    for the number of pupils transported.
25. Safe traffic patterns for approaching, parking on,   na 1 2 3 4
    and leaving school grounds are established.
26. Designated personnel are present in the bus   na 1 2 3 4
    loading area to assist and supervise loading.
27. District has written guidelines for reporting:
    (a) Students transported.   na 1 2 3 4
    (b) Student misconduct.   na 1 2 3 4
    (c) Complaints from community.   na 1 2 3 4
    (d) Bus conditions.   na 1 2 3 4
    (e) Route conditions   na 1 2 3 4
    (f) Accidents.   na 1 2 3 4
    (g) Injuries.   na 1 2 3 4
    (h) Overtime.   na 1 2 3 4
28. There is a definite and clearly understood   na 1 2 3 4
    procedure for handling requests for the use of
    buses for instructional trips and other nonroute
    uses.
29. Consideration has been given to staggering   na 1 2 3 4
    school starting times for convenience and
    economy of busing.
30. Parents and pupils are informed of the policies   na 1 2 3 4
    and rules that have been established regarding
    the transportation program.
31. Children who must cross the road after alighting   na 1 2 3 4
    from a bus are required to cross in front of the
    bus and then only after receiving a signal from
    the driver.
32. It is the policy of the transportation program   na 1 2 3 4
    that no child should be let off the bus for any
    reason except at his or her designated stop
    unless special instructions have been given by
    the proper authority.
33. Rules and regulations regarding their duties   na 1 2 3 4
    and responsibilities are given to drivers in writ-
    ten form or in a drivers' handbook.
34. When new drivers are employed, previous   na 1 2 3 4
    driving experience is investigated to assure that
    it has been safe and satisfactory.
35. Consideration is given to maturity and character   na 1 2 3 4
    of every individual before he or she is employed
    as a driver.
36. The board of education has established a mini-   na 1 2 3 4
    mum and a maximum age range for employment
    as a driver.

37. Substitute drivers are expected to meet the same general requirements as regular drivers. na 1 2 3 4

38. When school bus drivers are employed, a written contract is signed by the driver and school officials. na 1 2 3 4

39. A training program for drivers is required and includes both classroom instruction and demonstration and practice with the vehicle. na 1 2 3 4

40. Conferences with drivers and discussions of problems are held at regular intervals. na 1 2 3 4

41. Drivers are furnished with the names of pupils assigned to their routes. na 1 2 3 4

42. Buses are inspected regularly for cleanliness. na 1 2 3 4

43. Drivers are instructed in emergency procedures. na 1 2 3 4

44. All vehicles used for transporting children meet the minimum standards for construction of school buses adopted by the State Department of Education. na 1 2 3 4

45. School officials emphasize and make all necessary provisions for carrying out a preventive maintenance program. na 1 2 3 4

46. There is an easy and direct way for drivers to report apparent failure or unsatisfactory performance of the bus. na 1 2 3 4

47. Spare buses are available and can easily be assigned to a bus route in case of need. na 1 2 3 4

48. Every bus is inspected regularly by a mechanic for detecting mechanical defects. na 1 2 3 4

49. Vehicles are kept out of service if they are deemed unsafe. na 1 2 3 4

50. A record or written report is made of all inspections, maintenance and repair work on each bus. na 1 2 3 4

51. Records show maintenance costs directly resulting from accidents. na 1 2 3 4

Here is a major consideration that most boards of education will contend with at one time or another: Is it better to contract pupil transportation services with a private company or is it better to have a district-operated program? Of course, there is no answer to this question that will be applicable in every situation. However, the decision of the school board should be guided by the option that will provide the students of the district with the best and safest service at the most reasonable cost. The superintendent and his or her staff can certainly provide the school board with data about the cost of a district-operated program along with information about the safety of the operation and long-term concerns such as maintenance and vehicle replacement costs in addition to revenue projections for the program. At that point a school board may have the superintendent prepare specifications and take bids on contracting services. An analysis of the bids and a comparison of contracted services with a district-operated program can then be made by the board in determining which of the two options is best for the school district.

Two issues have arisen in the last five years that address the concern of school boards about becoming more cost effective with the pupil transportation program. First, the use of alternative methods of fueling school buses has received considerable attention, and experiments have been conducted using gasohol, propane, and diesel fuel. Every school board should require the administration to provide them with data and a compilation of the current literature dealing with alternative fuels so that the board can address this issue.

Secondly, computerized transportation programs have saved some districts a considerable amount of money, particularly by establishing routes and pupil pick-up points, in scheduling bus runs, and in monitoring and reporting costs. Such computerized programs are available from private companies on a contract or fee basis, while medium to large districts may have their own computer hardware necessary for developing such a system. The ultimate question a school board must ask is whether the capital outlay to convert vehicles for the use of alternative fuels, and the capital investment to purchase or contract for computer capabilities in pupil transportation will give the district a payback in a reasonable period of time to justify the expenditure.

THE SCHOOL FOOD SERVICE PROGRAM

There are three reasons why a school district should provide a food service program for children: (1) Pupils should have the opportunity to obtain nutritional food during the school day needed for physical, emotional, and intellectual development; (2) The school lunch program provides pupils with the opportunity to learn about the amount and kinds of food needed for good nutrition; (3) Eating in the school cafeteria provides pupils with the opportunity to practice desirable social behavior.

The school food service program includes much more than just a hot lunch program. Some school districts provide breakfast programs, especially in areas where family income severely limits the opportunity of a child to receive a nutritional breakfast at home. Many school districts have found that the food service program can provide the school district with a cost effective way of supplementing the extra-curricular and school-sponsored clubs/associations program. Every team and club member in the school district looks forward to culminating the season's activities with a banquet or dinner during which the teams and individual team members can be recognized for their accomplishments. The cost of a banquet served at school will be much less than the cost of such an event at a private restaurant.

Like the pupil transportation program, food service can be contracted for with a private company or the program can be district-operated. The guiding objective for the school board is the same as that of the pupil transportation program: The best option is the one providing the students in the district the most nutritional program at the most reasonable cost. In making this decision, a board of education can use the checklist in Figure 6-7, which lists a set of descriptions to analyze the adequacy of a school district's food service program. In addition, Figure 6-8 provides a "blueprint" for a food service program. Developed by the American Food Service Association, it presents a set of objectives that will produce an effective food service program.

FIGURE 6-7 Checklist to Determine the Adequacy of the School District's Food Service Program[9]

Indicate the degree to which the district conforms to the standards as follows: na = not applicable; 1 = unsatisfactory; 2 = fair; 3 = satisfactory; 4 = exceptional.

1. The objectives of the food service program have been defined in writing.   na   1   2   3   4

2. School food service is under the direction of a competent person considered an integral part of the total educational program.   na   1   2   3   4

3. Food service policies, procedures, and regulations are in written form and provided for all employees. (Example: Employees are not to bring food and supplies in or take any out.)   na   1   2   3   4

4. Lines of authority and responsibility are clearly defined in writing for proper administration, supervision, and management of the program.   na   1   2   3   4

5. The district has a policy regarding the sale of competitive food such as a la carte, packaged snacks, soft drinks, candy, etc.   na   1   2   3   4

6. The sale of all food items is under the direct management of the food service director and all receipts are deposited to the food service account.   na   1   2   3   4

7. The school has a policy for selling lunches and/or tickets that is flexible enough to take care of all the students in a time frame that avoids unnecessary delay.   na   1   2   3   4

[9]Department of Elementary and Secondary Education, *Checklist to Determine the Adequacy of the School District's Food Service Program* (Jefferson City, Mo.: the Department, 1980).

8. The district has developed a policy and procedures for providing meals to needy children.   na   1   2   3   4

9. The district follows an effective procedure for protecting the anonymity of children approved for free meals and free milk, and reduced price meals.   na   1   2   3   4

10. Scheduling of lunch periods is well planned and considers the needs of students with sufficient time allowed for students to eat.   na   1   2   3   4

11. Nutrition education in the classroom is correlated with school food service program.   na   1   2   3   4

12. Supervision is provided at lunch time so students will be encouraged to practice good food habits and social graces.   na   1   2   3   4

13. The district evaluates program participation on a continuing basis.   na   1   2   3   4

14. Attractive and clean uniforms are worn by all food service employees.   na   1   2   3   4

15. In-service training is provided food service personnel.   na   1   2   3   4

16. All personnel must furnish annually evidence of good health and negative TB test.   na   1   2   3   4

17. Food service personnel use the program planning aids that are available to them such as recipe cards, food buying guides, newsletters, etc.   na   1   2   3   4

18. The community is made aware of federal and state program requirements and the quality and quantity of the food that is served through written publication.   na   1   2   3   4

19. Menus are planned monthly and published weekly.   na   1   2   3   4

20. Menus are based on sound nutritional adequacy, attractiveness, student acceptance, and meet state and federal program requirements.   na   1   2   3   4

21. Maximum utilization is made of all food supplies.   na   1   2   3   4

22. Menus are planned that will provide an "in-season" price advantage in purchasing food.   na   1   2   3   4

23. The district is successful in keeping plate waste to a minimum.   na   1   2   3   4

24. Students are provided an opportunity to contribute in upgrading the food service program.   na   1   2   3   4

25. Food is properly handled, prepared, and served under sanitary conditions.   na   1   2   3   4

26. Equipment is effectively utilized in food preparation.   na   1   2   3   4

27. Food and equipment are arranged to permit the serving line to move quickly.   na   1   2   3   4

28. Inventory procedures are sufficient and effective to utilize older shelf foods first.   na   1   2   3   4

29. Security and protection of foods is sufficient and effective.   na   1   2   3   4

30. Storage space is adequate in size and free of excessive temperature and humidity.   na   1   2   3   4

31. Food storage areas, refrigeration, and freezers are inspected on a regular basis to prevent food spoilage.   na   1   2   3   4

32. Thermometer readings are taken daily in dry, refrigerator, and freezer storage areas.   na   1   2   3   4

33. Stock is handled with minimum unpacking, shelving, and repackaging.   na   1   2   3   4

34. Storage and inventory procedures are uniformly practiced in all school buildings.   na   1   2   3   4

35. All foods are stored on shelves or dunnage.   na   1   2   3   4

36. Kind and amount of equipment are adequate for the food service operation.   na   1   2   3   4

37. The inventory procedure provides information on consumption and frequency of use.   na   1   2   3   4

38. The dining area is clean, adequately lighted, well ventilated and attractive.   na   1   2   3   4

39. Approved dishwashing facilities are provided.   na   1   2   3   4

40. Garbage and refuse are disposed in adequate and sanitary containers.   na   1   2   3   4

41. Provision is made for insect and rodent control.   na   1   2   3   4

42. Machines are equipped with safety devices.   na   1   2   3   4

43. Immediate follow-up action is taken to correct deficiencies revealed by local, county, or state health and sanitation inspections.   na   1   2   3   4

44. Daily program records are kept for individual schools.   na   1   2   3   4

45. Periodic checks are made to determine whether the potential and actual income agrees.   na   1   2   3   4

46. The procedure for handling money is considered satisfactory.   na   1   2   3   4

47. Monthly profit and loss statements are prepared.   na   1   2   3   4

48. Food, labor, and other related costs are calculated full cost per meal.   na   1   2   3   4

49. The district is willing to supplement program operations with local funds to provide nutritious meals at a price within the means of the large majority of students.   na   1   2   3   4

FIGURE 6-8 American School Food Services Association: A Blueprint for School Nutrition Programs[10]

Reflecting the educational potential of proper school nutrition programs, it is hereby declared to be our philosophy that food service permitted in schools shall contribute to optimum learning ability through good nutrition, good example, and good instruction.

School nutrition programs should contribute to the education of the child in three ways: (1) to physical well-being; (2) to mental receptivity; and (3) to knowledge of food and application of good eating habits.

I. NUTRITION OFFERINGS

The school, with the assistance of medical personnel, should determine the nutritional status of the individual child and his or her school-day nutritional needs.

School food service should be expanded to those children presently excluded because of a lack of facilities and/or funds.

Provision should be made for:

A. A meal that contains 1/3 of the child's recommended dietary allowances should be provided by the schools to all pupils without cost to the individual.

B. Two meals, each containing 1/3 of the Recommended Daily Dietary Allowances, should be available daily in all schools.

II. NUTRITION CURRICULUM

A school nutrition program should provide:

A. A sequential curriculum plan of nutrition instruction for pupils from kindergarten through high school.

B. Innovative curriculum materials.

C. Nutrition counseling with parents and medical personnel.

D. Continuing nutrition education for teachers through regional and local workshops and courses.

III. PROFESSIONAL EDUCATION AND TRAINING

The state educational agency should:

A. Establish qualifications for personnel responsible for directing, supervising, and implementing school food service and a nutrition program.

B. Define criteria for preservice and in-service training programs.

[10] American School Food Service Association and Association of School Business Officials, *A Guide for Financing School Food and Nutrition Services* (Denver, Co.: the Association, 1970), pp. 69–71.

C. Cooperate with educational institutions and professional organizations in developing education programs.

IV. STAFFING

The local educational agency should provide:

A. Direction and supervision by certificated personnel professionally trained in nutrition and/or administration and food services.
B. Adequate staff, qualified through nutrition and food service training, to implement school food service programs.

V. TECHNOLOGY

School nutrition program design should reflect the best technological research and development available to produce an optimum product at minimum cost.

VI. RESEARCH AND EVALUATION

Continuing research and evaluation is essential to provide information which will enable school nutrition programs to define and apply practices of maximum effectiveness.

Organizations, industry, and government, should combine their resources toward this purpose as well as in defining means through which this information can be effectively disseminated.

VII. EXPANDED USE OF SCHOOLS

Reflecting the trend for schools to become community centers:

A. School nutrition programs should be expanded to meet the needs of all ages at all times whenever they are using school facilities.
B. Maximum use of school food service facilities and personnel may be anticipated in times of emergency.
C. School food service facilities and staff should be used for vocational training of youth and adults.

VIII. FUNDING

In fidelity to the premise that the school accept the responsibility for the child during the hours he or she is under its care, the school nutrition programs should meet the child's nutrition needs during the hours of the school's responsibility.

Such nutrition programs should be funded as a public responsibility, and therefore at no cost to the individual.

Taking cognizance that this goal far exceeds our present public commitment toward meeting school-day nutrition needs, a timetable is needed to reach the objective.

IX. PUBLIC INFORMATION

An effective school nutrition program must be understood and supported by the public. All agencies with a concern for the nutrition of children should cooperate to develop and implement a public information program.

The superintendent of schools and his or her staff can provide the board of education with data about pupil participation in the food service program; state and federal reimbursements; menus and nutritional requirements; direct costs such as salary information, maintenance costs, and food costs. The board may wish to have the superintendent prepare specifications and take bids on a contracted service if there is question concerning the effectiveness of the food service program.

A major concern with many programs is the level of pupil participation. A la carte items and alternative menus have proven in some districts to increase participation in the food service program.

SUMMARY

The importance of business operations and activities in school districts has been dramatically heightened over the last decade. Operational practices common to the business and industrial community have been adopted by school districts as they attempt to become more accountable to taxpayers. Such practices can help to demonstrate that the school board and the administration are providing educational programs that are meeting the needs of children and are still cost effective.

The financial management of school districts includes many interrelated functions, which ultimately demonstrate that the revenue and expenditures of the district support the best educational program possible, given the fiscal resources available.

The major components of financial management include: (1) budgeting procedures, (2) financial accounting procedures, (3) purchasing, warehousing, and distribution procedures, (4) investing procedures, and (5) auditing procedures.

The school district's budget is a plan for delivering the educational program and for projecting the revenue and expenditures that support this program.

Financial accounting is a system involving recording, classifying, summarizing, interpreting, and reporting the results of the school district's financial activities.

School districts are important buyers and consumers because the amount of supplies, materials, and services needed to conduct the educational enterprise reaches into the millions of dollars. Such large expenditures demand the creation of board policies and administrative procedures that will ensure the proper purchase and use of these goods.

Most school districts can significantly increase their nontaxable revenue by developing an investment plan that places idle cash in interest-bearing money instruments. The budgeting process and accounting system can provide the superintendent with data concerning the cash flow requirements of the school district. Comparing revenue receipts and expenditures on a monthly basis with previous years is especially helpful in projecting cash needs.

Auditing accounts and programs is a standard operating practice in private business and industry as well as in government agencies. The external audit is usually conducted by an outside certified public accounting firm at the end of a fiscal year. The audit covers the scope of the school district's operations and attempts to analyze the accuracy of the record of financial transactions and verify the financial books. The practices and procedures utilized in conducting the business activities of the school district also come under the auditor's scrutiny.

The educational program is supported by two other programs, usually managed from the business office—the pupil transportation and food service programs. In addition, all the programs of the school district are enhanced by the data processing program.

It is an understatement to say that we live in a computerized society. In most school districts data processing can be applied to the following areas: budgetary accounting, payroll, personnel, scheduling, grade reporting, pupil accounting, attendance accounting, inventory, and enumeration census.

The board of education has an obligation not only to provide students with the opportunity to be taught by competent professionals at school but also to help parents get their children to school by establishing and maintaining a safe and effective pupil transportation program. The pupil transportation program can also enhance curricular and extracurricular programs by providing transportation for field trips and interscholastic athletic events.

There are three reasons why a school district should provide a food service program: (1) pupils should have the opportunity to obtain nutritional food during the school day; (2) the school lunch program provides students with the opportunity to learn about the amount and kinds of food needed for good nutrition; and (3) eating in the school cafeteria provides pupils with the opportunity to practice desirable social behavior.

IMPLICATIONS FOR SCHOOL
BOARD MEMBERS

There are two implications for school board members that emerge from this presentation on the business operations of school districts.

First, school board members must become completely familiar and comfortable with the business operations of the school district because it will be impossible to make realistic decisions concerning the educational problem without this knowledge. The school board should require the superintendent and his or her staff to make a wide range of reports about the business and financial condition of the school district on an ongoing basis, and particularly at the regular monthly board meeting. Board members should also attend workshops and seminars presented by school board associations on school finance and business operations if they are in need of basic information about such activities.

Second, school board members must understand the importance of auxiliary programs to the success of the educational program. If children are unable to arrive safely at school and are unable to receive the nutrition needed to be attentive in the learning-instructional process, the potential for their failure at school will be significantly increased. Such programs must become integral components of school district operations.

SELECTED BIBLIOGRAPHY

AMERICAN SCHOOL FOOD SERVICE ASSOCIATION and ASSOCIATION OF SCHOOL BUSINESS OFFICIALS, *A Guide for Financing School Food and Nutrition Services.* Denver, Colorado: The Associations, 1970.

BENSON, CHARLES S., *The Economics of Public Education* (2nd ed.). New York: Houghton Mifflin Company, 1969.

BURRUP, PERCY E., *Financing Education in a Climate of Change* (2nd ed.). Boston: Allyn and Bacon, Inc., 1977.

GONDER, PEGGY ODELL, *How Schools Can Save $$: Problems and Solutions.* Arlington, Virginia: American Association of School Administrators, 1980.

JOHNS, ROE L. and EDGAR L. MORPHET, *The Economics and Financing of Education: A Systems Approach.* Englewood Cliffs, New Jersey: Prentice-Hall, Inc., 1975.

MUNICIPAL FINANCE OFFICERS ASSOCIATION OF THE UNITED STATES AND CANADA, *A Public Investor's Guide to Money Market Instruments.* Chicago: The Association, 1982.

NATIONAL SCHOOL PUBLIC RELATIONS ASSOCIATION, *PPBS and the School: New System Promotes Efficiency, Accountability.* Arlington, Virginia: The Association, 1972.

U.S. DEPARTMENT OF HEALTH, EDUCATION and WELFARE, *Principles of Public School Accounting.* Washington, D.C.: U.S. Government Printing Office, 1967.

CHAPTER SEVEN
THE ROLE
OF THE SCHOOL BOARD
IN DISTRICT
PROPERTY MANAGEMENT

The beliefs of a society will last beyond that society's existence through the monuments and buildings erected during its flourishment.

The importance of school buildings and facilities is often overlooked by citizens, teachers, administrators, and even board members. Every school should be designed to support and strengthen the learning-instructional process. This cannot be accomplished unless the board of education and the school district administrators understand the integral relationship between educating children and the physical surroundings where learning takes place.

Children have been the object of much research, which has provided us with a vast amount of data that must be taken into consideration when building, remodeling, and maintaining school facilities. For example, we know children have social needs that must be met in their educational experience if they are to be successful at school. A sense of belonging and companionship must, therefore, be developed at school. This cannot be easily accomplished if the school facilities lack a variety of spaces for group activities. In recent years the *commons* area, furnished with leisure seating and brightly decorated, has become one of many popular architectural methods for addressing the social needs of students.

How to build school facilities meeting the social, psychological, and educational needs of students is only one of many issues that school boards must learn about if they are to have a working knowledge of property management. This chapter, therefore, is divided into five sections, each dealing with an area that has a significant impact on school district property management.

ARCHITECTURAL PRINCIPLES
AND THE LEARNING
ENVIRONMENT

Historically, no recognizable schoolhouse structure appeared in the United States until the seventeenth century. When they did appear, these schoolhouses were neither attractive nor comfortable, consisting primarily of one room, long tables for the pupils, and a raised podium for the teacher. The basic philosophy that persisted into the 1850's was that schoolhouses were simply shelters in which pupils and teachers came together. Through the efforts of eminent educators such as Horace Mann and Henry Barnard, free public education became an accepted American institution. With this recognition, the design of schools began to attract the attention of the architectural profession.

Shortly after the acceptance of public education as an institution, another unrelated event occurred that had a significant effect not only on the design of schools but also on the entire field of architecture. In 1880, Louis Sullivan, an eminent American architect, enunciated the principle, "Form follows function." In fact, the planning of *functional* school buildings has been of primary concern not only to architects but also to educators since the 1940's. Before this period, American architecture was more concerned with imitating what was in vogue in Europe and particularly in England.

The function of educational institutions is to educate children and young people. Consequently, the design of school facilities began to be viewed within the context of educational concepts. Today all school construction and remodeling projects must be part of the process whereby fundamental educational concepts are formulated, developed, expressed, evaluated, and incorporated into the design of the school.[1] Hence there was the need to use educational specifications when designing a building. Such specifications should clearly describe the various learning activities, their spatial requirements, and any special features of the curriculum that will be housed in the school building.

There are four principles of school operation that mirror the human condition and must be considered when planning an educational facility in our contemporary times. First, the principle of gradualism dictates that teachers, administrators, students, and parents be ready for curricular changes that are also reflected in architectural design. The "open space" classroom concept is a case in point. Without proper preparation and readiness, a newly constructed school utilizing the open space classroom concept will gradually develop partitions made out of bookcases and other moveable objects.

Secondly, the principle of reversibility dictates that new dimensions required in the design of school facilities supporting a specific curricular approach can be implemented without extensive structural modification. Soundproof sliding par-

---

[1] Basil Castaldi, *Creative Planning of Educational Facilities* (Chicago: Rand McNally & Company, 1969), p. 143.

titions can be used to convert an open area into a more confined space for small group instruction or for that teacher who is more effective in a traditional classroom setting.

Third, with our highly mobile population, a decrease in our population, and the high cost of construction, school facilities should be designed for more than one use. Many school districts across the United States are closing school buildings because of decreasing enrollments. A school built for the sole purpose of being a school would require considerable structural modifications to convert it into, for example, an office building. A more universal design would give the school district the opportunity to recuperate its investment, which in turn could be put into other educational areas.

Finally, schools should be designed for people. Every child has physical, social, intellectual, and psychological needs that may or may not be enhanced because of the school building design. For example, mental fatigue will certainly retard a student's ability to learn. Thus, the physical conditions causing fatigue can be minimized if, for example, a building is well ventilated, has functional heating and air conditioning systems, and is decorated with bright colors and fascinating shapes.

STEPS IN A SCHOOL CONSTRUCTION OR REMODELING PROGRAM

There are four steps in the process of carrying out a school construction and/or remodeling program. Each step has a number of components implemented by various staff members. Each component has a number of procedures and subprocesses requiring a very detailed explication that is beyond the scope of this treatment. However, a school board member should be familiar with the overall process, which will provide him or her with a frame of reference when interacting with the administrative staff about construction and/or the remodeling of facilities.

Step One—Establishing Educational Goals and Objectives

It is absolutely imperative that the board of education establish a five-year plan consisting of educational goals and objectives that can be altered from year to year and incorporated into an ongoing, continuous five year plan. The school board needs the input of citizens, students, teachers, staff members, and administrators before deciding on district-wide goals.

These goals and objectives are subsequently converted into a curricular plan. The curriculum is a professional responsibility of the superintendent of schools and his or her professional staff. Certainly teachers, building level administrators, and curriculum specialists will also be engaged in the curricular planning process.

The curriculum is then translated into educational specifications, which present in great detail the kinds of spatial, equipment, and building requirements that will be needed to operationalize it. For example, the teaching of high school level chemistry will require a laboratory with specialized equipment. It is also the responsibility of the superintendent and other staff professionals to formulate these educational specifications. Teachers and building level administrators have on-the-line experience that will be invaluable to this task.

Step Two—Developing Architectural Plans

The first concern of the board of education in operationalizing this second step is the selection of an architect. Because architects are professionals who provide a service, one of the most successful ways of selecting them is to advertise that the board is accepting credentials and proposals for an architect. The credentials should include documentation of the successful school projects completed by the architect; the proposal should include how the architect will be paid. There are two traditional methods of paying an architect—a flat fee basis or a percentage of the project cost. The American Institute of Architects has established guidelines for members in setting compensation for professional services. It is the responsibility of the school board to select the architect.

The architect is then responsible for taking the educational specifications and developing preliminary sketches and cost estimates for the project. Once these sketches are reviewed by the superintendent, teachers, curriculum specialists, and the building principal who helped develop the educational specifications, the board of education should state their opinion and approve or reject the sketches.

Next, the architect should select a site for a new school project and develop working drawings and architectural specifications. The architect will require the services of other various professionals, such as electrical and mechanical engineers, in developing these plans. Of course, the school board exercises final approval of the school site and plans.

Step Three—Developing the Financial Plan

The superintendent and central office administrators are responsible for developing preliminary plans for a bond issue election. The campaign should be organized and coordinated by the director of community relations. If the bond issue passes, the board of education must select an attorney who specializes in bond issues. The process used in selecting an architect is applicable to all professionals and will suffice for a bonding attorney. The various aspects of floating a bond issue are outlined later in this chapter.

Step Four—Implementing the Construction and/or Remodeling

The architect is responsible for advertising and taking bids for a general contractor who will actually construct or remodel the building. It is more effective for the general contractor to handle the subcontracting with electrical contractors and all other construction specialists. The board of education approves the contract with the general contractor but should have the contract executed by the school district's attorney.

The superintendent, in conjunction with the building principal who will administer the new school, should prepare an equipment list. In many cases, the architect will be responsible for taking bids on heavy equipment that will be attached to the building, and for furniture.

The building should be inspected on a regular basis by the architect and someone designated by the superintendent of schools. Upon certification of the architect, monthly payments can be made to the general contractor from the money generated through the sale of the bonds. Final payment should be withheld until the board of education can make a final inspection of the new or remodeled facility.

PUBLIC BORROWING FOR CAPITAL PROJECTS

In recent years almost 80 percent of new U.S. corporation financing has been accomplished through the issuing of bonds. In the public sector, however, bonds are sold for limited purposes. State statutes closely regulate the process of flotation, debt limits, and all aspects of public borrowing. A distinctive characteristic of public borrowing is its voluntary nature. If the citizens of a school district do not wish to bind themselves and future generations to paying taxes for the retirement of the district's bonded indebtedness, they simply vote *no* in the bond issue election.

Bonds are formal I.O.U.s. Most state statutes permit boards of education to ask the citizens of a school district for approval (bond issue election) to borrow money by selling bonds to raise funds for capital projects. *Capital projects* usually refer to building schools, furnishing schools, remodeling programs, replacing roofs, buying boilers, and purchasing large, expensive equipment such as school buses. The critical aspect is voter approval, because without it, a school district cannot engage in public borrowing. However, when a bond issue election passes, the taxpayers have in essence said that they will pay yearly through a special tax the principal and interest on the bonds that the school district sells until the entire debt is retired.

Capital projects have traditionally been financed through public borrowing for three major reasons. First, capital projects are usually nonrecurring expenditures which should not be financed with funds generated through the operating tax levy. The operating levy is for paying salaries, fringe benefits, utilities, routine maintenance, and other ongoing expenses. Secondly, the large dollar outlay for capital projects would seriously effect the monies available to continue with daily operations if the funding was taken from the operating levy. Finally, the burden for financing capital projects should be spread out over many generations because these future generations will also benefit from the projects. Most municipal bonds are repaid over a twenty-year period.

The Process of Bond Flotation

The first step is for a board of education to determine what capital projects are and will be needed by the present and future generations of the school district. This must be accomplished by the superintendent and his or her administrative team. Enrollment projections are essential. Most capital projects are predicated on the number of students who will be occupying a place in the schools. If the student population is increasing, additional buildings will be needed. As a school district matures and the student population decreases or stabilizes, there will still be a need to remodel or refurbish existing buildings. Energy conservation modifications to older facilities have become a must in recent years. There are a number of existing techniques, such as the Cohort-Survival method of enrollment projecting, that can provide the school board with adequate data about pupil population trends.

The second step is to review the state statutes pertaining to municipal bonds and bond issue elections. For example, there is a significant statutory limitation in most states that could prevent a school district from even considering a bond issue election. A debt ceiling expressed as a certain percentage of the school district's assessed valuation can limit the bonding capability of the district. For example, if a school district has an assessed valuation of one hundred million dollars and the state statutes limit a district to a bonding capacity of ten percent of this assessed valuation, the school district can borrow only ten million dollars. If the district has already issued bonds worth nine million dollars and has retired one million dollars of this debt, the bonded indebtedness of the school district is eight million dollars, which leaves a bonding capacity for an additional capital project of only two million dollars. Two million dollars does not buy a very elaborate school building today. These restrictions are placed on school districts to prevent them from incurring a debt their tax base will not support.

The third step is to initiate a bond issue election campaign headed by the director of community relations if the board of education decides that a capital project is needed. Chapter five, Appendix B, outlines a process for conducting such a campaign.

If the bond issue passes, the fourth step is to initiate those procedures necessary to ensure the legality of the bonds. Because school district bonds are purchased and traded using the *bearer* form, legality is of primary importance. A board of education should always hire an attorney who specializes in bonds to review and to handle the entire process of *flotation*.

The following steps in the process of flotation will help to minimize confusion and maximize the potential in selling the bonds.

1. The board of education should pass a resolution approving the results of the bond issue election.
2. Obtain certification from the appropriate authority concerning the assessed valuation of the school district.
3. Have the treasurer of the school board certify the outstanding indebtedness of the district.
4. Prepare a bond maturity schedule.

5. The board of education should pass a resolution directing the sale of the bonds.
6. Prepare a notice that the bonds are for sale and advertise in the appropriate publications.
7. Notify Moody's Investors Service and/or Standard & Poor's Corporation about the bond sale.
8. Solicit bids for the printing of the bonds.
9. The board of education should accept bids for the sale and printing of the bonds.
10. The board of education should pass a resolution directing the issuance of the bonds.
11. Once the bonds are delivered to the school district, they should be signed by the secretary and treasurer of the board.
12. The bonds should then be registered with the appropriate state authority.
13. Deliver the bonds to the purchaser.
    a. A nonlitigation certificate must be signed by the clerk of the circuit court.
    b. A receipt for the funds obtained through the bond sale must be signed by the treasurer of the board.
    c. A verification of the president's and secretary's signature should be prepared and attested to by an official of the bank handling the school district's money.

Facts about Bonds

It is impossible to talk about municipal bonds in isolation from the bonds issued by corporations because both have similar characteristics. It is also important for school board members to have at least a rudimentary understanding of bonds. The following facts constitute the essential data necessary to that understanding.

1. The amount to be repaid by the school district is *principal amount, face value,* or *par value,* which is printed on the face of the bond.
2. The repayment date is the *maturity date.*
3. The interest rate paid by the school district to the person who owns the bond is the *coupon rate.*
4. The period of time that the bond is outstanding is the *term.* Municipal bonds usually have a term from one through twenty years.
5. Bond certificates either come with coupons which are *chipped* from the bond and presented for interest payments; or the bonds are *registered* with the issuing agent who mails the interest payments directly to the bond holder.
6. The *bearer* form is used with most municipal bonds, which means that the person who holds the bond is presumed to be the owner.
7. When the bonds are backed up by the collateral of a corporation, such as property, the bonds are referred to as *mortgage bonds.*
8. When the bond is issued on the full faith of the borrower, it is called a *debenture.*
9. *Municipal bonds* are issued by cities, states, and political subdivisions.
10. Municipal bonds differ from corporate bonds in the following ways:
    a. Municipal bonds are *tax exempt,* which means that the interest is exempt from federal income taxes, and, if the investor lives in the state of issue, the interest is also exempt from state and local taxes.

      b. Municipal bonds are issued in *serial* maturities rather than on a term basis. Therefore, a portion of the total issue matures annually, with each year in the series having its own interest rate. While the overall net interest might be 10 percent, the 1983 issue could yield 7.703, with the 1984 issue yielding 7.90, and the 1985 issue yielding 8.10, etc.

      c. Municipal bonds are generally issued in $5000 principal amounts and traded in the Over-the-Counter (OTC) market.

      d. There are three basic types of municipal bonds:

        (1) *General obligation* bonds, which are backed by the faith and taxing authority of the issuer.

        (2) *Revenue bonds,* which are backed by the earning power of the facility constructed. (A stadium would generate gate receipts which would be used to retire the bonds.)

        (3) *Special tax* bonds, which are backed by a special tax levied yearly to pay the principal and interest of a maturing series. This is the type generally issued by school districts.

11. Bonds are rated by the following two independent agencies, which measure the probability of a bond issuer being capable of repaying the principal amount at maturity and the interest schedule.

      a. Standard & Poor's Corporation uses the first four letters of the alphabet— AAA, AA, A; BBB, BB, B; CCC, CC, C; through D (default)—in rating bonds, with AAA being the most secure. At times a plus or minus may be added to a rating in order to more finely delineate the rating.

      b. Moody's Investor Service Incorporated also uses the alphabet but stops with C.

12. Bonds carrying the greatest risk also command the highest interest.

13. New bonds are issued at interest rates dictated by the economy. Therefore, the following explanation of *yield* is very important.

      a. Bonds are negotiable and are often traded among investors.

      b. Because the *interest is fixed,* adjustments in profit or loss are made through the price of the bond.

      c. *Current yield* is calculated through dividing the annual interest by the price of the bond.

      d. If a $1000 bond is *bought at par* and pays $90 interest, the yield is 9 percent ($90/$1000 = 9.00%).

      e. If a $1000 bond is *bought at a discount* of 10 percent and pays $90 interest, the yield is 10 percent ($90/$900 — 10.00%).

      f. If a $1000 bond is *bought at a premium* of 10 percent and pays $90 interest, the yield is 8.18 percent ($90/$1100 = 8.18%).[2]

RISK MANAGEMENT AND INSURING SCHOOL PROPERTY

The 1950s saw a significant advance in the commercial insurance industry. By drawing together all of a business's property and casualty insurance coverage into one *package,* a business could have a convenient, improved, and cost effective insurance

[2] Jeffery B. Little and Lucien Rhodes, *Understanding Wall Street* (Cockeysville, Maryland: Liberty Publishing Company, 1978), pp. 126–128.

program. However, insurance is only one aspect of a total risk management program. With the rising cost of all services, it is important for a board of education to require the superintendent of schools and his or her staff to develop an approach to school property management that incorporates the tenets of risk management.

Principles of Risk Management

The very act of living is a risk. No matter what you do or how careful you are, there is always the possibility that an accident will cause injury to yourself or damage to your property. There are, however, certain principles for handling risks that experience has identified and that have been operationalized for a considerable amount of time by large corporations.

First, identify and evaluate the school district's exposure to risks. It might be necessary to ask the insurance agent/broker or the underwriter for the district's insurance coverage to help the school district administration in conducting an audit of the school district's facilities to ascertain potential risks. If such services are not available from the underwriter and the district's agent or broker, it may be necessary to contract with a management consulting firm that employs *safety engineers* who can advise the administration on hazards. For example, steps may not have slip-retarding strips or adequate handrails to protect the students as they move from one floor to the next. Custodial and maintenance areas may need additional ventilation to prevent fumes from accumulating and possibly being sparked into an explosion. Drivers education cars should have dual steering mechanisms to prevent an accident if a student driver loses control of the vehicle. It is possible to give numerous additional examples; however, the following question summarizes the idea of identifying the school district's potential exposure to accidents: What are the sources, causes, and kinds of possible losses and how significant are these losses likely to be?

Second, attempt to eliminate or minimize the risk. Repairing defective handrails and installing slip-retarding strips on steps are easy and relatively inexpensive ways of minimizing potential risks; others requiring a major modification to a building will be more costly. However, the expense of installing a new and more effective fire alarm system is much more cost-effective than rebuilding a facility significantly damaged because of a fire. The co-insuring of buildings is an added incentive to administrators in developing and implementing a risk management program.

Finally, if it is impossible to eliminate or significantly minimize a risk, it is common practice to transfer that risk to another party. Purchasing insurance is the most common method of transferring a risk. There are circumstances, however, when a school district should transfer a risk to another party through a contractual agreement. It is not uncommon for school districts in metropolitan areas to have experienced decreasing enrollments, which has eventuated in the closing of schools. Many of these facilities have been leased to private firms and other public institutions. The lease agreement should have a provision requiring the lessee to protect the property and the school district from liability through insurance. A second example of transferring risk through a contractual agreement involves the usual requirement of a performance bond from a contractor who is building or remodeling a school facility.

The Value of Deductibles

In purchasing insurance, the premium paid by the school district is a measure of the transferred risk. The greater the risk, the more it will cost the district in premium. If the risk assumed by the insurance company is reduced, not only will the premium be reduced but the competition for the premium will be increased.

Besides having a reduced premium, there are many reasons for using deductibles. It is good management for a business or institution to retain some portion of a risk because it encourages a continual concern for safety. In addition, deductibles eliminate nuisance claims, preserve a market for the district's coverage, broaden that coverage and reduce internal administrative costs.

There is no magic formula for determining the appropriate size for a deductible. However, there are a few guidelines that can be used in analyzing a school district's situation to settle on a deductible. First, determine the district's loss expectancy from past history; second, determine how much loss can be absorbed by the district per location and occurrence or in the aggregate; finally, determine how much money can be saved in reduced premium costs if the district assumes a portion of the loss.

There are many different types of deductibles, ranging from a *straight* dollar amount to *percentage, disappearing, franchise,* and *time* deductibles. It is most important for school board members to review the school district's deductible approach from time to time and especially when a current insurance contract is up for rebidding.

Commercial Package Insurance Policies

Before 1960, packaged commercial insurance policies were nothing more than separate property and liability exposures brought together under one cover. The true commercial package combines both property and liability coverages and has three distinct advantages to school districts: lower premium, convenience, and broader-based protection.

Property insurance. This is, of course, the most extensive aspect of the school district's exposure. Direct damage to property and building contents can be disastrous. The basic property coverage will insure both buildings and contents against damage caused by fire, lightning, windstorm, hail, smoke, vandalism, riot, explosion, vehicles, and aircraft. Through endorsements, this coverage can be extended to include such additional perils as glass breakage, ice and snow, water damage, and even earthquakes. A more common approach today in providing property coverage is, however, the *all-risk* policy, which is broader than the most inclusive *named-peril* policy. All-risk protection means that a loss is covered unless it is clearly excluded in the policy.

Most property insurance policies limit the amount of recovery on losses to *actual cash value,* which is commonly defined as the current replacement cost minus actual physical depreciation. It is possible, however, to have property insurance endorsed to provide coverage on a *replacement cost* rather than the *actual cash value* basis. A school district will probably be required to carry insurance equal to 80 percent of replacement value with such an endorsement. Most insurance companies will also cover furniture, machinery, and equipment on a replacement cost basis.

Liability insurance. The liability portion of a package policy should be written on a *comprehensive* basis, which provides automatic coverage for newly acquired or rented premises. The standard liability protection covers proven claims of bodily injury or property damage arising out of the facility. For example, if a student slips on a loose floor tile and breaks an arm and/or damages a wrist watch, the hospital bills, physicians' fees, and a new watch should be covered under the liability portion of the property insurance coverage. The limits of coverage are determined by the history of claims, but protection under one million dollars in the aggregated claim is very risky for a school district.

Additional types of coverage. There are many different types of insurance coverage that can be included in a package. Some of the more common types included in a school district package are: (1) crime coverage for loss of money occurring inside or outside the premises; (2) boiler and machinery insurance for losses and injuries occurring in a boiler explosion or failure of major machinery such as a a high voltage electrical panel; (3) automobile and vehicle insurance coverage for drivers education cars and school district owned vehicles; (4) inland marine insurance on such items as musical instruments.

Selecting an Agent or Broker

Insurance constitutes a legal contract between the insurance company and the insured person or organization. This contract is facilitated through a third party, the insurance agent or broker. A majority of insurance companies operate under the American Agency System by which the company contracts with an individual who is authorized to issue policies, collect premiums, and solicit renewals within a given territory. *Independent* agents may represent several companies while *exclusive* agents usually limit their practice to a single company's products. In either case, the agent is a legal representative of the insurance company and can act for the school district on the company's behalf.

Brokers are not tied to a specific insurance company by contract and act on a freelance basis to buy coverages for clients. The broker may place business through an agent or go directly to an insurance company. The significant difference between an agent and a broker lies in the *legal* character of the agent. As the legal representative of an insurance company, if the agent says that the school district is covered, it is. The broker must first obtain verification from the insurance company.

Selecting an Insurance Company

There are literally thousands of insurance companies selling property and casualty insurance in the United States. These companies differ significantly in their capacity to handle risks. A good reference about the ability of an insurance company to cover the possible losses of a school district is the rating service, A. M. Best Company, Incorporated. Because insurance companies are competitive in establishing premiums, it is imperative for a board of education to select their insurance package through a public bidding process initiated by the central office administrative staff. The directory published by A. M. Best can be used by school district administrators and school board members when they analyze the bids from various insurance companies before awarding a contract.

It will be necessary for a school district to have an up-to-date appraisal of the school buildings and their contents before initiating the bidding process. A land appraisal is, of course, not necessary for insurance purposes but could be necessary for those school districts wishing to sell excess schools abandoned because of decreasing enrollment. The services of a professional appraiser are easily obtained but the school board should thoroughly understand the procedures criteria the appraiser will use in establishing values. This will have a significant effect on a school district if a catastrophe occurs and the district needs to replace a building. The co-insurance provisions in most insurance packages by which a school district is required to retain ten to twenty percent of the property and content value, make it imperative for a school district to keep its appraisal values consistent with replacement value. Otherwise, a school district may be underinsured.

There are certain questions that the school district's administrative staff should ask the insurance companies submitting bids on the insurance program. First, does the insurance company write all the forms of coverage needed by the school district? Second, is the insurance package flexible enough to include optional coverages not available under conventional packages? Third, does the insurance company have nearby offices satffed by professionals who can handle all lines? Fourth, are the company's adjusters qualified to deal with all types of claims? Fifth, is the company's underwriting philosophy progressive enough to consider new types of insurance risks? Figure 7-1 represents an instrument developed by the Missouri Department of Elementary and Secondary Education but modified for this presentation and meant to be used by a board of education as it evaluates its school district's insurance program. Each description is a criteria for evaluating the management of the program. The degree to which the school district's management procedures conform to each descriptor is evaluated on the following scale: na = not applicable, 1 = poor or missing, 2 = fair, 3 = good, and 4 = excellent.

SELECTED ISSUES IN PROPERTY MANAGEMENT

There are three significant issues currently facing public school districts that will persist into the next two decades and present boards of education with major challenges: adapting school facilities to meet the needs of handicapped students and

FIGURE 7-1 Checklist to Determine the Adequacy of a School District's Insurance Program[3]

LEGAL REQUIREMENTS

The school district has developed policies and procedures which comply with common under-standings of the state statutes as they apply to school insurance.	na	1	2	3	4
The school district utilizes open competition to determine who carries their insurance; also the board accepts the lowest responsible bid.	na	1	2	3	4
The school district's total insurance program is open for inspection.	na	1	2	3	4

ORGANIZATION AND ADMINISTRATION

Responsibility

The school district has developed a policy which places the responsibility for managing the insurance program with the central office administration.	na	1	2	3	4
The school district maintains adequate records on the total insurance program.	na	1	2	3	4
The school district utilizes professional assist-ance as needed in evaluating the total insurance pro-gram.	na	1	2	3	4
The school district reviews the total insurance program annually.	na	1	2	3	4

Procedures

The school district has developed a standard operating procedure utilizing a definite set of writ-ten criteria for awarding insurance on the basis of competition.	na	1	2	3	4
The school district recognizes that the con-tinuity of the insurance program is important and changes in the program or carriers are made on the basis of substantial improvement of coverage or cost reduction.	na	1	2	3	4
The school district utilizes acceptable business principles in developing its risk management pro-gram.	na	1	2	3	4

[3]Department of Elementary and Secondary Education, *Checklist to Determine the Adequacy of a School District's Insurance Program* (Jefferson City, Mo.: The Department, 1980).

The school district has developed procedures   na   1   2   3   4
to follow on insurance losses.

The school community in general and interested   na   1   2   3   4
local insurance agents and brokers in particular are
well aware of the objectives of the program.

The school district's policy on insurance matters   na   1   2   3   4
neither favors nor discriminates against local in-
surance representatives.

RISK MANAGEMENT

Identification

The school district has a clearly defined, written   na   1   2   3   4
and legally defensible policy on liability coverage.

The school district has developed a clearly de-   na   1   2   3   4
fined, written policy on providing for adequate
protection for all school properties.

The school district's policy provides for a   na   1   2   3   4
definite procedure for periodically appraising replacement cost and the insurable value of buildings
and contents.

The school district keeps a current listing of all   na   1   2   3   4
buildings and/or additions for insurance purposes,
including such details as dates of construction,
condition, and square footage.

The school district, for insurance purposes,   na   1   2   3   4
classifies as building-fixed equipment laboratory
tables, built-in cabinets, and other items that are
attached to the building.

The school district keeps a current inventory of   na   1   2   3   4
all school supplies and equipment classified as
contents for insurance purposes, including such
details as current market value, date of purchase,
and condition.

The school district keeps a current listing of all   na   1   2   3   4
school vehicles for insurance purposes, including
details such as model, purchase price, and current
value.

The school district has a standard procedure to   na   1   2   3   4
account for depreciation on the various types of
property.

The school district's vehicle coverage includes   na   1   2   3   4
comprehensive, liability, personal injury, property
damage, fire, theft, collision, and insured motorist
types where applicable.

The school district provides a bond on the   na   1   2   3   4
treasurer.

The school district provides burglary insurance.	na	1	2	3	4
The school district provides broad form coverage on money and securities.	na	1	2	3	4
The school district carries broad form boiler insurance.	na	1	2	3	4
The school district's boiler insurance includes a provision for regular inspection and reports.	na	1	2	3	4
The school district reports crimes and vandalism to the proper police authorities.	na	1	2	3	4
Employees and supervisors are familiar with reporting procedures in the event of accidents.	na	1	2	3	4
The school district is prepared to cover all of the risks which have been determined as responsibilities of the school system, i.e., fire and extended, floater, boiler, liability, Workmen's Compensation, vehicle, crime, athletics, honesty bond, health and medical for employees, student, builder's risk, sprinkler.	na	1	2	3	4

Reduction

The school district has cooperated with outside agencies such as the insurance carriers, fire department, police department, and others in developing policy and procedures to eliminate hazards to human life and property and for possible reductions in insurance premiums.	na	1	2	3	4

Assumption

The school district is aware of all coverage which is not transferable and also limitations on insurance coverage.	na	1	2	3	4
The school district utilizes coinsurance coverage on property.	na	1	2	3	4
The school district includes a deductible clause in its insurance policy or policies where the premium difference is favorable.	na	1	2	3	4

Transfer

The school district has considered the possibility of transferring some risks to contractors or lessors. Transportation is an area where this might be considered.	na	1	2	3	4
The school district's policy statement on insurance outlines an approach which provides effective coverage at a minimum cost for those risks which have been classified as responsibilities to be transferred from the district.	na	1	2	3	4

The school district schedules premium payments in such manner that approximately equal amounts are paid each year and insures that policies are written for a specified period of time.	na	1	2	3	4
The school district has insured property on the basis of insurable value and/or replacement cost.	na	1	2	3	4
The school district includes an agreed amount clause in the carrier's written policy or policies if co-insurance is utilized.	na	1	2	3	4
The school district has considered a package plan which combines coverages.	na	1	2	3	4
The school district utilizes blanket coverage, schedule coverage, and/or specific coverage plan in its insurance program.	na	1	2	3	4
The school district endeavors to engage a minimum number of agencies and companies in its insurance program.	na	1	2	3	4
The school district uses services such as Best's Rating Guide to determine the managerial and financial status of the insurance companies with which it deals.	na	1	2	3	4

employees; designing and modifying school buildings that are energy-efficient; closing, selling, and/or leasing school buildings because of decreases in pupil enrollments.

Title V of the Rehabilitation Act of 1973 contains five sections. Section 504, Subpart C, applies to school facilities and requires that they be accessible to the handicapped. Its provisions state that all new construction is to be barrier-free and all programs are to be accessible within three years. School districts are not obliged to make each school accessible to the handicapped, but the district must make such accommodations allowing the programs "as a whole" to be accessible. All non-structural accommodations were to be completed within sixty days after these regulations went into effect. Outside ramps, however, were to be immediately built after June 1, 1977, and all structural changes completed no later than three years after this date.

A board of education must be energy conscious today from a very practical perspective—energy costs the district a large amount of money, a portion of which could be redirected to other needed areas if savings could be realized through initiating an energy conservation program. A skilled director of buildings and grounds with help from other central office administrators in the Administrative Services Department can analyze the district's energy efficiency by examining (1) utility bills; (2) lighting systems; (3) major energy loads; (4) walls, doors, windows, roofs, and other outer shell features; and (5) heating, ventilating, and air conditioning systems. Such an audit will point out areas of immediate concern.

However, an organized energy conservation program is the only long-term solution to escalating costs. Such a program will be successful only if it is people-centered. Figure 7-2 presents an outline of how all members of the school community can be part of an energy conservation program.

FIGURE 7-2 Outline: Staff Involvement in an Energy Conservation Program[4]

I. DISTRICT LEVEL
   A. School Board
      1. Commit school district to energy conservation ethic
      2. Establish basic energy usage policy for school district
      3. Authorize energy audit
      4. Set goals for energy savings
      5. Evaluate energy conservation efforts and results
   B. Superintendent
      1. Initiate and lead commitment to energy conservation ethic
         a. Provide philosophy and rationale
         b. Be aware of applicable funding and compliance legislation
         c. Demonstrate impact of energy dollars exported from school district
         d. Develop district-wide, long-range energy conservation in-service educational program
         e. Visibly reward persons and programs that meet or exceed energy conservation objectives
         f. Set personal example of energy conservation
      2. Establish persuasive district-wide energy conservation task force or committee
         a. Solicit energy policy suggestions
         b. Help establish energy conservation priorities
         c. Provide data on energy conservation performance of district
         d. Utilize members in public information efforts
      3. Assign specific energy conservation responsibilities to specific district individuals
         a. Monitor their performance
         b. Examples: building level energy manager, district public information officer
      4. Realize energy consumption is a political and an economic matter
   C. Assistant Superintendent for Business Affairs
      1. Prepare technical reports for school board, superintendent, energy conservation task force, principals, physical plant staff
      2. Monitor and report on applicable energy conservation funding and compliance legislation

[4]Dale E. Kaiser and James C. Parker, "Staff Involvement in Energy Programs," *School Business Affairs,* Vol. 47, No. 7 (June 1981), pp. 10, 11, 23.

   3. Evaluate energy usage and provide factual record
      a.   Identify source, quantity, and cost of each district energy source
      b.   Inspect facilities, equipment and supplies usage
      c.   Present data in comparable forms
      d.   Establish tough yet realistic and measurable energy objectives to support district goals and priorities
      e.   Assess progress toward meeting objectives
   4. Purchase and construct with energy savings in mind
   5. Identify and recommend expert consultant help
   6. Demonstrate cost effectiveness of any energy measures
   7. Work with building engineers in scheduling operations, maintenance and repairs to reduce energy consumption
   8. Convey energy usage progress to school publics by:
      a.   district and by individual school buildings
      b.   monthly, weekly, or daily energy consumption charts for principals, teachers, and pupils
      c.   less complex charts and graphs for mass media
   9. Attend conferences and workshops on energy conservation

II.   BUILDING LEVEL
   A.   Principals
      1. Program and schedule to conserve energy
      2. Participate in district-wide energy conservation conferences and workshops
      3. Establish building energy audit and operations oversight committee
      4. Survey teachers and staff regarding their suggestions for energy conservation in their rooms and/or building areas
      5. Compare and compete with similar school concerning energy conservation
      6. Report in meetings and in bulletins at least monthly about comparative energy conservation effectiveness
      7. Prepare individual classroom energy checklists
      8. Encourage teachers to attend conferences on energy usage
      9. Demonstrate commitment to energy conservation ethic by setting a personal example
   B.   Teachers
      1. Heighten pupils' awareness of energy topics in imaginative ways
      2. Put energy conservation in appropriate course materials
      3. Program and schedule to conserve energy
      4. Follow operational guidelines for building and district energy conservation
   C.   Physical Plant Staff
      1. Lead or assist in collecting energy audit data
         a.   Keep accurate records
         b.   Analyze bus routes and field trip requests
         c.   Assess food services energy usage

2. Read and follow operational and maintenance manuals
3. Read and follow school district guidelines for energy conservation
4. Monitor and report compliance with district energy reduction objectives
5. Investigate alternative energy sources—especially solar—may be used to conserve conventional sources
6. Suggest both short and long-term operational and maintenance guidelines modifications which promise energy conservation
7. Monitor trade journals and catalogs for energy saving tips, supplies, and equipment
8. Help all fellow personnel to be familiar with equipment, installations, and distribution systems
9. Assist in developing energy efficient purchase specifications
10. Participate in hands-on training opportunities

D. Pupils
1. Form committees for energy conservation awareness
2. Act through Student Council projects
3. Plan competition between classes, buildings
4. Present student forums
5. Instill awareness through curriculum projects

One of the most highly charged issues that a school board can be faced with is the closing of a school. Parents, students, and teachers usually have very strong emotional ties to individual schools and will not immediately see the wisdom of closing "their school." There is no *right* way to proceed. However, there are some things a board of education can do to minimize the potential disruption. First, form a committee composed of teachers, administrators, parents, citizens, and students charged with formulating a criteria to be used in deciding which schools will be closed and which schools will remain open. It is important for the school board to ask the various constituents of the school community to designate who will serve on the committee. For example, the teacher unions (NEA, AFT, etc.) should appoint the teacher representatives, and the PTA/PTO organizations can choose the parent representatives. The criteria should include such considerations as the age of the schools, maintenance and janitorial costs, classroom size, location of the schools, repair requirements, energy costs, and the quality of education.

Once the criteria are established, it is the task of the administrative staff to apply them to the schools under consideration. Before the board of education makes a final decision, a public hearing should be conducted during which the criteria and administrative staff analysis are presented to those in attendance. The public should then be allowed to provide further input. The board of education is advised to consider all of this data and make a final decision at an official board meeting held at a different time than the public hearing.

SUMMARY

The importance of school buildings and facilities to the success of the instructional program is often overlooked by citizens, teachers, administrators, and even board members. The function of educational institutions is to educate children and young people. Consequently, the design of school facilities must be viewed within the context of educational concepts.

Historically, schoolhouses as designated structures did not appear until the seventeenth century and consisted primarily of one room, long tables for the pupils, and a raised podium for the teacher. In 1880, Louis Sullivan, an eminent American architect, enunciated the principle, "Form follows function." The planning of functional school buildings has been the continual concern not only of architects but also of educators.

There are four principles of operation that mirror the human condition and must be considered when planning an educational facility: (1) gradualism, (2) reversibility, (3) dual purpose design, (4) people-centered design.

In addition, there are four steps in the process of carrying out a school construction and/or remodeling program. First, establish educational goals and objectives; second, develop architectural plans; third, develop a financial plan; fourth, implement the construction and/or remodeling project. Each of these steps has a number of components implemented by various staff members. Each component has, in turn, a number of procedures and subprocesses.

In the public sector, financing capital projects is usually accomplished through public borrowing, in the form of bond issues. Bonds may be sold to build schools, furnish schools, remodel schools, replace roofs, and purchase large, expensive equipment. Voter approval is necessary through a bond issue election in order for a board to be authorized to sell bonds. State statutes closely regulate the process of flotation, debt limits, and all aspects of public borrowing.

Capital projects have traditionally been financed through public borrowing because they are nonrecurring expenses that should not be financed from the operating fund levy. In addition, the burden of financing capital projects should be spread out over many generations because these future generations will also benefit from the projects.

There are four steps in the process of bond flotation. First, the board of education must determine what capital projects are and will be needed by the present and future generations of the school district. Second, the board must become familiar with the state statutes pertaining to municipal bonds and bond issue elections. Third, the board of education needs to initiate a bond issue election campaign. Fourth, if the bond issue passes, the board must initiate those procedures ensuring the legality of the bonds.

The 1950s saw a significant advance in the commercial insurance industry, the packaging of multiple insurance coverages. However, insurance is only one aspect of a total management program. There are three principles of operation in risk management that should be implemented by the administration. First, identify and evaluate the school district's exposure to risks; second, attempt to eliminate or minimize the risk; third, if it is impossible to eliminate or significantly minimize a risk, transfer it to another party.

In purchasing insurance, the premium paid by the school district is a measure of the transferred risk. If the risk assumed by the insurance company is reduced by the use of deductibles, the competition for the premium will be increased. Deductibles also encourage a continual concern for safety, eliminate nuisance claims, and reduce internal administrative costs.

The commercial package combining property and liability coverages usually will provide the district with a lower premium, more convenience, and broader-based protection. Property coverage should be "all risk," which is a broader protection than the most inclusive named-peril policy. All-risk protection means that a loss is covered unless it is clearly excluded in the policy.

Insurance constitutes a legal contract between the insurance company and the insured party or organization. This contract is facilitated through a third party, the insurance agent or broker. A majority of insurance companies operate under the American Agency System by which the company contracts with an individual agent who is authorized to issue policies, collect premiums, and solicit renewals within a given territory, whereas brokers are not tied to a specific company by contract and act on a freelance basis to buy coverage for clients.

There are literally thousands of insurance companies selling property and casualty insurance in the United States. A service that rates the ability of an insurance company to cover the possible losses of a school district is the A. M. Best Company, Incorporated.

It will be necessary for a school district to have an up-to-date appraisal of the school buildings and the contents before initiating the bidding process.

There are three significant issues currently facing public school districts which will persist into the next two decades: (1) adapting school facilities to meet the needs of handicapped students and employees, (2) designing and modifying school buildings which are energy efficient, (3) closing, selling, and/or leasing school buildings because of decreases in pupil enrollments.

IMPLICATIONS FOR SCHOOL
BOARD MEMBERS

There are four implications for boards of education indicated from this presentation of school district property management and allied issues.

First, board members should be concerned with appropriating sufficient dollars in the school district budget to maintain school facilities that are safe, healthy, pleasant, and stimulating because such environments have a significant effect upon the quality of the learning-instructional process.

Secondly, boards of education should finance capital projects through public borrowing—bond issues. This method will keep the operating levy from being overburdened and will spread out the responsibility of paying for capital projects over the many generations benefitting from the improvements.

Third, boards of education should require periodic audits from the superintendent concerning the scope and adequacy of the school district's risk management program. The potential loss to a school district in property and liability could bankrupt a district through underprotection if a catastrophy occurred.

Fourth, school board members must evaluate the school facilities and appropriate funds to make them accessible to the handicapped and to make them energy efficient.

SELECTED BIBLIOGRAPHY

CASTALDI, BASIL, *Creative Planning of Educational Facilities.* Chicago: Rand McNally & Company, 1969.

COUNCIL OF EDUCATIONAL FACILITY PLANNERS, *Guide for Planning Educational Facilities.* Columbus, Ohio: The Council, 1982, Revised Edition.

_____ , *Surplus School Space: The Problem and the Possibilities.* Columbus, Ohio: The Council, 1978.

RESEARCH CORPORATION OF THE ASSOCIATION OF SCHOOL BUSINESS OFFICIALS, *Energy Conservation and Management.* Park Ridge, Illinois: The Association, 1981.

_____ , *Schoolhouse Planning.* Park Ridge, Illinois: The Association, 1980.

CHAPTER EIGHT
THE ROLE OF THE SCHOOL BOARD IN DEVELOPING THE INSTRUCTIONAL PROGRAM AND IN PUPIL RELATIONS

Learning will occur if students are presented with a well planned course of studies and if they are held responsible for their education.

This chapter deals more directly with pupil-related issues than the other chapters in the book. The first section on the instruction program presupposes an acquaintance with the learning-instructional process and attempts to provide school board members with a frame of reference for analyzing how responsibilities are delegated in relation to program development. The various steps for program development as presented are applicable not only to the regular instructional program but also to remedial programs and programs for the gifted, as well as extracurricular programs. Appendix A presents a glossary of terms that should be helpful in understanding the instructional program and its implementation.

The second part of this chapter deals specifically with the rights and responsibilities of students—information necessary for the school board as it creates policies and makes decisions concerning pupil behavior.

THE INSTRUCTIONAL PROGRAM

The instructional program is, of course, the central concern of every school district because it is through this program that the mission of the school system, to educate students, is fulfilled. The instructional program is also a rather elusive entity. In order to more thoroughly understand the instructional program, it is necessary to begin by defining and clarifying a set of concepts.

Through the ages of time, human beings have sought to gain a greater knowledge and understanding of the world in which they live. History, in fact, can be viewed from the perspective of human achievements—such as taming the elements and harnessing them in such a manner that the quality of life is enhanced. Countless scientists and explorers have attempted to quantify and categorize the physical world. Others have sought to understand the interactions of the human condition as expressed through communication and socialization. In developing the process for this quantification and study of reality, there have emerged bodies of organized knowledge commonly referred to as subject matter *disciplines*. Physics, mathematics, biology, and all the other related physical sciences are attempts to isolate a segment of reality and to understand it in terms of quantity and category. Languages and the fine arts attempt to interpret an aspect of reality in terms of creative human expression and communication. The social and historical sciences isolate human events and interpret their meaning in relation to the socialization process. Physical health and skills enhance an individual's perception of reality.

While this is an oversimplification of the development of subject matter disciplines, it does exemplify the existence of organized bodies of knowledge that have, in turn, been developed into curricula by educators interested in transmitting this knowledge to others. The facts, concepts, formulas, and processes constituting a discipline can never be completely transmitted to any given individual at any level of instruction because that body of knowledge known as a discipline is constantly expanding. Human communication will never be sophisticated enough nor will any human being be capable of assimilating such a totality of knowledge.

Therefore, a selection must be made by educators as to what will be taught to students at what level and in what sequence. Teaching is the process of deciding on and implementing the most effective method for transmitting the facts, concepts, formulas, and processes that are to be learned by a specific group of students. The psychology of human development teaches that learning occurs in a building block configuration. New skills, concepts, processes, and ideas are assimilated by the learner in relation to previously learned skills, concepts, processes, and ideas going back to the existential encounters of childhood. Learning is defined as a change in human capability that is retained and is not simply ascribable to the process of growth. That which is taught is the *curriculum*.

A curriculum is taken by teachers and subsequently organized into *instructional units*, each composed of lesson plans stating how the curriculum is taught. For example, a high school economics curriculum could be organized and offered in two one-semester courses. Instructional units for the first semester might deal with: (1) defining land, labor, and capital; (2) describing the type and quantity of these resources necessary for production in the U.S. economy; and (3) how this production generates income for spending, saving, and investing. Lesson plans set forth the instructional methods the teacher will employ to transmit the concepts in an instructional unit. Articles from *The Wall Street Journal* about the American auto industry and its relationship to foreign oil prices could be used when discussing the types and quantity of resources necessary to the health of the U.S. economy. Skills in analyzing the U.S. economy become a primary objective for this lesson plan.

The instructional program is thus composed of the curriculum, which is derived from subject matter disciplines organized into instructional units and presented to students through lesson plans.

Steps in Developing
the Instructional Program

The instructional program should reflect the desires and values of the school community. Educators in some school districts tend to believe that the instructional program and its development are the prerogative of the professional staff. While the professional staff plays a significant part in developing this program, the expertise of the professional staff essentially centers around constructing instructional units and lesson plans and in carrying out the instructional process. The following steps should clarify and bring into focus not only the various steps in developing the instructional program but also identifying who is responsible for each step in the process.

First, schools belong to the people and as such must reflect the values and beliefs of the people within the parameters established by federal and state constitutions, federal and state laws, and court decisions. The board of education, as the elected representatives of the people living within a school district's boundaries, is, therefore, directly responsible for translating the values and beliefs of the community into educational goals and objectives. Ongoing input from students, parents, teachers, administrators, and other citizens is essential if the school board is going to truly understand the needs and desires of the school district's constituents. The director for community relations can help gather much of the needed input through surveys. In addition, state departments of education and the U.S. Office of Education have a great deal of material available to assist school boards as they attempt to formulate local goals in harmony with national and state educational objectives. Educational goals are usually formulated around the following five categories: (1) intellectual development; (2) physical development; (3) social development; (4) emotional development; and (5) career development. The board of education should formally promulgate educational goals for the school district and should review the relevance of these goals on a continual basis and, when necessary, revise them. It is necessary to have formal educational goals in order to give direction to the professional staff so that they can carry out their responsibilities.

Second, the assistant superintendent for curriculum, curriculum coordinators, other administrators, and teachers under the direction of the superintendent are responsible for translating the educational goals established by the school board into a curriculum, which is the body of knowledge, skills, and values that are to be taught. Curriculum in this sense, therefore, not only includes the concepts, formulas, facts, and processes of a discipline such as geography but also those human values permeating our society, such as freedom, respect for individual rights, and the free enterprise system of economics. Furthermore, curriculum includes providing opportunities for students to develop their potential in such a way that they are able to make a choice after completing high school to either go on to other educational institutions or to enter the work force. Thus, vocational as well as college preparatory programs are necessary aspects of an effective instructional program. Extracurricular and athletic programs enhance and actualize certain values and skills acquired through the instructional program.

Third, curriculum coordinators, teachers, and building level principals are responsible for organizing the curriculum into instructional units and lesson plans. *Site specific curriculum* is a term which is often used by educators to designate the adaptation of the curriculum to the specific needs of the students living in a given attendance area.

Fourth, measuring the effectiveness of the instructional program is essential if modifications are to be made in how the curriculum is organized and presented to students through instructional units and lesson plans. Two vehicles providing the board of education, administration, and instructional staff with a great deal of information and insight are (1) minimum competency testing and (2) standardized achievement testing.

"A minimum competency test is designed to determine whether an examinee has reached a prespecified level of performance relative to each competency being tested."[1] Many states have developed, and require students to pass, a minimum competency test in order to demonstrate that they have acquired certain basic skills.

Standardized achievement tests measure the skills and acquired knowledge of students by comparing their performance with national and regional standards.

Nonobjective methods may also be used to determine if the instructional program is meeting the needs of students and the desires of parents. Parents and presently enrolled students can be surveyed concerning perceptions about the quality of education being offered by the school district. In addition, alumni can be contacted and asked to comment on how well the instructional program prepared them to meet the challenges of their post high school life.

Supervising the Instructional Program

The instructional program is implemented by teachers and other professionals through the learning-instructional process, which takes place in and outside the classroom. It should be no great surprise to anyone that the success of the instructional program depends upon the quality of instruction provided by teachers and the quality of support services provided by other professionals such as guidance counselors.

Monitoring the quality of teaching and services is the responsibility of the building principal. This monitoring process usually includes the formal evaluation of employee performance using an evaluation instrument such as the one exhibited

---

[1] Ronald K. Hambleton and Daniel R. Eignor, "Competency Test Development, Validation, and Standard Setting," in *Minimum Competency Achievement Testing: Motives, Models, Measures, and Consequences,* eds. Richard M. Jaeger and Carol Kehr Tittle (Berkeley, Calif.: McCutchan Publishing Corporation, 1980), p. 369.

in Appendix A. Chapter nine outlines a due process procedure for terminating teachers and other professional employees who consistently perform at a substandard level.

It is very important to the success of the instructional program for a board of education to make an attempt to retain quality teachers and other professional employees by providing the best possible salary compensation and fringe benefit packages. Reasonable working conditions will also help retain good employees, and thus the school board should consistently evaluate and try to improve conditions. The pupil-teacher ratio, the quantity and quality of instructional materials, and the maintenance level of facilities are also important to employee satisfaction.

Special Education Programs

The 1970s saw the passage of two laws by the U.S. Congress that have had a direct effect upon the instructional program as it relates to handicapped children. The thrust of all civil rights legislation is equal treatment under the law. Minority groups and females have succeeded in getting legislation ensuring their civil rights. The difference between these civil rights laws and the two laws dealing with the handicapped lies in implementation regulations. In order for a handicapped person to receive the same treatment as other students, he or she must receive special consideration. For example, access to educational programs for the handicapped might require modifying existing school facilities.

Section 504 of the Rehabilitation Act, 1973, specifically addresses the accessibility requirements of educational facilities to handicapped students, teachers, and other employees. Chapter seven deals, to a great extent, with the implementation of Section 504.

Public Law 94-142, the Education for All Handicapped Children Act of 1975, stipulates that public schools must educate handicapped students in the "least restrictive environment." Further, an "individual educational program" must be developed and implemented for each handicapped student.

In order for a student to be designated as handicapped, he or she must be tested to determine the specific nature of the handicap and, before being placed in a special class, the school officials must:

> First, notify the parents or guardians of the child, in their primary language if it is not English, that the school intends to change the student's educational placement, including a full explanation of the reasons for the change;
> Second, provide an opportunity for the parents or guardians to receive an impartial due process hearing and the opportunity to examine all relevant records and to obtain an independent evaluation of the student;
> Third, provide an individual who is not a school employee to act as a surrogate parent when the natural parents or legal guardians are unavailable;
> Fourth, make provisions which will ensure that the decision rendered in the due process hearing is binding and subject only to judicial review;
> Fifth, proceed to develop an individual educational program for the handicapped student, which should include *mainstreaming* the child whenever possible into programs and activities with nonhandicapped children.

The director of special education should be held responsible for ensuring that test materials and other vehicles for identifying, classifying, and placing students in special education programs are selected and administered in a nondiscriminatory manner in terms of race, sex, and national origin.

THE RIGHTS
AND RESPONSIBILITIES
OF STUDENTS[2]

The children and youth of our nation are of vital concern to every level of government and have received considerable attention, particularly in the legislative actions of the U.S. Congress and the federal judiciary. The underlying principle that must guide the policy-making activities of school boards as they address pupil behavior is that children are *citizens,* having rights and privileges under the law. The difference between an adult and a child in the legal sense is that children are not required to exhibit the same level of responsibility as an adult. This does not mean that children are free from responsibility for their actions, but rather, possess limited responsibility. The intent of this section is to clarify the rights and responsibilities of students as defined by legislation and case law. Boards of education should consider these rights and responsibilities to be the minimal level required in dealing with pupil behavior, a level that may be expanded in future state and federal legislation and/or case law. It is most unlikely that these rights and responsibilities will be diminished through the legislative or judicial process.

Religion.   All students have the right to observe or not to observe a religion. The school cannot interfere with the right by requiring, establishing, or conducting religious services. Further, the school board and administration are forbidden to create policies or administrative procedures favoring one religion over another or religion over nonreligion.

In enjoying this right, students have the responsibility of not interfering with the rights of others as they observe their religious beliefs.

This right to religious noninterference is clearly outlined in the following court cases: *Engel* vs. *Vitale,* 370 U.S. 421, 431 (1962); *Abington School District* vs. *Schempp,* 374 U.S. 203 (1963); *Epperson* vs. *Arkansas,* 393 U.S. 97, 107–108 (1968).

Speech and expression.   There are four areas under this section that must be considered. First, students have a right to express their viewpoint through the spoken word or through other forms of expression, such as wearing arm bands

---

[2]The content for this section was gleaned from *The Rights and Responsibilities of Students: A Handbook for the School Community,* by the U.S. Department of Health, Education, and Welfare (Washington, D.C.: U.S. Government Printing Office, 1979), pp. 1–46.

decorated with symbols espousing a cause or belief. In exercising this right, students have the responsibility of not *materially or substantially* disrupting school operations and interfering with the rights of others. Further, students are responsible under the law for the legal consequences of slanderous speech. This decision was rendered in *Tinker* vs. *Des Moines Independent Community School District,* 393 U.S. 503, 514 (1969).

Second, students have the right to publish and distribute literature written independently from school-related courses and activities. However, students have the responsibility of following the rules established by school officials as to the time, place, and manner for distributing such literature. Further, students are responsible under the law for the legal consequences regarding libel. *Riseman* vs. *School Committee of Quincy,* 439 F. 2d 11-8 (1st Cir. 1971) applied the disruptive test of the Tinker case to the distribution of literature in establishing this right.

Third, students have a right to dress and groom themselves in accordance with their own taste or in accordance with the taste of their parents. School district officials may restrict this right only if there is a legitimate health or safety reason and if less drastic measures are inadequate in protecting the health or safety of the student and/or others. Further, school officials must be cautious not to discriminate on the basis of sex in applying the health and safety restrictions, and cannot require a more restrictive code to participate in extracurricular activities. However, students have the responsibility of dressing and grooming themselves in such a manner that they are not immodest or provocative, which might cause material or substantial disruption to school operations. *Breen* vs. *Kahl,* 296 F. Supp. 702 (W.D. Wis.), aff'd, 419 F. 2d 1034 (7th Cir. 1969), helped to establish this student right.

Fourth, students have the right not to participate in saluting the American flag or in saying the Pledge of Allegiance, if so doing violates their beliefs. It is not necessary for the students to leave the classroom when such activities occur, and they may be required to be seated quietly during the ceremony. Students who are not participating in such ceremonies have the responsibility of not being disruptive to those students who wish to participate. This right of nonparticipation was set forth in *West Virginia State Board of Education* vs. *Barnette,* 319 U.S. 624, 634 (1934) and further refined in *Goetz* vs. *Ansell,* 477 F. 2d 636 (2nd Cir. 1973) and *Banks* vs. *Board of Public Instruction,* 314 F. Supp. 285 (S.D. Fla.), aff'd 450 F. 2d 1103 (5th Cir. 1973).

Press. Students have the right to gather, write, and editorialize on the news and to distribute official and/or unofficial school newspapers. This right should be exercised without prior censorship and without the fear of reprisal for the content of the published material. Faculty advisors may intervene only when material may be libelous or legally prohibited on the grounds of obscenity. In such a situation, the principal of his or her designee should consult with the school district's attorney, who should render a legal opinion as to whether the material is in violation of contemporary legal standards within five school days after the material was suppressed. The decision is immediately binding but subject to an appeal and grievance procedure.

Students have the responsibility not only of conforming to the law in regards to libel and slander but also to adhere to sound journalistic ethics. In addition, student newspapers should allow the expression of opinions contrary to editorials through publishing letters to the editor and guest columnists.

There is some ambiguity on the legal issues surrounding student journalism. However, there have been lower federal court decisions upholding students' rights to publish an official newspaper without prior censorship as in *Zucker* vs. *Panita,* 299 F. Supp. 102 (S.D.N.Y. 1969).

Assembly.   Students have the right to peacefully assemble in order to express their views on issues that are related or unrelated to school affairs. As with rights previously discussed, assembling students have a responsibility to do so in such a way as not to materially and substantially disrupt school operations. When determining if an assembly interferes with school operations, only the conduct of the demonstrators must be taken into consideration and not the conduct of the audience which, if disruptive, is subject to disciplinary action. Further, students must adhere to those administrative rules governing the time, place, and manner of assembly. In exercising the right of assembly, the test of disruptiveness established in the Tinker case is applicable with the refinements of *Gebert* vs. *Hoffman,* 336 F. Supp. 694 (E.D. Pa. 1972).

Grievance and appeal procedures.   Students have the right to a grievance procedure and the right of appeal when there arises a question concerning the scope of their rights. Such a grievance procedure should follow the line authority of the school district. For example, a grievance involving a teacher should be made to the building principal; a grievance involving a principal should be made to the superintendent of schools; and a grievance involving the superintendent should be made to the board of education. The appeal process should also follow this same line authority. Thus, a decision concerning a grievance involving a teacher, and rendered by the building principal could be appealed to the superintendent and then go to the school board if the superintendent's decision is unacceptable.

The grievance and appeal procedure should be outlined in writing and perhaps incorporated into a student handbook. This procedure should also have time constraints to ensure a speedy resolution of the grievance. For example, a student should file a grievance with the building principal within ten days after the occurrence of an incident. The principal should have at least five days to investigate the grievance and render a decision, whereupon the student might have five days to appeal the decision of the principal to the superintendent of schools.

It is the responsibility of the students to know and follow the grievance and appeal procedure. The following constitutes the major legal sources of authority for establishing such procedures: 42 U.S.C. 1983 (1970) (Codification of the Civil Rights Act of 1971); *Strickland* vs. *Inlow,* 348 F. Supp. 244 (W.D. Ark. 1972); *Strickland* vs. *Inlow,* 485 F. 2d 186, 191 (8th Cir. 1973); *Wood* vs. *Strickland,* 420 U.S. 308, 322 (1975).

The right to an education. Students have a right to receive an education that will allow them the opportunity to develop their intellectual, social, emotional, and physical potentials to the extent that they are able to become productive citizens of their community, state, and nation. Furthermore, no student shall be denied access to educational programs or extracurricular activities or be discriminated against in any manner on the basis of race, color, national origin, sex, handicap, marital status, or because of pregnancy.

Students have the responsibility of attending school punctually and on a regular basis; of adhering to all school rules and procedures; and of respecting the rights of others by not engaging in behavior disruptive to the educational process.

A considerable amount of legislative activity and case law bear directly on issues related to equal access of educational opportunities. What follows is a partial listing of those sources that should be consulted for a thorough understanding of students' right to an education:

Title VI, Civil Rights Act, 1964, 42 U.S.C. 2000d. (1970)

HEW Reg. 45 C.F.R. 80.3 (1976)

35 Fed. Reg. 11595 (1970)

Title IX of the Educational Amendments of 1972, 20 U.S.C. 1681 (1970) as amended 20 U.S.C. 1681 (a) (6) (Supp. V, 1975)

P.L. 94–482, 412 (October 12, 1976)

20 U.S.C. 1681 (a) (1970)

45 C.F.R. 86 (1976)

HEW Press Release, Statement by Casper W. Weinberger, Secretary of Health, Education and Welfare, June 3, 1975

45 C.F.R. 86.3 (1976)

45 C.F.R. 86.34 (a) (1976); HEW Press Release, supra note 51 at 3

Brown vs. *Board of Education,* 349 U.S. 294, 301 (1955)

Griffin vs. *County School Board,* 377 U.S. 218 (1964)

Green vs. *County School Board,* 391 U.S. 430 (1968)

Runyon vs. *McCracy,* 427 U.S. 160 (1976)

Lau vs. *Nichols* 414 U.S. 563 (1974)

Student records. Students who have attained the age of eighteen years, and the parents of younger students have a right to review their own or their children's official school records and the right to a hearing for the purpose of challenging the appropriateness and validity of such records. Students and parents have the responsibility of following the administrative rules of time and place for reviewing such records and for participating in a hearing. In addition, students should exercise discretion in discussing their records with other students.

The Family Educational Rights and Privacy Act of 1974 and the accompanying regulations (HEW Reg. 45 C.F.R. 99, 1976) present a detailed explanation of this right and outline certain exceptions to the law.

Search, seizure, and police interrogation. Students have the right to be free from unreasonable searches of their person, school locker, and personal property. The following constitutes minimal requirements of a reasonable search: (1) A designated school official shall be the only individual authorized to search a student, his/her locker, or personal property; (2) The search must be based on probable cause, which is defined as facts leading a prudent person to believe that some item subject to seizure is in the student's possession; (3) A reasonable attempt must be made to allow the student to be present when searching his or her locker or personal property. The concept of probable cause has created some concern on the part of school officials. Certain factors, however, should be considered when applying the probable cause criteria, including the student's age, record in school, seriousness of the problem, and exigency to make the search. Further, when a law enforcement official requests to interrogate a student, that student has a right to have his or her parents or guardian present for such an interrogation. If a parent or guardian is unavailable, a teacher or some other school official should be present and the student should be advised of his or her right to legal counsel and to remain silent.

It is the responsibility of all students to adhere to the law and not to have illegal items stored in a locker or on their person. The legality of search and seizure and its limitation have been tested in the following cases: In re W. 29 Cal. App. 3d 777, 105 Cal, Rptr. 775 (1973); *People* vs. *D.*, 34 N.Y. 2d 483 358 N.Y.S. 2d 403, 407 (1974); *Katz* vs. *United States,* 389 U.S. 347, 351 (1967); *Mapp* vs. *Ohio,* 367 U.S. 643, 651–57 (1961).

Discipline. Students have rights in areas involving discipline, suspension/ expulsion, and corporal punishment. To deprive a student of an educational opportunity even for a short period of time is a very serious issue. Suspension and/or expulsion should be invoked only as a last resort for a serious infraction after other means of handling the problem have proven to be ineffective. Students should be provided with a written discipline code that outlines those offenses that may result in suspension and/or expulsion.

There are procedural rights of students involving suspension from school for a short period of time. In an informal conference, the building principal or his or her designee should (1) provide the student with oral or written notice of charges; (2) provide an explanation of the charges to the student if he or she denies them; and (3) allow the student to tell his or her understanding of the events that may result in suspension. Of course, the principal may suspend a student without this due process if there is a clear and present danger of physical injury to school personnel or students. The due process should be afforded the student as soon as practicable in such a case. Time constraints should be placed upon the use of suspension. For example, the building principals might be given the authority to suspend a student for up to five school days. When a student returns to school, he or she should be given the opportunity to make up the classwork and examinations missed while suspended from school.

The procedural rights of students involving long-term suspensions and expulsion from school by the superintendent or school board include: (1) The student is entitled to a hearing on the charges during which he or she may be represented by an attorney; (2) The student shall have the right to call witnesses, present documentary evidence, and may cross-examine witnesses. Upon appeal to the courts, the student should be provided, at no expense, with a copy of the proceedings. Of course, time limits must be placed on the superintendent or school board in rendering a decision. For example, a decision based on the facts presented at the hearing could be required within five days after the hearing. If the superintendent conducted the hearing, the student must appeal the decision to the board of education before going to the courts for review.

Students also have the right to be free from physical violence. Physical force may be used against a student when that student is threatening physical injury to others, in self-defense, or for the protection of property. The amount of force used must be reasonable enough to prevent injury or property destruction.

Students are responsible for following the disciplinary code of their school and for observing all administrative rules and procedures. Students must also respect each other and the adults who interact with them, if there is going to be a positive and caring atmosphere in the school.

Two significant court cases dealing with discipline, which provided a basis for the above discussion are: *Lopez* vs. *Williams,* 372 F. Supp. 1249 (S.D. Ohio 1973) and *Goss* vs. *Lopez,* 419 U.S. 565 (1975).

Developing a Code of Student Rights and Responsibilities

No code of conduct will be effective unless it is developed with input from all members of the school community. Teachers, parents, administrators, and students must be actively involved in the research and formulation process. If a code is created solely by the administration and mandated to the student body, the ingredients necessary for effective school discipline, which involve understanding and cooperation, will be lacking. There are five major steps which, if followed, will ensure that an effective code is established.

First, a committee of students (at the middle, junior high school, and high school levels), parents, teachers, and administrators should be commissioned by the school board through the superintendent to study the need to develop or update a code of student rights and responsibilities. Each segment of the school community could be allowed to choose its own representative on the committee. For example, the student council could appoint student representatives; the PTA could select parent representatives; and the faculty could choose teachers for the committee. Experience has shown that very large committees are ineffective, consequently, a committee of five, seven, or nine members would be desirable. To avoid deadlocks on issues, an uneven number of members is appropriate. A survey of the students, parents, teachers, and administrators would be very helpful in analyzing the needs of a given school.

Second, the committee should conduct a review of the literature dealing with student rights and responsibilities. Other schools should be contacted about their codes and if possible, copies received from these schools could be reviewed by the committee. Local, state, and federal agencies, educational associations, and civil liberties organizations can also provide valuable information on the possible content for such a code.

Third, the committee can then proceed to draft a code using the data researched and the suggestions provided by members of the school community. There are certain critical questions that should be addressed by the committee as the members work through the task of codification. The following questions can serve as a checklist focusing attention on aspects of the new code that are essential if it is to be an effective disciplinary vehicle: (1) Are the provisions of the new code precise and easily understood by parents, students, and all members of the school community? (2) Is the format and construction of the code manual convenient and serviceable? (3) Does the code contain rules necessary to the effective operation of the school?

Fourth, a public hearing could be held on the code to receive comments and suggestions on how to improve its provisions. Publishing the time and place of the hearing in local newspapers along with an outline of the draft code and information on where to receive the complete draft would help to generate public awareness and interest in attending the hearing.

Finally, because the board of education commissioned the committee to review and write the code on student rights and responsibilities, it is necessary for the board to approve the final document and to promulgate its provisions, probably in the form of a student handbook.

One additional comment should be made at this point. Because new legislation will be passed, because case law may modify previous decisions, and because the composition of society and the student body will change, the code should be reviewed and possibly updated at least every five years.

SUMMARY

The instructional program is the central concern of every school district because it is through this program that the mission of the school system, to educate students, is fulfilled. Throughout the ages of history, man has sought to gain a greater knowledge and understanding of the world in which he lives. In developing the process for quantifying and studying reality, there have emerged bodies of organized knowledge commonly referred to as subject matter disciplines. The facts, concepts, formulas, and processes constituting a discipline can never be completely transmitted to any given individual at any level of instruction, because that body of knowledge known as a discipline is constantly expanding. A selection must therefore be made by educators as to what will be taught to students at what level and in what sequence. That which is taught is the curriculum.

This curriculum is then taken by teachers and organized into instructional units and lesson plans. Thus the instructional program is composed of the curriculum derived from subject matter disciplines organized into instructional units and presented to students through lesson plans.

There are four steps in developing the instructional program: (1) The school board must translate the values and beliefs of the community into educational goals and objectives; (2) The administrative and instructional staff are responsible for translating these educational goals into a curriculum, which is the body of knowledge, skills, and values to be taught; (3) The instructional staff and building level administrators should organize the curriculum into instructional units and lesson plans; (4) Measuring the effectiveness of the instructional program is essential if modifications are to be made in how the curriculum is organized and presented to students.

The instructional program is implemented by teachers and other professionals through the learning-instructional process, which takes place inside and outside the classroom. Monitoring the quality of teaching and support services offered to students is the responsibility of the building principal. This monitoring process usually includes the formal evaluation of employee performance using an evaluation instrument.

The 1970's saw the passage of two laws, The Rehabilitation Act of 1973 and The Education for All Handicapped Children Act of 1975, which have had a direct effect upon the instructional program as it relates to handicapped children. Section 504 of the Rehabilitation Act specifically addresses the accessibility requirements of educational facilities. The Education for All Handicapped Children Act stipulates that public schools must educate handicapped children in the "least restrictive environment" and must develop an "individual education program" for each handicapped student.

The U.S. Congress and the federal judiciary have addressed the rights and responsibilities of students. These rights and responsibilities cover the following areas: (1) freedom to observe or not observe a religion; (2) freedom of speech and expression; (3) freedom of the press; (4) freedom of assembly; (5) the right to a grievance and appeal process; (6) the right to an education; (7) the right to inspect school records; and (8) freedom from search, seizure, and interrogation.

In creating an effective code of conduct on student rights and responsibilities, the board of education must actively involve teachers, parents, administrators, and students.

IMPLICATIONS FOR BOARD MEMBERS

There are three implications for school board members that emerge from this presentation on the instructional program and pupil relations.

First, school board members should require the superintendent and his or her administrative staff to provide them with information on a continual basis concerning curriculum guides, instructional materials, course descriptions, course enrollments, and standardized test scores. Such data and information will help the school board in analyzing the effectiveness of the instructional program.

Second, school board members should require the superintendent and his or her administrative staff to continually provide the board with data concerning the types, scope, and severity of pupil behavior problems and the steps taken to rectify such problems.

Third, school board members should make an attempt to keep abreast of research and innovations in curriculum and instruction. Recent court cases and legislation affecting the rights and responsibilities of students should also be noted. The National School Boards Association and state board associations have programs, materials, newsletters, and journals helpful to board members in relation to this responsibility.

APPENDIX A
TEACHER EVALUATION REPORT[3]

LINDBERGH SCHOOL DISTRICT
4900 SO. LINDBERGH BLVD.
ST. LOUIS, MO 63126

Teacher Evaluation Report

TEACHER _____ SCHOOL _____ YEAR _____

SUBJECT OR GRADE _____ YEARS IN SYSTEM _____

STATUS OF TEACHER   ( ) PROBATIONARY   ( ) TENURED

PHILOSOPHY: Evaluation is a means of improving the quality of instruction.

PURPOSES:
1. To improve the quality of teaching and service to students.
2. To enable the teacher to recognize her/his role in the total school program.
3. To assist the teacher in achieving the established goals of the curriculum.
4. To help the teacher identify her/his strengths and weaknesses as a personal guide for her/his improvement.
5. To provide assistance to the teacher to help correct weaknesses.
6. To recognize the teacher's special talents and to encourage and facilitate their utilization.

[3]Lindbergh School District, *Teacher Evaluation Report* (St. Louis, Mo.: The District, 1983).

7. To serve as a guide for renewed employment, termination of employment, promotion, assignment, and unrequested leave for tenured teachers.
8. To protect the teacher from dismissal without just cause.
9. To protect the teaching profession from unethical and incompetent personnel.

IMPLEMENTATION: The evaluation is to be made by the building principal, grade principal, assistant principal, or acting principal.

If a teacher does not agree with an evaluation, she/he may request an additional evaluation to be made by another administrator of her/his choice.

Evaluation of a probationary (nontenured) teacher's services will be made semi-annually during the probationary period with one of the evaluations completed during the first semester, and both completed before March 15. Each evaluation must be preceded by at least one classroom visit.

Evaluation of a permanent (tenured) teacher's services will be made every year with the evaluation completed before March 15. Each evaluation must be preceded by at least one classroom visit.

DEFINITION OF TERMS:

1. *Superior:* consistently exceptional.
2. *Strong:* usually surpasses the standards of Lindbergh School District.
3. *Average:* generally meets standards of Lindbergh School District.
4. *Improvement needed:* occasionally does not meet standards of Lindbergh School District.
5. *Unsatisfactory:* does not measure up to standards of Lindbergh School District.

Rating of Unsatisfactory or Improvement Needed must include a written comment describing the cause for the rating.

NOTE: The space at the end of this form marked "Principal's Comments" may be utilized to record the observations of the teacher's exceptional performances and/or to record the principal's recommendations for improvement.

The space at the end of this form marked "Teacher's Comments" may be utilized by the teacher to record any comment or comments which she/he wishes to make.

I. TEACHING PERFORMANCE

	Superior 1	Strong 2	Average 3	I-N 4	Unsatisfactory 5
A. Plans and Organizes Carefully					
1. Lesson is well planned					
2. Sets definite goals including student participation					
3. Makes clear, specific assignments					
4. Is familiar with appropriate guide and adapts to the recommendations therein					
5. Provides for individual and group instruction					
B. Is Skillful in Questioning and Explaining					
1. Asks thought provoking questions					
2. Gives clear explanation of subject matter					
3. Exposes students to varying points of view					
4. Is aware of both verbal and non-verbal acceptance or rejection of students' ideas, and uses this skill positively					
C. Stimulates learning through innovative activities and resources					
1. Encourages class discussion, pupil questions and pupil demonstrations					
2. Uses a variety of teaching aids and resources					

D. Displays knowledge of and enthusiasm for subject matter

E. Provides a classroom atmosphere conducive to good learning

   1. Maintains a healthy and flexible environment . . . .

   2. Observes the care of instructional material and equipment . . . .

F. Keeps adequate and accurate records

   1. Records sufficient quantitative and qualitative data on which to base pupil progress reports . . . .

G. Has wholesome relationship with pupils

   1. Knows and works with pupils as individuals . . . .

   2. Encourages relationships that are mutually respectful and friendly . . . .

   3. Uses positive language with students which is devoid of sarcasm . . . .

H. Initiates and preserves classroom and general school management and discipline

   1. Rules of pupil conduct have been developed and teacher requires observance of these rules . . . .

   2. Rules of safety have been developed and teacher requires observance of these rules . . . .

   3. Emphasizes importance of both developing and maintaining self-respect and respect for others . . . .

II. PROFESSIONAL QUALITIES

	Superior 1	Strong 2	Average 3	I-N 4	Unsatis-factory 5
A. Recognition and acceptance of out-of-class responsibilities					
1. Participates in the general and necessary school activities					
2. Sometimes volunteers for the "extra" duties					
3. Serves on school committees					
B. Intra-school relationship					
1. Cooperates effectively and pleasantly with colleagues, administration and nonprofessional personnel					
C. Public Relations					
1. Cooperates effectively and pleasantly with parents					
2. Practices good relationships between school and community					
D. Professional Growth and Vision					

E. Utilization of Staff Services

   1. Makes proper use of available special services . . . .

F. Understands the growth patterns and behaviors of students at various stages of development and copes satisfactorily with situations as they occur

G. Ethical Behavior

   1. Protects professional use of confidential data . . . .

   2. Supports the teaching profession . . . .

DEFINITION OF TERMS FOR PERSONAL QUALITIES

S— *Satisfactory:* meets or surpasses standard for Lindbergh School District teachers.

I— *Improvement needed:* does not measure up to standards Lindbergh School District teachers meet.

	S	I

III. PERSONAL QUALITIES

A. Health and Vigor

1. Has a good and reasonable attendance record . . . .

2. Is cheerful . . . .

3. Displays a sense of humor . . . .

B. Speech

1. Is articulate . . . .

2. Can be heard and understood by all pupils in the
room . . . .

3. Speaks on the level of pupils' understanding . . . .

C. Grooming and appropriateness of dress

1. Practices habits of good grooming . . . .

D. Promptness in meeting obligations

1. Reports to classes on time . . . .

2. Performs assigned tasks properly . . . .

3. Completes reports on time . . . .

A copy of the written evaluation will be submitted to the teacher at the time of the conference following the observation(s). The final evaluation report form is to be signed and retained by the principal, and a copy is to be retained by the teacher. In the event the teacher feels the evaluation was incomplete, inaccurate, or unjust, she/he may put the objections in writing on the back of this form. Teacher's signature acknowledges that the conference has taken place.

DATE OF OBSERVATION(S) _____

TIME OF OBSERVATION(S) _____

LENGTH OF OBSERVATION(S) _____

DATE EVALUATION MADE _____

PRINCIPAL'S COMMENTS _____

OVERALL EVALUATION _____

PRINCIPAL'S SIGNATURE _____ DATE _____

TEACHER'S COMMENTS _____

TEACHER'S SIGNATURE _____ DATE _____

SELECTED BIBLIOGRAPHY

DEPARTMENT OF HEALTH, EDUCATION, AND WELFARE, *The Rights and Responsibilities of Students: A Handbook for the School Community.* Washington, D.C.: U.S. Government Printing Office, 1979.

FOSHAY, ARTHUR W., ed., *Considered Action for Curriculum Improvement.* Alexandria, Va.: Association for Supervision and Curriculum, 1980.

JOYCE, BRUCE R., *Selecting Learning Experiences: Linking Theory and Practice.* Alexandria, Va.: Association for Supervision and Curriculum Development, 1978.

POSNER, GEORGE J., ALAN N. RUDNITSKY, *Course Design: A Guide to Curriculum Development for Teachers.* New York: Longman Inc., 1978.

TURNBULL, H. RUTHERFORD, ANN TURNBULL, *Free Appropriate Public Education: Law and Implementation.* Denver: Love Publishing Co., 1978.

YARD, GEORGE J., *Exceptionalities of Children and Adults.* St. Louis: Midwest Regional Resource Center, 1978.

CHAPTER NINE
THE ROLE
OF THE SCHOOL BOARD
IN DISTRICT
PERSONNEL MANAGEMENT

As a service rendering institution, the school will be successful in direct proportion to the effectiveness of school board policies to attract and retain quality employees and staff members.

In every school district people must be recruited, selected, placed, appraised, and compensated. These tasks may be performed by a central office unit or assigned to various administrators within the school district.

The goals of the personnel function are basically the same in all school systems—to hire, retain, develop, motivate personnel, assist individual members of the staff to reach the highest possible levels of achievement, and maximize the career development of personnel.

These goals must be implemented through the following dimensions of the personnel function:

—*Manpower Planning.* Establishing a master plan of long- and short-range personnel requirements is a necessary ingredient in the school system's program, curricular, and fiscal planning processes.

—*Recruitment of Personnel.* Quality personnel are, of course, essential for the delivery of effective educational services to children, youth, and adults.

—*Selection of Personnel.* The long- and short-range manpower requirements are implemented through selection techniques and processes.

—*Placement and Induction of Personnel.* Through appropriate planning, new personnel and the school system accommodate each other.

—*Staff Development.* Development programs help personnel meet school district objectives and also provide individuals with the opportunity for personal and professional growth.

—*Appraisal of Personnel.* Processes and techniques for appraisal help the individual grow professionally and help the school district attain its objectives.
—*Compensation of Personnel.* Establishing programs that reward quality performance helps to motivate personnel.
—*Collective Negotiations.* The negotiating process gives personnel an opportunity to participate in matters that affect their professional and personal welfare.

Unfortunately, many school systems still see the personnel function only as the hiring of competent teachers. These eight dimensions of the personnel function are not discrete, isolated entities, but rather, integral aspects of the same function.

PERSONNEL ADMINISTRATORS

Many school districts have seen the need in recent times to delegate a major share of the personnel function to a specialized central office unit. In this type of organization, an assistant superintendent (personnel director) administers personnel functions and aids the superintendent in solving personnel problems. *Personnel administrator* is usually a staff position that exists to service line administrators. Line positions include the assistant superintendents for secondary education and elementary education, administrators of certain support services, and building principals. These administrators have been granted authority to make decisions in the supervisory process as it relates to staff, faculty, and students.

A major question facing school districts with increasing enrollments is: When does it become necessary to establish a central office personnel administrator position? Castetter suggests a formula:

> One way of examining the problem of whether or not to include a central staff position for personnel in a school system is through the staff adequacy assumption. Simply stated, this assumes that for every 1,000 pupils enrolled, there should be a minimum of 50 professional personnel. Thus, a hypothetical school district with an enrollment of 4,000 pupils should have at least 200 professional employees. When classified personnel are taken into consideration, this district would have 300 members. If one considers the ramifications of performing, without proper organization (central office positions) all of the personnel processes . . . for this number of school employees, the conclusion is inescapable that the function will be inefficiently handled.[1]

Not only does the personnel function have an impact on the continual staffing of positions, which in turn directly affects the quality of educational programs, but it also has a significant effect on the budget. Approximately 80 percent of all school district expenditures are for personnel salaries and benefits. Inefficiency in

---

[1] William B. Castetter, *The Personnel Function in Educational Administration,* 2nd ed. (New York: Macmillan Publishing Co., Inc., 1976), p. 41.

the personnel function can—potentially—cost the taxpayer unnecessarily large sums of money.

Boards of education and administrators are seldom fully aware of the pervasive effect their personnel decisions have on the planning process. Every position within a school system generates a series of decisions as to the type of work to be performed, the qualities needed for its proper performance, and its economic value. A variety of actions are required for the proper recruiting, selecting, inducting, developing, and appraising of personnel. Policies and procedures must also be established regarding academic freedom, tenure, health, grievances, leaves of absence, and retirement. In all but the very smallest districts the movement of personnel into and out of a school system requires the attention of personnel specialists.

The number of strikes by public school teachers has dramatically increased over the last ten years. Salaries, fringe benefits, and working conditions constitute the major issues that may lead to an impasse at the bargaining table and subsequently cause a strike. Education, however, is a relative newcomer to the negotiations process.

Collective negotiation is traditionally a personnel function and correctly belongs under the jurisdiction of the assistant superintendent for personnel. Because of the magnitude of the issues involved in this process, most school districts should consider establishing the position of employee relations. The American Association of School Administrators sponsored the publication of a monograph in 1974 entitled, "Helping Administrators Negotiate," with the prophetic subtitle, "A Profile of the Emerging Management Position of Director of Employee Relations in the Administrative Structure of a School System."

The knowledge explosion and the constantly changing social milieu has also produced a major issue in the area of personnel administration. In the past, staff development was viewed primarily from the in-service training model, which concentrated on providing a few workshops on instructional materials. The last quarter century, however, has ushered in federal legislation and litigation that has more clearly defined the rights of racial minorities, women, students, and the handicapped. This, coupled with the deluge of new instructional technologies, the differing attitudes of the new professionals entering teaching, and the changing values of our society as manifested by parents and students, has created a need for an ongoing staff development program for administrators and teachers alike. This function is so specialized that it, also, like collective negotiations, requires the attention of a new personnel specialist, the director of staff development.

The avalanche of federal legislation and litigation on minority rights has made it necessary to establish a central-office administrative position, usually entitled director of affirmative action. Most federal legislation contains an equal opportunity clause which, in turn, dictates the organization of a detailed program for carrying out the intent of the law in all phases of the personnel function. This organized program is more commonly called "affirmative action." A unique feature of this administrative position in the organizational structure is that the director of affirmative action reports directly to the superintendent of schools. This provides for integrity in the school district's compliance with civil rights legislation because the director is independent of the influence of other administrators.

If a school district of 4,000 students needs the position of assistant superintendent for personnel, a school system of over 5,000 pupils certainly can justify hiring these additional personnel administrators.

MANPOWER PLANNING

Planning is a process common to all human experience. Before embarking on a journey an individual must understand where he or she is, know where he or she wants to go, and decide how best to get there. In an elementary form this exemplifies the essence of the process even as it is applied to educational organizations.

Through the process of manpower planning a school district ensures that it has the right number of people, with the right skills, at the right place, at the right time, and that these people are capable of effectively carrying out those tasks that will aid the organization in achieving its objectives. If a school district is to achieve its objectives, it needs financial resources, physical resources, and people. Too often the people are taken for granted, and yet they are the force that directly effects the main objective of a school district—to educate children. Manpower planning thus translates the organization's objectives into human resource terms.

In some school districts long- and short-range objectives are couched in ambiguous language and often known only by central office administrators. This makes it difficult to involve building principals in the hiring process when unexpected vacancies occur, when replacements are needed because of natural attrition, or when new programs must be staffed.

Manpower planning, as a process, ensures the smooth development of an organization. "We assess where we are; we assess where we are going; we consider the implications of these objectives on future demands and future supply of human resources; and we attempt to match demand and supply so as to make them compatible with the achievement of the organization's future needs."[2]

Assessing Manpower Needs

The process of assessing human resource needs has four aspects. First, manpower inventories must be developed to analyze the various tasks necessary to meet the school district's objectives; these tasks are then matched against the skills of current employees. Second, enrollment projections must be developed for a five-year period. The extreme mobility of the American population has made this aspect increasingly important over the past ten years. Third, the overall objectives of the school district must be reviewed within the context of changing needs. At a time of high inflation and shrinking revenue, all but the wealthiest districts must establish

---

[2]Stephen P. Robbins, *Personnel: The Management of Human Resources* (Englewood Cliffs, N.J.: Prentice-Hall, Inc., 1978), p. 53.

priorities in meeting objectives. Fourth, manpower inventories, enrollment projections, and the school district's objectives must be organized into a manpower forecast, which becomes the mandate of the personnel administrator.

Implementing this manpower mandate becomes more involved, however, when viewed in the light of compliance with federal legislation, potential litigation, and the staff reductions brought on by decreasing enrollment. Because both issues have had such a tremendous impact on the personnel function, they have been given particular emphasis in this chapter.

Manpower planning is sometimes understood only within the confines of the instructional program. However, for every teacher there is usually a support employee. The contemporary school district employs not only teachers and administrators but also cooks, custodians, maintenance personnel, secretaries, computer programmers, telephone switchboard operators, warehouse personnel, distribution truck drivers, and other specialists who the average citizen thinks are employed only in the private business sector.

The future objectives of a school district determine future manpower needs. The number and mix of human resources is determined by the types of services called for by these organizational objectives. Establishing objectives is the prerogative of the board of education. The board, however, must rely on the experience and expertise of the school administrators to formulate objectives that will best meet the educational needs of the community.

The review of current objectives in light of future educational needs is a cooperative task. In a district working under the organizational structure presented in chapter one, the assistant superintendents for secondary education, elementary education, and instructional services would have the primary responsibility for determining future objectives. The assistant superintendent for personnel would develop a manpower forecast to meet the projected objectives developed by the three curriculum-related assistant superintendents. The assistant superintendent for administrative services would then translate the objectives and manpower needs into fiscal resource data. The superintendent of schools is finally charged with prioritizing objectives for school board approval.

This review of objectives is not a one-time task but rather a continual process. The objectives, however, should be established for at least a five-year period, and if the need occurs, will be revised into a new five-year plan. Thus a set of objectives is always in effect for a set period of time.

Manpower forecasting. Once the objectives have been reviewed and an overall manpower forecast has been established, a more explicit projection of future manpower needs must be developed. There are five commonly accepted methods for computing future needs.[3]

---

[3]See Bruce Coleman, "An Integrated System for Manpower Planning," *Business Horizons*, October, 1970, pp. 89–95.

1. *Expert Estimate.* Those staff members in the school district most familiar with employment requirements use their experience and judgment to estimate future needs.
2. *Historical Comparison.* By this method, past trends are projected into the future.
3. *Task Analysis.* Each person in each type of position is reviewed to determine demand. This method is sometimes effective in uncovering specific quality shortages within a school system.
4. *Correlation.* Manpower requirements fluctuate in relation to such variables as decreasing enrollment, fiscal resources, and new programs. A correlation of these variables can be statistically formulated.
5. *Modeling.* This usually refers to decision-making models. However, it may be broadened to include reviewing the programs and how they are organized in other school systems, which in turn may serve as a model for staffing.

Whatever method or combination of methods is used, the manpower inventories on current human resources will be used to provide data on the age, sex, education, certification, and position held within the school district.

The supply of human resources.   An increase in a school system's supply of human resources can come from two sources—newly hired employees and individuals returning from leaves, such as maternity, military, and sabbatical leaves. Both types of increases are relatively easy to incorporate into a manpower forecast because hiring is controlled and leaves are usually for set periods of time.

Decreases in a school system's supply of human resources, however, are more difficult to predict. Deaths, voluntary resignations, and dismissals are unpredictable except in the broadest sense, as through statistical averaging. Some decreases, such as sabbatical leaves, can be controlled; others, such as retirement, are easier to predict when the school district has a mandatory retirement age.

The available labor force has a significant effect on manpower forecasting. Graduates from high schools, colleges, and universities continually replenish the supply of labor necessary to carry out the mandate of public education. In recent years, however, educational organizations have experienced a decrease in the number of applicants for mathematical and science teaching positions because of the higher wages and employment opportunities available in private business and industry.

Entrants into the work force other than recent graduates include women seeking full-time or part-time employment either to supplement family income or to provide primary income. Divorce rates and high inflation are key factors contributing to the number of women reentering the labor force.

Matching needs with supply.   A final activity in manpower forecasting is to match the school district's future human resource needs with supply. This will pinpoint shortages, highlight areas of potential overstaffing, and identify the number of individuals who must be recruited from the labor force to satisfy current and future needs. In the final analysis, human resource planning ensures that we have the right number and mix of human resources to meet the school district's future needs as determined by its future objectives.

Reduction in Force

A pressing problem facing metropolitan areas is decreasing pupil enrollments, which has led to a surplus of teachers. Declining enrollments have particular significance in the manpower planning process and have caused the initiation of a procedure commonly referred to as a reduction in force, or RIF. Excess employees are usually placed on involuntary leave according to the seniority system, which follows the principle of "last in, first out." Retained employees may be transferred within the school system to balance a particular staff or faculty. Such changes are certain to create anxiety among individuals who have become accustomed to the atmosphere and procedures of a particular school. Because many school districts have only recently attempted to equalize minority groups in their work force, the use of seniority-based reduction procedures usually means that minority employees are among the first to go. Court-mandated desegregation in hiring practices and the legislative demand for affirmative action calls for the introduction of alternatives to RIF whenever possible.

Two of the most successful alternatives to RIF have been early retirement incentive programs and retraining individuals for positions that will become vacant through attrition or will be created because of program development.

Teacher negotiations have in recent years centered on the job security issue, and many contracts now call for teachers in excessed areas to be transferred to other positions, hired as permanent substitutes, or retrained for new assignments at school district expense.

The Role of the Principal

A key person in manpower planning is, of course, the building principal. He or she is usually the first to spot dwindling enrollments. The principal can provide the central office staff with up-to-date and projected enrollment figures, with projected maintenance and capital improvement costs, and with projected staffing needs.

The principal also has front-line contact with staff members, students, and parents and therefore will be responsible for preparing teachers who may suffer job loss and easing the concerns of parents and students. To perform these tasks effectively, the principal must become an integral part of the manpower planning process—being relied on for data and input. He or she must in like manner be constantly kept informed of central office decisions before such decisions are announced to the staff and public.

FEDERAL INFLUENCES
ON MANPOWER PLANNING

A hallmark of our contemporary American society is the avalanche of federal legislation and court decisions delineating and more clearly defining civil rights. The term civil rights is somewhat misunderstood and is most often applied to the constitutional rights of racial minority groups. However, it correctly refers to those constitutional and legislative rights that are inalienable and applicable to all citizens. In manpower planning the master plan should provide direction for the recruitment and selection processes. In so doing, the plan must not violate the civil rights of job applicants or lead the school district into an indefensible position.

What follows is an explanation of major federal legislation, executive orders, and court decisions that should provide direction in the development of a manpower plan. It is not meant to be exhaustive because the legislative and judicial processes are organic in nature; therefore, modifications and change will undoubtedly occur. The underlying concept of equality, however, has universal application.

As a prelude to this information, however, the important concept of affirmative action must be clearly understood because it is a requirement incorporated or implied in civil rights legislation and executive orders.

Affirmative Action

Definition. The sometimes-quoted cliché, "There can be justice for none if there is not justice for all," captures the intent of civil rights legislation, while the familiar yet authorless motto of many women that "in business we must all be like our fathers" correctly highlights affirmative action programs.

Affirmative action programs are detailed, result-oriented procedures, which, when carried out in good faith, result in compliance with the equal opportunity clauses found in most legislative and executive orders.[4] Affirmative action, therefore, is not a law within itself but rather a set of guidelines that organizations may use to ensure compliance with legislative and executive orders. Thus, an organization does not "violate" affirmative action; it violates the law.

Brief history of affirmative action. Although the term, *affirmative action,* is of recent origin, the concept of an employer taking specific steps to utilize fully and to treat equally minority groups can be traced to President Franklin D. Roosevelt's Executive Order 8802, issued in June, 1941. This executive order, which has the force of law, established a policy of equal employment opportunity in defense contracts. President Roosevelt issued a new order in 1943 extending the order to all

---

[4] See "Labor Law Reports—Employment Practices," Office of Federal Contract Compliance Programs Manual, 2nd ed., Report 86, No. 580, July 3, 1975 (New York: Commerce Clearing House, Inc.), foreword.

government contractors and for the first time mandating that all contracts contain a clause specifically forbidding discrimination.

In 1953 President Dwight D. Eisenhower issued Executive Order 10479, which established the Government Contract Compliance Committee. This commitee received complaints of discrimination by government contractors but had no power to enforce its guidelines.

The period of voluntary compliance ended in 1961 when President John F. Kennedy issued Executive Order 10925. This order established the President's Committee on Equal Employment Opportunity and gave it the authority to make and enforce its own rules by imposing sanctions and penalties against noncomplying contractors. Government contractors were required to have nondiscrimination clauses covering race, color, creed, and national origin.

In September, 1965 President Lyndon B. Johnson issued a very important executive order giving the secretary of labor jurisdiction over contract compliance and creating the Office of Federal Contract Compliance, which replaced the Committee on Equal Employment Opportunity. Every federal contractor was required to include a seven-point equal opportunity clause, agreeing not to discriminate against anyone in hiring and during employment on the basis of race, color, creed, or national origin. Further, the contractor had to also agree in writing to take affirmative action measures in hiring. President Johnson's Executive Order 11375 in 1967 amended Executive Order 11246 by adding sex and religion to the list of protected groups.

The secretary of labor issued Chapter 60 of Title 41 of the Code of Federal Regulations for the purpose of implementing Executive Order 11375. The secretary delegated enforcement authority to the Office of Federal Contract Compliance (OFCC), which reports to the assistant secretary of the Employment Standards Administration.

The Office of Federal Contract Compliance provides leadership in the area of nondiscrimination by government contractors and also coordinates with the Equal Employment Opportunity Commission (EEOC) and the Department of Justice on matters relating to Title VII of the 1964 Civil Rights Act as amended.

The EEOC was established by Title VII of the Civil Rights Act to investigate alleged discrimination based on race, color, religion, sex, or national origin. The EEOC was greatly strengthened in 1972 by the passage of the Equal Employment Opportunity Act. It extended coverage to all private employers of fifteen or more persons, all educational institutions, all state and local governments, public and private employment agencies, labor unions with fifteen or more members and joint labor-management committees for apprenticeships and training. This act also gave the Commission the power to initiate litigation against an organization that engages in discriminatory practices.

Equal Employment Opportunity Commission. A major failing of many school administrators is their lack of understanding about EEOC and its influence on human resource administration. This five-member commission has from time to time established affirmative action guidelines that, if adopted by school districts, can minimize liability for claims of discrimination. To further aid employers, on December 11, 1978, the EEOC adopted additional guidelines that can be used to avoid liability from claims of "reverse discrimination" resulting from affirmative action to provide employment opportunities for women and racial and ethnic minorities. The following compilation from several sources will provide a framework for affirmative action compliance.

Eight steps have emerged from federal guidelines:

First, a district's board of education must issue a written equal employment opportunity policy and affirmative action commitment to be enforced by its chief executive officer, the superintendent. Some of the areas covered in such a statement might be a determination to recruit, hire, and promote for all job classifications without regard to race, creed, national origins, sex, or age (except where sex or age is a bona fide occupational qualification); to base decisions on employment solely on individual qualifications as related to the requirements of the position for which he or she is being considered; and to ensure that all personnel actions such as compensation, benefits, transfers, layoffs, return from layoffs and continuing education will be administered without regard to race, creed, color, national origin, sex, or age.

Second, the superintendent must appoint a top official directly responsible to him or her with the responsibility and authority to implement the program. The affirmative action officer should develop policy statements, write affirmative action programs, initiate internal and external communications, assist other administrators in the identification of problem areas, design and implement audit and reporting systems, serve as a liaison between district and enforcement agencies, and keep the superintendent informed of the latest developments in the area of equal opportunities.

Third, a school district should disseminate its affirmative action program both internally and externally. The board policy should be publicized through all internal media channels, such as at meetings and on bulletin boards. External dissemination might take the form of brochures advertising the district; written notification to recruitment sources; clauses in purchase orders, leases, contracts; and written notification to minority organizations, community agencies, and community leaders.

Step four begins with a survey and analysis of minority and female employees by school and job classification. The percentage and number of minority and female employees currently employed in each major job classification should be compared to their presence in the relevant labor market—that is, the area in which you can reasonably expect to recruit. This will determine "underutilization," defined as having fewer minorities or women in a particular job category or school than could be reasonably expected; and "concentration," defined as more of a particular group in a job category than would reasonably be expected. A survey should also be conducted of transferable females and minorities who have the credentials to handle other positions.

With this information, the school district administration should proceed to step five, developing measurable and remedial goals on a timetable. Once long-range goals have been established, specific and numerical targets can be developed for the hiring, training, transferring, and promoting of personnel to reach goals within the established time frame. During this step the causes of underutilization should be identified.

Step six calls for developing and implementing specific programs to eliminate discriminatory barriers and to achieve goals. This is the heart of an affirmative action program and must be discussed under several subheadings, which will be further expanded in subsequent chapters. All persons involved in every aspect of the hiring process must be trained to use objective standards that support affirmative action goals. Recruitment procedures must be analyzed and reviewed for each job category to identify and eliminate discriminatory barriers. Recruitment procedures might include contacting educational institutions and community action organizations that represent minorities.

Reviewing the selection process to ensure that job requirements and hiring contribute to affirmative action goals is a vital part of step six. This includes making certain that job qualifications and selection standards do not screen out minorities unless the qualifications can be significantly related to job performance and no alternate nondiscriminatory standards can be developed.

Upward mobility systems such as assignments, promotions, transfers, seniority, and continuing education play an important role in step six. Through careful record keeping, existing barriers may be identified and specific remedial programs initiated. These programs might include targeting members of minorities and women by identifying those currently qualified for upward mobility and providing training for those who are not.

Wage and salary structures, benefits, and conditions of employment are other areas of investigation. Title VII of the 1964 Civil Rights Act and the Equal Pay Act require fiscal parity for jobs of equal skill and responsibility. All fringe benefits such as medical, hospital, and life insurance must be equally applied to personnel performing similar functions. Even in instances where states have "protective laws" barring women from hard and dangerous work, the courts have generally found that the equal employment requirements of Title VII supersede state law. Courts have also barred compulsory "maternity leave" or discharge of pregnant teachers.

Under affirmative action programs the criteria for deciding when a person shall be terminated, demoted, disciplined, laid off, or recalled should be the same for all employees. Seemingly neutral practices should also be reexamined to see if they have a disproportionate effect on minority groups. Special considerations, such as job transfers or career counseling, should be given to minorities laid off because of legitimate seniority systems.

Step seven is to establish internal audit and reporting systems to monitor and evaluate progress in each aspect of the affirmative action program. Quarterly reports based on the data already outlined should be available to all administrators, enabling them to see how the program is working and where improvement is needed. The issue of keeping records on employees and potential employees by sex, race, or national origin is a very sensitive concern. Such record keeping has been used in the past as a discriminatory device, and some states have outlawed the practice. In certain litigation they have even been used as evidence of discriminatory practices. On the other hand, this data will be demanded by enforcement agencies, and it is necessary for affirmative action record keeping. The EEOC suggests that such information be coded and kept separate from personnel files.

Developing supportive district and community programs is the last step in an affirmative action program. This may include developing support services for recruiting minority and female employees and encouraging employees to further their education to qualify for promotion.

The EEOC administrative process. Alleged discrimination charges can be filed with any of EEOC's regional or district offices. In 1976 the Equal Employment Opportunity Commission received an average of six thousand charges each month.

Bona fide occupational qualification. Discrimination by sex, religion, or national origin is allowed by the Equal Employment Opportunity Act under one condition, referred to in the law as follows:

> Notwithstanding any other provision of this title, (1) it shall not be an unlawful employment practice for an employer to hire and employ employees, for an employment agency to classify, or refer for employment any individual, for a labor organization to classify its membership or to classify or refer for employment any individual, or for an employer, labor organization, or joint labor management committee controlling apprenticeship or other training, or retraining programs to admit or employ any individual in any such program, on the basis of his religion, sex, or national origin in those certain instances where religion, sex, or national origin is a bona fide occupational qualification reasonably necessary to the normal operation of that particular business or enterprise, and (2) it shall not be an unlawful employment practice for a school, college, university, or other educational institution or institution of learning to hire and employ employees of a particular religion if such school, college, university, or other educational institution or institution of learning is, in whole or in substantial part, owned, supported, controlled, or managed by a particular religion or by a particular religious corporation, association, or society, or if the curriculum of such school, college, university, or other educational institution or institution of learning is directed toward the propagation of a particular religion.[5]

Therefore, a school district's personnel administrator has the right to specify a female for the position of swimming instructor when part of the job description includes supervising the locker room used by female students. In like manner, a

---

[5]The Equal Employment Opportunity Act of 1972 (Washington, D.C.: U.S. Government Printing Office, 1972), p. 4.

Lutheran school official may hire only those applicants who profess the Lutheran creed because the mission of the school is to propagate that particular faith.

In certain school districts the national origin of teachers is extremely important. One out of every twenty persons in the United States is now of Spanish-speaking origin, making this group the nation's second largest minority, after blacks.[6] If in a particular school district over thirty percent of its student population has Spanish surnames, being of Latin origin would be a bona fide job qualification for certain teaching positions in that school system.

Judicial review of affirmative action. Court decisions have further modified affirmative action laws and regulations. Although the courts will continue to refine the interpretation of the Civil Rights Act and the Equal Employment Opportunity Act, certain basic conclusions have emerged and provide direction to school districts in their efforts to construct and implement an affirmative action program.

First, discrimination has been broadly defined, in most cases including a class of individuals rather than a single person. Where discrimination has been found by the courts to exist, remediation must be applied to all members of the class to which the individual complainant belongs.

Second, it is not the intent but rather the consequences of the employment practice that determines if discrimination exists and dictates the remedy.

Third, even when an employment practice is neutral in text and impartially administered, if it has a disproportionate effect upon members of a protected class (those groups covered by a law) or if it perpetuates the effects of prior discriminatory practices, it constitutes unlawful discrimination.

Fourth, statistics that show a disproportionate number of minorities or females in a job classification relative to their presence in the work force constitute evidence of discriminatory practices. Where such statistics exist, the employer must show that this is not the result of overt or institutional discrimination.

Fifth, for an employer to justify any practice or policy that creates a disproportionate effect on a protected class, he or she must demonstrate a "compelling business necessity." The courts have interpreted this in a very narrow sense to mean that no alternative nondiscriminatory practice can achieve the required result.

Finally, court-ordered remedies not only open the doors to equal employment but also require employers to "make whole" and "restore the rightful economic status" of all those in the affected class. In practice, courts have ordered fundamental changes in all aspects of employment systems.

Two recent U.S. Supreme Court decisions have an indirect effect upon affirmative action programs in school districts. The first case dealt with admission quotas to a medical school; the second, with a voluntary race-conscious affirmative action plan in private industry. Both cases addressed the issue of reverse discrimination. They are important not only because of the issue involved but also because

[6]See Carlos J. Orvando, "School Implications of the Peaceful Latino Invasion," *Phi Delta Kappan*, 59 (December, 1977), pp. 230, 231.

of the precedent established in each case, which may be used in a similar action involving public school districts. For these reasons, each case will be briefly summarized.

Regents of the University of California vs. *Bakke.* This case has been heralded as the most important civil rights case since *Brown* vs. *Board of Education* outlawed racial segregation in public schools in 1954 and, ultimately, in all American life. The question before the Supreme Court was perplexing and emotionally charged: Is it fair to give preference to blacks over whites in order to remedy the evils of past discrimination?

Allen Bakke graduated from the University of Minnesota with a degree in engineering and an academic average close to "A." He entered the Marines after graduation and spent seven months in Vietnam as commander of an anti-aircraft missile unit. On his return to civilian life Mr. Bakke earned a master's degree in engineering at Stanford University. He developed a deep interest in medicine and in his spare time became a hospital emergency-room volunteer. In the fall of 1972 at the age of thirty-three he applied to the medical school of the University of California at Davis. Although he scored in the ninetieth percentile in the Medical School Admissions Test, he was rejected. Mr. Bakke filed a lawsuit that eventuated in the Supreme Court.

The University of California at Davis had enacted an admissions program that reserved sixteen out of one hundred openings of the first-year medical class for disadvantaged minority students.

By a five-to-four decision the Supreme Court in July, 1978 affirmed a lower court order admitting Allen Bakke to the medical school at Davis. The Court stated that the admissions program for minorities violated Title VI of the Civil Rights Act, which prohibits racial discrimination in any program receiving federal funds. While rejecting a rigid quota system based solely on race, the Court offered a Solomonic compromise by further stating that race might legitimately be an element in judging students for admission.

United Steelworkers vs. *Brian F. Weber.* In June, 1979 the United States Supreme Court issued a decision that appeared to modify the Bakke decision. In 1974 the Kaiser Aluminum and Chemical Corporation had entered into a collective bargaining master contract with the United Steelworkers of America (USWA). The agreement covered terms and conditions of employment at fifteen plants and contained an affirmative action plan designed to eliminate the racial imbalance in Kaiser's predominately white craft work force.

At each of Kaiser's plants a goal was established, calling for the recruitment and hiring of black craft workers equal to the percentage of blacks in the respective local labor force. To help meet this goal the company initiated an on-the-job training program for unskilled production workers. The plan specified that 50 percent of the openings in the training program were to be reserved for black employees.

This case arose out of the operations at Kaiser's plant in Gramercy, Louisiana.

Until 1974 only persons with prior craft experience were hired as craft workers at Gramercy. Blacks had long been excluded from craft unions in that region and, as a consequence, few had the credentials necessary to apply for craft positions. Only 5 out of 273 workers were black, while the population of Gramercy was 39 percent black.

Pursuant to the national labor agreement, Kaiser began the training program at Gramercy. Workers were selected for the program on the basis of seniority, with the provision that 50 percent of those selected would be black until the percentage of black craft workers in the Gramercy plant approximated the percentage of blacks in the labor force.

During the first year of the affirmative action program, thirteen production workers were selected as trainees from the Gramercy plant; seven were black and six were white. The junior blacks selected had less seniority than several whites who were rejected for admission. Brian Weber, one of the rejected production workers, subsequently instituted a class action suit in the United States District Court for the Eastern District of Louisiana. The complaint alleged that the affirmative action program at Gramercy resulted in discrimination against Mr. Weber and similarly situated white employees in violation of Title VII of the Civil Rights Act, which prohibits racial discrimination in employment.

The district court held that the plan did violate Title VII and entered a judgment in favor of the plaintiff class. The court further issued a permanent injunction prohibiting Kaiser and the United Steelworkers of America from denying access to on-the-job training programs on the basis of race. The Court of Appeals for the Fifth Circuit affirmed this decision.

By a five-to-two vote, the U.S. Supreme Court overturned the lower courts' decisions and ruled that employers may take race-conscious steps to eliminate manifest racial imbalances in traditionally segregated job categories. Further, the Court declared that the law does not condemn all private, voluntary, race-conscious programs.

Although the Bakke and Weber decisions did not apply to personnel management practices in public school districts, reverse discrimination has become the most controversial area of affirmative action programs, and the lower courts have had a difficult time dealing with this issue. The implication for human resource management is that quota system policies in hiring and promotions can be defended only if there is clear evidence of racial imbalance because of job-category segregation.[7]

Equality for the Handicapped

Title V of the Rehabilitation Act of 1973 contains five sections, four of which relate to affirmative action for handicapped individuals and one of which deals with voluntary actions, remedial actions, and evaluation criteria for compliance with the law. The congressional intent of the Rehabilitation Act is identical to other civil

---

[7] See *The Chronicle of Higher Education*, July 2, 1979, pp. 1, 12.

rights legislation, such as the Civil Rights Act (covering discrimination based on race, sex, religion, or national origin) and Title IX of the Educational Amendments (discrimination based on sex). However, the U.S. Department of Health, Education and Welfare (HEW) emphasized in the Federal Register promulgating the law that it also contains a fundamental difference:

> The premise of both Title VI (Civil Rights Act) and Title IX (Educational Amendments) is that there is no inherent difference of inequalities between the general public and the persons protected by these statutes and, therefore, there should be no differential treatment in the administration of federal programs. Section 504 (Rehabilitation Act), on the other hand, is far more complex. Handicapped persons may require different treatment in order to be afforded equal access, and identical treatment may, in fact, constitute discrimination. The problem of establishing general rules as to when different treatment is prohibited or required is compounded by the diversity of existing handicaps and the differing degree to which particular persons may be affected.[8]

Subpart B of Section 504 specifically refers to employment practices. It prohibits recipients of federal financial assistance from discriminating against qualified handicapped individuals in the recruitment, hiring, compensation, job assignment/ classification, and fringe benefits provided. Employers are further required to provide reasonable work environment accommodations for qualified handicapped applicants or employees unless they can demonstrate that such accommodations would impose an undue hardship on the employer. The law applies to all state, intermediate, and local educational agencies. Finally, any agency that receives assistance under the Education of the Handicapped Act must take positive steps to employ and promote qualified handicapped persons in programs assisted under that Act.

Equality for Women

The French writer Stendhal believed that granting women equality would be the surest sign of civilization and would double the intellectual power of the human race. Although he wrote over one hundred years ago, equality for women continues to be a significant issue in our society.

In educational organizations the question of equal employment opportunity for women traditionally applies to a specific job classification—administration. It is obvious to all observers that women are well represented in teaching, custodial, food service, and bus driving positions. Skilled trade jobs, such as carpenters, electricians, or plumbers, when incorporated into a school district maintenance staff, however, are frequently dominated by males, as are industrial arts teaching positions. In such cases, the norms of affirmative action previously outlined in this

---

[8]Department of Health, Education, and Welfare, "Nondiscrimination on the Basis of Handicap," *Federal Register,* Vol. 41, No. 96 (May 17, 1976).

chapter would become applicable. The critical issue, however, is the need to have women better represented in administrative ranks.

The legal mandate of equal employment opportunity for women emanates primarily from two federal laws: Title IX of the Educational Amendments of 1972, which prohibits sex discrimination in educational programs or activities including employment when the school district is receiving federal financial assistance; and, of course, Title VII of the Civil Rights Act of 1964, as amended in 1972, which prohibits discrimination on the basis of sex as well as religion, national origin, race, or color.

Potential areas of employment discrimination concerning women. As a general rule school districts—and all employers—are prohibited from establishing job qualifications that are derived from female stereotyping. The courts have uniformly required employers to prove that any restrictions are indeed bona fide occupational qualifications.

Some of the most common forms of discrimination against females in the business-industrial community are even less defensible in educational organizations. Females have been denied employment because of height and weight limitations. In such situations, a woman who is capable of performing the job-related tasks has clearly established case law precedent to bring the employer to court. However, it is sometimes still the case that an exceptionally talented woman may not be hired for an administrative position because she is a "nice and petite" person who does not measure up to the image of a strong leader. Discrimination is much harder to prove in this latter situation.

The Equal Employment Opportunity Commission prohibits discriminating against women because of their marital status, being pregnant, not being the principal wage earner in a family, or having preschool age children.

The preferences of customers and clientele are also not bona fide occupational qualifications. Thus the preference of parents, teachers, and even students for male principals and administrators in a given school district does not permit the district to discriminate against females for these positions.

Maternity as a particular form of discrimination. On October 31, 1978, President Carter signed into law a pregnancy disability amendment (PL95-555) to Title VII of the Civil Rights Act of 1964. The law had the effect of eliminating unequal treatment for pregnant women in all employment-related situations. The EEOC issued guidelines for implementing this law, indicating that it is discriminatory for an employer: to refuse to hire, train, assign, or promote a woman solely because she is pregnant; to require maternity leave for a predetermined time period; to dismiss a pregnant woman; to deny reemployment to a woman on maternity leave; to deny seniority credit to a woman on maternity leave; and to deny disability or medical benefits to a woman for disabilities unrelated to but occurring during pregnancy, childbirth, or recovery from childbirth.

Equality by Age

Peter Drucker, the nationally recognized expert in management theory and practice, predicts that "flexible retirement is going to be the central social issue in the U.S. during the next decade. It is going to play the role that minority employment played in the 1960s and women's rights played in the seventies.[9] Drucker's prediction is, however, only one aspect of an even larger issue—we are rapidly becoming a nation whose population is by percentage mostly middle-aged.

The Age Discrimination in Employment Act of 1967, as amended, is taking on ever-increasing importance for personnel administrators. This act was passed by Congress to promote the employment of the older worker based on ability rather than age by prohibiting arbitrary discrimination. Also, under this act the Department of Labor has consistently sponsored informational and educational programs on the needs and abilities of the older worker. The "Statement of Findings and Purpose" in the Age Discrimination in Employment Act sets forth a rationale for its passage that is a true reflection of current societal trends towards older workers:

> Sec. 2.(a) The Congress hereby finds and declares that
> (1) in the face of rising productivity and affluence, older workers find themselves disadvantaged in their efforts to retain employment, and especially to regain employment when displaced from jobs;
> (2) the setting of arbitrary age limits regardless of potential for job performance has become a common practice, and certain otherwise desirable practices may work to the disadvantage of older persons;
> (3) the incident of unemployment, especially long-term unemployment, with resultant deterioration of skill, morale, and employer acceptability is, relative to the younger ages, high among older workers; their numbers are great and growing; and their employment problems grave;
> (4) the existence in industries affecting commerce of arbitrary discrimination in employment burdens commerce and the free flow of goods in commerce.

Conclusion

This section has dealt with four major federal influences on the manpower planning process. Although affirmative action and the legislation on equality for the handicapped, women, and individuals by age represent central trends in personnel administration, these are by no means the only federal considerations that affect personnel processes.

The following laws enacted by Congress in the nineteenth and twentieth centuries constitute the national public employment policy that directly or indirectly affects the employment policies of public and private educational institutions.

1883   Pendleton Act (Civil Service Commission)
1931   Davis-Bacon Act

---

[9] Peter F. Drucker, "Flexible-Age Retirement: Social Issue of the Decade," *Industry Week*, May 15, 1978, pp. 66–71.

1932	Anti-Injunction Act
1935	National Labor Relations Act
1935	Social Security Act
1936	Walsh-Healey Public Contracts Act
1938	Fair Labor Standards Act
1947	Labor-Management Relations Act
1959	Labor-Management Reporting and Disclosure Act
1962	Work House Act of 1962
1963	Equal Pay Act of 1963
1967	Reemployment of Veterans
1968	Garnishment Provisions, Consumer Credit Protection Act
1974	Employee Retirement Income Security Act

BOARD OF EDUCATION POLICY ON EQUAL EMPLOYMENT OPPORTUNITY AND AFFIRMATIVE ACTION

The following sample policy has been developed to illustrate more clearly how school districts can comply with the intent and practices of federal legislation and litigation set forth in this chapter.

The board of education further recognizes that implementation of its responsibility to provide an effective educational program depends on the full and effective utilization of qualified employees regardless of race, age, sex, color, religion, national origin, creed, or ancestry.

The board directs that its employment and personnel policies guarantee equal opportunity for everyone. Discrimination has no place in any component of this school system. Therefore, all matters relating to the recruitment, selection, placement, compensation, benefits, educational opportunities, promotion, termination, and working conditions shall be free from discriminatory practices.

The board of education further initiates an affirmative action program to be in compliance with Title VII of the Civil Rights Act of 1964 and the Equal Employment Opportunity Act of 1972. This program shall ensure: proportional minority and female representation and participation in all employment opportunities; that civil rights will not be violated, abridged, or denied; that recruitment and selection criteria will be unbiased; that information relative to employment and promotional opportunities will be disseminated on an equal basis; and finally that every employee has a right to file an internal or external complaint of discrimination and to obtain redress therefrom based on the finding of facts that substantiate the complaint.

The following school district administrators are responsible for the effective implementation of the affirmation action program:

Superintendent of Schools. As the chief executive officer of the school system, the superintendent is directly responsible for exercising a leadership role in formulating and implementing procedures that are in keeping with this policy.

Director of Affirmative Action. Under the supervision of the superintendent, the director is responsible for the formulation and administration of the affirmative action program.

RECRUITMENT OF PERSONNEL

After the manpower planning process identifies current and future staffing needs, the next step is to recruit qualified personnel. However, certain constraints on recruitment must be taken into consideration in program development. Affirmative action requirements, the reputation and policies of a school district, the enormous responsibilities of positions in education, the salary and fringe benefits offered in certain school districts—all have an influence on how a district will implement the recruitment process.

To carry out a recruitment program effectively, personnel administrators must have a good understanding of vocational development theory. The following principles are common to many theories and can be used to formulate recruitment strategies. First, people have different interests, abilities, and personalities, which will qualify them for a number of occupations. Second, the occupational preferences, competencies, and the self-image of people will change with time and experience, making personal adjustment a continuous process. Third, both life and work satisfaction depend on how well individuals can utilize their abilities and find outlets for their interests, personality traits, and values. Fourth, the process of occupational choice is influenced by employment variables such as salary, fringe benefits, location, the opportunity for advancement, and the nature of the work to be performed. Finally, vocational development is essentially a compromise between personal characteristics, such as interests and abilities, and external factors, such as the type of work to be performed.

Experience shows that certain recruiting methods produce the best candidates for a particular job vacancy. Therefore, before initiating the recruitment process, each job vacancy should be analyzed to ascertain what method will be most effective. The most common methods include: internal search; referrals; contacting employment agencies; advertising vacancies with college and university placement services; advertising in newspapers and in the publications of professional organizations; following up on unsolicited applications; and contacting community organizations that promote the interests of minority groups.

When a school district wishes to communicate that it has a vacancy, it usually relies on a formal advertisement. The content of an advertisement is dictated by the job description and criteria to be used in selecting the most qualified candidate for the position. An effective advertisement must accurately reflect the major responsibilities of the position and the minimum qualifications an individual must possess to become a candidate for the job.

In terms of content and style, the most effective advertisement will include the title of the position, information about the school district, information on how to apply, and qualifications for candidates. Listing subjective qualifications and using "blind ads" are generally not appropriate. It is also more effective for a school district to place only a few vacancies in a given advertisement and, when possible, to advertise each position by itself.

A special type of advertisement is the recruitment brochure. Its purpose is to provide potential candidates with enough information to allow candidates to determine if they wish to apply for the job and if they possess the minimum requirements for it. The brochure should include the announcement of the vacancy, the procedure for applying, a description of the qualifications that the successful candidate must possess, information about the community served by the school or school district, and financial, personnel, and curricular data about the school and/or school district.

General information brochures containing data about the community and school district could be used when recruiting teachers and support personnel. The more extensive brochure is usually limited to school executive positions because the cost of printing such brochures for each vacancy would be prohibitive.

SELECTION OF PERSONNEL

The objective of the selection process is to hire individuals who will be successful on the job. The cost of this process is a major expenditure for most school districts. It includes advertising the position, printing and mailing applications, interviewing candidates, and checking references. This process should be implemented through a series of activities that will minimize the chances of hiring individuals who are inadequate performers. The following steps constitute the selection process:

1. *Write the Job Description.* The job description is the end product of another process known as the "job analysis." This process gathers information about each job through observations, interviews, questionnaires, consulting, and the diary method. The job description outlines specific details of a position and establishes the minimal qualifications needed to perform the job successfully.

2. *Establishing the Selection Criteria.* Criteria instruments delineate those ideal characteristics that, if possessed by an individual to the fullest extent possible, will ensure the successful performance of the job. Selection criteria can also be used to quantify the expert opinion of those who will be interviewing candidates.

3. *Writing the Job Vacancy Announcement and Advertising the Position.* The advertisement is based on the job description and provides interested individuals with sufficient information to decide whether to apply for the position. The advertisement must clearly identify the job title, major responsibilities, name and

location of the school district, application procedure, and the minimal job qualifications.

4. *Receiving Applications.*   A central office staff member should be assigned to receive all applications for a given vacancy. As the applications are received, they should be dated and filed in a designated folder. This will provide integrity to the process and establish a method of monitoring the progress towards filling the vacancy.

5. *Selecting the Candidates to be Interviewed.*   The application form should contain a statement requesting the applicants to have their placement papers, transcripts, and letters of reference sent to the personnel department. The form should provide sufficient information to evaluate each person against the selection criteria and against the minimal requirements for the job. A selected group of applicants are then interviewed for the position.

6. *Interviewing the Candidates.*   Interviewing candidates is a school responsibility shared by the personnel department and other school district employees. It is important to include not only those who will supervise the new employee but also others who have expert knowledge about the duties that will be performed by the successful candidate. An interview is essentially a conversation between two or more individuals conducted to generate information about the respondent. Interviewing is a learned skill; it also has profound legal implications.

7. *Checking References and Credentials.*   "Credentials" refers to such items as a college or university transcript, teaching certification, and a physician's verification of health. These credentials along with letters of reference should, whenever possible, be sent directly to the personnel department by the issuing source.

8. *Selecting the Best Candidate.*   The personnel administrator who is responsible for implementing the selection process for a particular vacancy must organize all relevant data in such a manner that a choice may be made by the superintendent of schools.

9. *Implementing the Job Offer and Acceptance.*   For professional positions, a contract must be approved by the board of education and signed by the finalist before this step can be considered completed. For classified positions, once the candidate affirms that he or she will accept the offer, employment may commence at a mutually acceptable time.

10. *Notifying the Unsuccessful Candidates.*   This step is initiated only after the offer of employment has been accepted by the desired candidate because there may be a need to offer the position to another individual if the candidate selected first refuses the offer.

The first formal task in applying for a position is filling out the application form. There are two basic formats in constructing the forms. The first emphasizes detailed factual information; the second, the applicant's attitudes, opinions, and values.

The basic principle in constructing application forms is, "Only ask for information you need to know!" The information requested on most applications falls under one of the following headings: personal data, education and/or professional preparation, experience, and references. The physical layout of the form should have sufficient space for answering the questions and providing the requested information.

The business and industrial community uses two techniques as part of the selection process that are seldom used by school districts: employment tests and assessment centers. Aptitude and ability tests can be successfully used as part of the selection process for most classified jobs in school districts. In fact, they are necessary for some positions. Assessment centers are places where supervisors have an opportunity to observe candidates for a particular job. Candidates are taken through a series of simulations dealing with administrative problems that will probably be encountered on the job. Large metropolitan school districts could find this technique beneficial in selecting and promoting teachers into the principalship and other administrative positions.

PLACEMENT AND INDUCTION
OF PERSONNEL

The last phase in procuring a new employee for the school district is the individual's assignment and orientation to the school community.

The placement of employees within the school system is the responsibility of the superintendent of schools. The planning required in making assignments is a very complicated task, demanding the full-time attention of at least one personnel administrator in most metropolitan-area school districts. It is to the advantage of the school district to make assignments that are in harmony with the wishes of its employees. A staffing survey is one method of systematically gathering information on the placement preferences of employees.

Other variables that the personnel department must take into consideration in making assignments include staff balancing, certification requirements, experience, and working relationships. The welfare of students and implementation of the school district's instructional program are the primary considerations. When there are a number of requests for reassignment, seniority is a defensible criteria after the other variables are considered. A due process should be established to give employees the opportunity to have an assignment reviewed by the appropriate administrator.

Induction is the process designed to acquaint newly employed individuals with the school system and the relationships he or she must develop to be a successful employee. An effective induction program must have well-defined objectives that will help the employee to feel welcome and secure, to become a member of the "team," to be inspired towards excellence in performance, to adjust to the work environment, and to become familiar with the school community.

Induction programs fall into one of two major categories: informational and personal adjustment programs. Informational programs are concerned with either initial material or updating information. Initial data consist primarily of information about the school system, the community it serves, and the school where a new employee will work. Updating informational programs is geared to the employee who is reassigned; they concentrate on a particular school and community. Personal adjustment programs are designed to help the newly hired or reassigned employee interact with the other people for whom and with whom they will work.

In effectively orienting new employees to the school district, policies and services must be thoroughly explained and system-wide personnel identified. Orientation to the community must convey to employees a knowledge and understanding of the social, cultural, ethnic, and religious makeup of the community. How people make a living, customs, clubs and organizations, church denominations, museums, libraries, colleges and universities, and social services are all within the scope of this program.

Orienting new employees to a particular school and program begins by introducing new employees to their colleagues. A tour of the facility and an explanation of administrative procedures along with an orientation to the instructional program are also important aspects of induction.

Personal adjustment orientation includes encouraging new employees to establish working relationships with their colleagues. Organized activities such as faculty meetings with time for socialization, Christmas parties or dinners, serving on faculty and district committees, and membership in professional organizations are effective methods of establishing desired relationships among the professional staff.

Evaluating the effectiveness of the induction process is extremely important in order to develop the necessary data for improving the program.

An area of special concern in the induction process centers around first-year teachers. Many potentially excellent teachers are lost to the education profession because they are not properly inducted. A number of suggestions and models have been developed. They all recognize the importance of giving first-year teachers time to consult with colleagues and feedback concerning their performance.

STAFF DEVELOPMENT

Change is a constant condition of our American way of life. Improved communications place before students and educators advances in politics, economics, and science almost as soon as they occur.

School districts have a mandate to educate the youth of our country. To do so successfully, schools need well-qualified teachers, administrators, and support personnel. No employee will remain qualified in the face of accelerating change without some form of ongoing education and training. This is the impetus behind the recent emphasis on staff development programs.

Adult learning usually consists of two processes, training and education. Training is designed to teach a sequence of programmed behaviors; education seeks to impart understanding and an ability to interpret knowledge. Both types of learning occur through a staff development program based on the objectives to be reached.

In all learning environments four basic components must be present to ensure success: stimulus, response, reinforcement, and motivation.

Creating a staff development program consists of six separate but sequential processes: (1) establishing school district goals and objectives, which become the foundation of the program; (2) assessing the needs of the school district employees to determine if there is a discrepancy between the competencies of the staff and the requirements of the organization; (3) establishing staff development goals and objectives; (4) designing a program that will meet staff development requirements; (5) implementing the designed plan in such a way that effective learning can occur; and (6) evaluating the program to ascertain if it is meeting its objectives, which in turn will affect future program designs.

A staff development program for the instructional staff will focus on updating subject area skills and knowledge, outlining societal demands and changes, presenting the findings of research on teaching methods and practices, and updating teachers on the advances in instructional materials and equipment.

In assessing the needs of teachers, four sources of information may be helpful: (1) the teacher needs assessment surveys, (2) community surveys, (3) certification information coupled with the manpower master plan, and (4) research and curriculum studies.

In the last decade school principals have experienced multiple challenges brought on by such trends as cultural pluralism, community involvement, special education, student rights, and collective bargaining. A recent study conducted in California identified the following areas as appropriate for principal development programs: instructional skills, management skills, human relations abilities, political and cultural awareness, leadership skills, and self-understanding.

Besides the traditional model of staff development for principals, which includes workshops and seminars, many school districts are taking a more personalized approach directed at helping principals acquire skills that relate to their job and personal development.

Staff development programs have been limited to the professional staff in many school districts. However, all employees can profit from development programs, and classified employees should have the opportunity to increase their skills and to participate in personal growth activities. Newly hired and promoted classified employees are usually inducted into the responsibilities of their positions through a staff development program. The three most commonly used methods are: on-the-job training, off-the-job training, and apprenticeship training.

APPRAISAL OF PERSONNEL

During this century, three stages of development occurred concerning the process of teacher evaluation. In the 1920s, efforts were primarily centered around analyzing if a given teaching style correlated with the philosophy and psychology of William

James and John Dewey. The second stage was concerned with ascribing certain personality traits as being related to excellence in teaching. In the 1960s the final stage, which emphasized generic teaching behaviors, appeared.

The last five years have ushered in a dramatic change in evaluation procedures. The traditional concept of teacher evaluation has been replaced by the broader concept of appraisal management. In this approach an employee is evaluated within the context of attaining certain preestablished objectives.

The reasons that justify the establishment and implementation of an appraisal process for all school district employees include: to foster self-development, to identify a variety of tasks which an employee is capable of performing, to identify staff development needs, to improve employee performance, to determine if an employee should be retained and what his or her salary increase should be, and to help in the proper placement or promotion of an employee.

A significant aspect of an appraisal process is measuring an employee's performance against his or her job responsibilities as outlined in a job description.

In developing an appraisal process, a board of education should establish a policy on employee appraisal that will give direction to the various divisions within a school district. These divisions are responsible for developing objectives aimed at implementing the goals of the school board. Each employee is then responsible for developing personal objectives that further the divisional objectives. Consequently, employee performance is measured against the degree to which each individual has attained his or her objectives. Feedback data is then available to analyze if divisional objectives have been reached. The actual appraisal procedures for implementing this process are best developed by involving representatives of the employees who will be evaluated.

As with the development of appraisal procedures, evaluation instruments are more appropriately constructed by the committee process. There are two basic categories of evaluation instruments: trait forms and result forms. The trait approach rates an employee against a predetermined list of traits to ascertain overall performance. The results approach involves comparing an employee's performance against objectives that were developed by the employee and agreed to by the supervisor. Using both types of instruments helps to identify areas where improvement is needed.

Developing Termination Procedures

A universal reason for evaluating an individual's performance is to make a determination concerning the desirability of retaining the person as an employee of the school district. A decision to dismiss an employee, of course, is extremely difficult to make because of the importance of employment to a person's welfare and also because of the effects on the employee's dependents.

Employment counselors have seen the devastating financial and psychological effects that "getting fired" has on a person's life. In fact, the trauma usually centers on the individual's self-concept. Feelings of inadequacy, failure, self-contempt, and anger are common to people who have their employment terminated. Although most individuals are able to cope with such a situation, others never fully recover from such an experience. Consequently, it is not only good personnel management but also a humane responsibility for school district administrators to develop termination procedures that are objective and fair, and that incorporate a due process that gives an employee the opportunity to modify or defend his behavior. The following presentation is meant to explicate the nuances of due process and the grounds for terminating employment. It is based upon a compilation of state statutes and court decisions; it can serve as a model for school boards as they apply statutes from their particular state covering termination procedures.

Grounds for terminating the employment of tenured teachers. A tenured teacher may have his or her employment terminated for one or more of the following causes: physical or mental condition making him or her unfit to instruct or associate with children; immoral conduct; insubordination, inefficiency, or incompetency in the line of duty; willful or persistent violation of the published policies and procedures of the school board; excessive or unreasonable absence from work; conviction of a felony or a crime involving moral turpitude.

The first cause listed must be understood within the context of the Rehabilitation Act of 1973. A handicap does not constitute a physical condition that may in any way be construed as unfitting an individual from associating with children or students. In fact, the prevalent interpretation of the law is that an aide must be hired to assist an employee if the employee's handicap interferes with the instruction or supervision of the children. The only possible physical condition that would prevent an employee from associating with children is the contracting of a contagious disease. This would be a potential cause for dismissal only if the individual refused to get medical treatment and insisted on working. Emotional illness that produces dangerous or bizarre behavior is also a potential cause for dismissal if the employee refuses to receive medical treatment and insists on working. In both cases, the documentation of a physician is necessary to proceed with the termination process. The school district is, of course, responsible for all expenses incurred in securing the expert opinion of the physician.

Immoral conduct must be judged within the context of local standards but also must be reasonable and consistent with recent court decisions. A number of significant court cases have been cited and form the foundation for the following principles that should be used in judging employee conduct. First, the health of the pupil-teacher relationship is the criterion for judging employee behavior. A teacher or other employee who establishes a relationship with a student that goes beyond friendship and is exhibited in some form of "dating" is unacceptable. Second, illegal sexual acts are cause for immediate suspension. If an employee is convicted of such an act, his or her employment with the district must be terminated. Suspension is a justifiable practice while investigating allegations of sexual misconduct if the employee receives his or her salary during this period. Third, private nonconventional sexual life styles are not a cause for employee dismissal. Such practices as wife swapping, homosexuality, and a couple living together outside of matrimony may be unacceptable to the majority of people in the community, but such practices do not inherently affect an individual's performance in the work place. These and other practices are publicly displayed on television and in other media, which has, to an extent, nullified their impact on students. Fourth, if an employee advocates non-conventional sexual life styles at school, the employee has placed himself or herself in a position where termination is possible because such life styles are in direct conflict with local standards.

Insubordination in the line of duty is always a cause for dismissal. Although the interpretation of what constitutes insubordination may appear to be self-evident, this situation has restricted application. Employees can be insubordinate only if they refuse to comply with a directive of their supervisor that is clearly within their job expertise. If a principal asks a teacher to supervise the children on the playground during the teacher's preparation time and the teacher refuses, the teacher is insubordinate because teachers have the job responsibility of supervising children. On the other hand, if the principal were to direct a custodian to supervise the children on the playground and he or she refused, the custodian would not be guilty of insubordination because this is not within his or her occupational expertise. Nor would it be insubordination if a teacher refused to fill in for the principal's secretary who was absent from work because of illness. The teacher was not hired to perform secretarial functions and may refuse this directive. The manner in which an employee responds to a directive does not usually constitute insubordination, if the employee performs the task. Thus, if a teacher responds in a sharp tone to the principal when assigned to playground duty but obeys the directive, the teacher is not guilty of insubordination.

Inefficiency is relatively easy to document. It usually refers to the inability of an individual to manage those tasks that are integral to a job responsibility. A teacher who never takes class attendance or who cannot account for the equipment, books, or materials assigned to his or her class is obviously inefficient. A principal who is always late in turning in building budgets or other reports also falls into this category.

Incompetency is perhaps the most difficult reason to document in terminating an employee. It also directly is related to the formal evaluation process. If a tenured teacher is performing in an incompetent manner, it means that he or she is hindering the instructional-learning process. The evaluations made by the principal must clearly indicate that major deficiencies have been identified and that objectives to remediate these deficiencies have not been met.

Claiming willful or persistent violation of state school laws or board of education policies and procedures as a cause for termination presupposes that school district employees have been informed of these. An effective method of notifying employees about these laws, policies, and procedures is through the publication and distribution of a handbook or manual that clearly outlines the employees' responsibilities.

Excessive or unreasonable absence from work is a relative circumstance that can operate only through a policy defining what is meant by *excessive* or *unreasona-*

ble. Local school boards will probably rely on patterns of absences in making their determination. Five consecutive days per month over a year's span, for example, could be considered excessive if the employee is not suffering from a chronic physical condition that interferes with attendance at work.

Conviction of a felony is obviously a reason to terminate the employment of an individual. The conviction for a crime involving moral turpitude, however, requires some explanation. Prostitution is usually classified as a misdemeanor, but because it involves morally offensive conduct according to most community standards, it is a reason to terminate a tenured teacher. The selling of pornography or a conviction for the use or sale of drugs also falls within the definition of moral turpitude.

Notification of charges against a tenured teacher. After a behavior that could result in the termination of an employee has been identified, the next step in a due process procedure is notification. This is a formal process of serving the employee with written charges specifying the alleged grounds that, if not corrected, will eventuate in dismissal. It must be kept in mind that notification with an opportunity to correct behavior is applicable only to charges arising out of incompetency, inefficiency, or insubordination in the line of duty. Physical or mental conditions as described above, immoral conduct, violation of education laws or board of education policies and procedures, excessive absences, and conviction of a felony or crime involving moral turpitude require a hearing before termination of employment, but they obviously do not require a period of time to correct the behavior. The behavior has already gone beyond what is rectifiable in an educational setting. A hearing is required, however, to determine if the facts substantiate the allegation.

Notification of charges, an extremely formal process, must not be confused with evaluation procedures that permit an employee the right to disagree with a written evaluation. As a normal course of action, employees may attach a written rebuttal to the evaluation instrument, setting forth points of disagreement and including any documentation to support their position.

Time periods are an essential component of the notification process. Three time periods are specified in most statutes: for example a thirty-day period during which time the employee has an opportunity to modify his or her behavior; a twenty-day period before a hearing is held, which allows the employee time to gather evidence supporting his or her position; and a ten-day period after service on the teacher of a hearing during which time he or she must respond to the notification that he or she wishes to have the hearing. If the employee does not wish to have a hearing on the charges, the board of education may terminate his or her employment with the school district by a majority vote of the board members. The teacher may be suspended with pay after notice of a hearing until the board of education makes a determination concerning the employment of the teacher.

Termination hearing on charges against a tenured teacher. This procedure should be followed in conducting a hearing that might eventuate in the dismissal of a tenured teacher. Once again this model is applicable to all termination proceedings and include the following provisions:

1. The hearing shall be held in a public forum. There is a distinction between a public hearing and a hearing held in public: at a public hearing those in attendance are usually allowed to address those conducting the hearing according to preestablished procedures; at a hearing held in public only those representing the party making the allegation and those representing the party against whom the allegation is made are allowed to speak and participate in the hearing.
2. Both parties may be represented by an attorney, who may cross-examine witnesses.
3. The testimony given at a hearing shall be under oath. Government agencies such as school districts are usually allowed the privilege of administering oaths in official proceedings. The president or secretary of the board of education is normally the official so empowered.
4. The board of education may subpoena witnesses and documentary evidence requested by the teacher. As with the power to administer oaths, school districts usually have subpoena rights and may limit the number of witnesses called on behalf of the teacher or school district administrators.
5. The proceedings at the hearing should be recorded by a stenographer employed by the school district. A tape recording of the hearing is usually acceptable in lieu of a stenographer. A transcript of the proceedings must be made available not only to the school board but also to the teacher. The transcript of a hearing held in public should be open to public inspection.
6. Except for the fee paid to the attorney representing the teacher, all expenses for conducting the hearing should be paid by the school district.
7. The decision by the board of education should be reached within a preestablished time period to ensure fair treatment to the employee.

The board of education is exercising judicial authority in conducting the hearing and reaching a decision on the possible dismissal of a tenured teacher. This is a unique circumstance because the school board acts in two capacities: prosecution, in the sense that the charges are brought against the employee in the name of the school board; and judicial, because the school board renders the decision. In this respect the board of education is reviewing its own action in alleging charges. Consequently, it is extremely important to maintain, as much as possible, an impartial structure to the hearing. The evidence should be presented by an attorney representing the building principal and other line administrators up to the superintendent of schools because these administrators have the responsibility for evaluating and reviewing employee evaluations.

The room should also be structured to clearly delineate the roles that will be exercised at the hearing. The board of education will occupy a central place in the room seated at a table. A second table could be set up perhaps ten to fifteen feet in front of and facing the board members where witnesses will give testimony. To either side of the board table and facing each other should be two tables: seated at one, the teacher and his or her attorney, and at the other the appropriate administrator with the school district's attorney. Those in attendance should be seated in a manner that clearly indicates that they must not interfere with the proceedings.

Another mechanism sometimes used in lieu of a formal hearing when discussing the possible termination of any employee is the executive session of the school board. Most state statutes permit a government body to hold private meetings at which public attendance is excluded when personnel matters are discussed. If a teacher or any employee is confronted with documentation that could possibly result in his or her termination and given notice that his or her behavior must be modified, it may be possible to invite the employee to discuss a lack of improvement at an executive session of the school board. If the employee resigns in the face of this documentation, the expense and potential embarrassment of a public hearing is avoided.

Appeal by a tenured teacher to a termination decision issued by the board of education. Because school districts are state government agencies, appealing the decision of a school board is a matter for the state circuit court, which is the court of original jurisdiction in state civil and criminal matters. In most states this appeal must usually be made within a set period of time. All evidence, documentation, records, and the transcript of the hearing will probably be requested by the court. Of course, the employee has the right to appeal the decision of the circuit court, as in any civil action, to the court of appeals and Supreme Court if there is a justifiable reason.

Figure 9-1, *Evaluation of a Permanent Teacher,* schematically represents the procedure outlined in this section.

Termination procedures for probationary teachers. A distinction must be made from the very beginning of this section between terminating the employment of a probationary teacher and not renewing a probationary teacher's contract. In the latter situation no formal due process is necessary; the employer-employee obligation simply ceases to exist with the expiration of the contract. This may occur if a probationary teacher is not performing at a level acceptable to the administration. A probationary teacher may have difficulty interacting with the students, staff, and parents in the school district or may be teaching at a minimal level. It is not only to the district's but also to the teacher's benefit not to renew the contract since the teacher might be more successful in another school district. Not renewing a contract presupposes that evaluations have been made by the supervisor, deficiencies have been pointed out, and advice and help have been offered on how to improve performance or remove the stated deficiencies. If such a process has occurred, nonrenewal of the teacher's contract is justified.

In terminating a probationary teacher before contract expiration, the employee must be given a written statement setting forth the allegations along with a reasonable time period to remove deficiencies or improve performance. If such corrections or improvements are not made within the specified time, the employee may be dismissed by action of the board of education.

Grounds and procedure for revocation of a teacher's license to teach. A final formal procedure must be briefly alluded to when discussing termination pro-

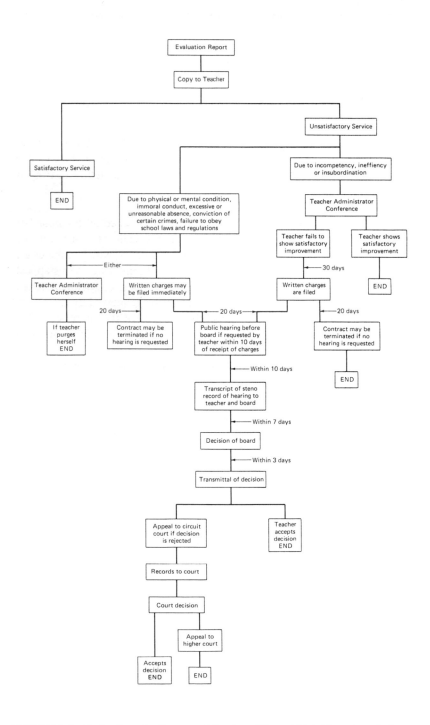

FIGURE 9-1 Evaluation of a Permanent Teacher, Missouri State Department of Education, November, 1970[10]

[10]Department of Elementary and Secondary Education, *Evaluation of a Permanent Teacher* (Jefferson City, Mo.: the Department, 1980).

cedures. A teacher's license to teach may be revoked if it can be proven that he or she has exhibited incompetency, cruelty, immorality, drunkenness, neglect of duty, or the breaking of a written contract with the board of education. As with the cause for terminating a tenured teacher, these reasons have a very narrow application.

Incompetency means that the teacher seriously hinders the instructional learning process. A chronic mental illness or sociopathic behavior that has been diagnosed by a psychiatrist is an example of incompetency that could result in revocation of a teacher's license.

Cruelty refers not only to physical but also to mental or emotional abuse of children. The conditions that constitute cruelty may be summarized as follows: any act that is meant to injure or bring serious ridicule and embarrassment to a child is abusive and cruel.

Immorality is, of course, an extremely sensitive issue. For practical considerations, this cause is commonly interpreted to mean that an individual has been convicted of an illegal sexual offense or a crime involving moral turpitude. The examples provided earlier in this chapter are applicable to immorality as a cause for a revocation of a teacher's license.

Drunkenness as a cause for revocation of an individual's license is usually interpreted to mean that the employee either is intoxicated or drinks alcoholic beverages while working. This situation is further complicated by the fact that drinking alcoholic beverages in a government building such as a school is a misdemeanor in most states. A second complicating factor is how drunkenness relates to the issue of alcoholism. Because alcoholism is considered to be a disease by the medical profession, the same considerations should be afforded the alcoholic as are granted to other employees with a medical problem. These considerations usually involve granting sick leave to an employee receiving medical treatment or reassigning the employee to a position with limited responsibilities during treatment. If an employee is not a diagnosed alcoholic and if he or she persists in drinking alcoholic beverages at work or arrives at school intoxicated, license revocation is in the best interest of a school district's clientele, the children.

Neglect of duty presupposes that an employee has been informed about the responsibilities that are integral to his or her position with the school district. This is usually accomplished by written job descriptions or in policy manuals and handbooks specifying these responsibilities. Neglect of duty as a cause for revoking a teacher's license requires that the teacher be given an opportunity to rectify his or her behavior. Thus, evaluations that set forth the employee's deficiencies are necessary to such a situation. It must also be remembered that the revocation of license is extremely serious and the neglect of duty must be, in like manner, extremely serious and chronic. A teacher who leaves young children unattended on a field trip—behavior that could result in an injury to a child—and who continues such irresponsible behavior after being informed of the danger by the principal—has exhibited a lack of understanding that seriously affects his or her ability to supervise children. This is a reason not only to terminate the employment of the individual but also to safeguard against this teacher's potential employment with another school by proceeding to have his or her license revoked.

Sometimes a teacher or other employee is offered a position with another school district or in private business or industry. If that teacher neglects to request a contract annulment from the school board and assumes another position, the board of education may proceed to have his or her license revoked. Most school boards are not resistant to annulling a contract except in those cases when the education of the students would be seriously affected. A teacher who tenders a resignation the day before the opening of school in September may not receive a contract annulment until a suitable replacement is obtained.

It should be clearly understood that boards of education usually do not have the authority to revoke a license; rather, it may follow a statutory procedure that could eventuate in the revocation of a teacher's license. The state board of education, which issues teaching licenses, has the authority to revoke them.

Finally, revocation of a teacher's license is usually irreversible unless the statutory procedures were neglected or unless the evidence was faulty. It is therefore, a very serious matter that should be initiated only if the education or health and safety of children would be significantly jeopardized not only in present but also in future situations. Terminating the employment of an individual obviously removes him or her from injuring the children presently in his or her care. Revocation of license prevents the teacher from bringing such injury to children if he or she were to be employed in another school district. A classic example involves the teacher who is convicted of child molestation and subsequently is fired from his or her position but who manages to get hired in another school district and commits a similar crime because his or her license was not revoked.

Humane considerations in the termination process.   The procedures described in this section may appear to overemphasize the legal and negative side of the appraisal process. It is, however, an aspect of appraisal that is seldom addressed and that is extremely important. Confusion over appropriate and fair termination procedures could result in a school district being saddled with an employee who hinders the instructional-learning process or who, in fact, may place children in an unsafe situation.

The educational welfare of children is the primary mandate of a school district. The hiring, retaining, development, and termination of personnel should be guided by this mandate. However, employees also have rights that must be taken into consideration when developing appraisal procedures and dealing with employee evaluation. Due process is one right that has long been a fundamental principle in English common law and is basic to the legal procedures of American democracy.

REWARDING PERFORMANCE

Psychologists have long recognized that satisfaction of needs is the primary motivation behind all human actions. In satisfying their needs, individuals will act in ways that they perceive to be in their own best interest. A manager who understands human motivation and what employees believe to be in their best interest is able to develop a unique rewards system.

School district administrators should attempt to utilize an "expectancy model" as the vehicle for developing a rewards system. With this model, rewards are linked to employee behavior that both meets the objectives of the school district and satisfies the needs of the employees.

Five variables must be taken into consideration in a rewards program: employee performance, employee effort, seniority, employee skills, and job requirements. The rewarding of performance, however, must be the primary objective of a rewards program.

An effective program must include both intrinsic and extrinsic rewards. Intrinsic rewards are those that pertain to the quality of the job situation; they may include participation in the decision-making process, increased responsibility, and greater job discretion. Extrinsic rewards are divided into direct, indirect, and non-financial compensation. Direct compensation is commonly referred to as salary or wages; indirect compensation is frequently referred to as fringe benefits. Non-financial rewards are limited only by the imagination of the administration and are tailored to meet the needs of individual employees. For example, a very status conscious employee might consider the services of a private secretary and a reserved parking place as a reward for exceptional performance.

Direct compensation, salary and wages, can be effectively administered only if the following principles are incorporated into the pay policy: skills required in various positions must be recognized; salaries must be competitive; the primary focus of salary increases must be improved performance; and salary schedules must be reviewed annually.

An important question central to any pay policy is, "Does money motivate?" A reasonable conclusion, supported by experience and research, is that money does affect performance if it is clear that performance is rewarded by a salary increase.

There are a number of other issues in salary and wage management that must command the attention of personnel administration. These issues will have an effect on pay policy development and include: public disclosure of salaries, compensation packaging, equity of pay with performance, techniques for collecting community wage data, methods of making salary recommendations to the school board, payroll deductions, employee reactions to salary decisions, appropriate pay periods, annual wage review, and salary schedule construction.

Indirect compensation, or fringe benefits, may be defined as benefits available to all employees that help a school district to attract and retain good employees. Certain fringe benefits are required by law—these include social security, state retirement programs, unemployment insurance, and workmen's compensation.

Voluntary fringe benefits may be divided into insurance programs, time away from the job, and services. Group insurance programs are available for almost every human need including medical and hospitalization insurance, dental insurance, term life insurance, errors and omissions insurance, and optical insurance.

A fringe benefit often taken for granted by employees is time away from the job, including sick leave, vacation time, paid holidays, and sabbatical leave. In like

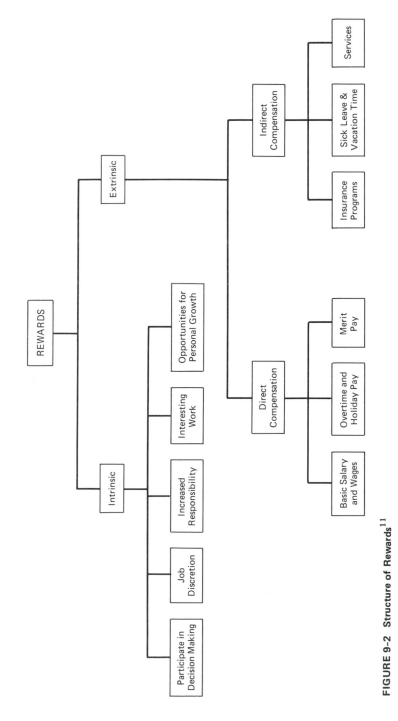

FIGURE 9-2 Structure of Rewards[11]

[11] Ronald W. Rebore, *Personnel Administration in Education* (Englewood Cliffs, N.J.: Prentice-Hall, 1982), p. 241.

manner, certain services offered by school districts are in reality fringe benefits. These include expenses paid for attendance at workshops, professional meetings, and conventions; tuition reimbursement; and free lunches and coffee. Central office administrators are usually given use of a school district automobile or receive mileage compensation. With decreasing enrollments, many school districts arc offering career counseling services to teachers who will be looking for a job outside education. Fringe benefits will continue to play a significant role in compensating employees as an alternative to large salary and wage increases.

CONTRACT MANAGEMENT

Teachers and administrators usually work under the provisions of an individual contract. Classified personnel such as secretaries, bus drivers, and custodians are employed at an hourly rate or for an annual salary. In school districts where a master contract has been negotiated by a union, teachers and administrators belonging to the bargaining units do not have individual contracts but rather work under the provisions of the master agreement. There are exceptions to these general statements but, for all practical purposes, these are the alternative methods by which employees arc hired to work in a school system.

The question may legitimately be asked, "What is the purpose of issuing individual contracts to teachers and administrators?" The most accurate response is tradition. As professionals, teachers and administrators are employed to perform a service for which they receive a certain amount of financial compensation. The performance of the service may require a teacher to take student projects home to be graded or may require a teacher to remain after the school day to talk with the parents of a student having problems in school. The time it takes to perform the service or the amount of work involved is not a consideration under the contract method of employment.

Classified employees are also paid to perform a service, but the time and work involved does make a difference in the amount of money received. When such employees are required to work after the regular eight-hour day, they receive overtime pay. If they are required to perform a task not specified by the categories outlined in the job description, they receive additional compensation.

Those professional employees who are covered by the terms of a master agreement work under conditions more like those of classified employees than teachers and administrators with individual contracts. Their working conditions are spelled out in the master agreement.

Board of education policies sometimes address working conditions, but these policies are usually not as specific as the terms of a master agreement. Teacher and administrator handbooks may also contain references to working conditions, but these are more concerned with internal procedures.

Using individual contracts for teachers and administrators is, therefore, a matter of tradition and is mandated by statutes in some states. Individual contracts also distinguish an individual's working conditions from those termed "classified." A teacher's or administrator's contract must meet the requirements of general contract law. Because school districts are legal entities with a corporate character, they may sue and be sued, purchase, receive, or sell real and personal property, and make contracts and be contracted with. The contracts entered into by a school district must not only conform to contract law but also to state statutes governing contracts and to the precedents established through case law.

A contract is defined as "an agreement between two or more competent persons for a legal consideration on a legal subject matter in the form required by law."[12] Every valid contract, therefore, has five basic components: offer and acceptance, competent persons, consideration, legal subject matter, and proper form. Each of these components will be discussed individually.

Offer and Acceptance

A valid contract must contain an offer and an acceptance. In the selection process, therefore, it is poor procedure to notify unsuccessful candidates for a position that the job has been filled until after the prospective employee has accepted the offer of employment. If the board of education approves a contract for a specific person to teach high school English, there is no agreement until the contract is executed, which constitutes acceptance.

A few other facts about the legal nature of an agreement must be kept in mind. First, an offer can be accepted only by the person to whom it was made. The husband of a candidate for a teaching position, for example, cannot accept the offer for his wife. Second, an offer must be accepted within a reasonable time after it is made. If an individual does not sign and return a contract within a few weeks in the hope that another job offer will be made by a different school district, the board of education may offer the contract to another candidate. Finally, a newspaper advertisement is not an offer of a position but rather an invitation to become a candidate for a job.

Competent Persons

A contract is not valid unless it is entered into by two or more competent persons. This means that the persons have the legal capacity to enter into a contract. As a corporate entity, the school district has the power, through the legal action of the school board, to enter into a contract. The most commonly identified classes include minors, mentally ill persons, and individuals who are intoxicated.

If a person was mentally ill or intoxicated at the time of entering into a contract to the extent that he or she did not understand the significance of the action, he or she may have the contract set aside because there was no agreement, which is essential to the validity of every contract.

[12] Ken Alexander, Ray Corns, and Walter McCann, *Public School Law: Cases and Materials* (St. Paul: West Publishing Co., 1969), p. 389.

Consideration

For a contract to be valid, it must be supported by a consideration, which is usually defined as something of value. The type of consideration found in an employment contract is referred to as "a promise for an act." For example, in a teacher's contract the board of education promises to pay an individual $15,000 to teach third grade for one year. The teacher fulfills the act by teaching during the designated time period.

Legal Subject Matter

In all fifty states an individual may teach only if he or she possesses a license to teach issued by the state department of education. Consequently, if a board of education enters into a teaching contract with a person who does not possess a license, such a contract would involve illegal subject matter and would be invalid.

Proper Form

For a contract to be enforceable, it must be in the form required by law. The courts recognize both oral and written contracts. However, most states have statutory provisions that require teachers' and administrators' contracts to be in writing and even specify the proper wording for the contract.

SUMMARY

Every school system performs a personnel function whether it is accomplished by a central office unit or assigned to various administrators within the system. The goals of the personnel function are to achieve the objectives of the school system while helping individual staff members maximize their potential and develop their professional careers. These goals are implemented through manpower planning, recruitment, selection, placement and induction, staff development, appraisal, compensation, and collective negotiations.

All but the very smallest school districts should delegate the personnel function to an assistant superintendent. The complexity of this function in our schools and the great impact it has on total school operations necessitates the hiring of a personnel specialist.

Collective negotiation has also created a need in most school districts for another specialist, the director of employee relations, who reports to the assistant superintendent for personnel and who is charged with managing the negotiations process.

The knowledge explosion, increased federal legislation and litigation, and the changing attitudes of parents, students, and educators have necessitated an ongoing staff development program for administrators and teachers. Like collective negotiation, this area is so specialized that most districts should consider establishing the position of director of staff development, who also reports to the assistant superintendent for personnel.

This avalanche of federal legislation and litigation has also mandated the creation of a central office administrative position, director of affirmative action. Most federal legislation requires that a detailed compliance program be established under the direction of an administrator who will be free from the influence of other administrators. Thus, the director of affirmative action reports directly to the superintendent of schools. Planning is a process common to all human experience. It encompasses an understanding of the present condition, future objectives, and methods for reaching these objectives.

Manpower planning as a process in personnel management is undertaken to ensure that a school district has the right number of people, with the right skills, in the right place, and at the right time.

The first step in the manpower planning process is to assess human resource needs, which includes the following four aspects: developing manpower inventories, developing a five-year enrollment projection, developing school district objectives, and developing a manpower forecast.

One of the most pressing problems facing metropolitan areas, one with a particular significance in manpower planning, is declining pupil enrollments. Two of the most successful alternatives to reduction in work force have been early retirement incentive programs and the retraining of individuals for positions that will become vacant through attrition or will be created through program development.

A hallmark of our contemporary American society is the avalanche of federal legislation and court decisions, which in turn have had a definite influence on the manpower planning process. Incorporated or implied in all civil rights legislation is the important concept of affirmative action. Affirmative action is not a law itself but rather a set of guidelines that organizations may use to comply with legislation and executive orders.

The Equal Employment Opportunity Commission was established by Title VII of the Civil Rights Act to investigate alleged discrimination in employment practices based on race, color, religion, sex, or national origin. The five-member commission has also from time to time established affirmative action guidelines.

Alleged discrimination charges can be filed with any of EEOC's regional or district offices. The administrative process includes an individual's filing a charge, investigation of the charge, determination of the charge, and the process of conciliation.

Limited discrimination is allowed by the Equal Employment Opportunity Act under one condition: when there is a bona fide occupational qualification mandating the employing of an individual of a particular sex, religious affiliation, or national origin. Therefore, a school district personnel administrator has the right to employ a female rather than a male applicant for the position of swimming instructor when part of the job description includes supervising the locker room used by female students.

Two recent U.S. Supreme Court decisions have had an indirect effect on affirmative action programs in school districts. Regents of the *University of California* vs. *Bakke* and *United Steelworkers* vs. *Brian F. Weber* both dealt with reverse discrimination. Their implication for human resource management is that quota-system policies in hiring and promotions can be defended only if there is clear evidence of racial imbalance because of job category segregation.

The Rehabilitation Act of 1973 prohibits recipients of federal financial assistance from discriminating against qualified handicapped individuals in the recruitment, hiring, compensation, job assignment/classification, and fringe benefits provided. Employers are further required to provide reasonable accommodations for qualified handicapped applicants or employees.

Equality in employment opportunities for women is a central issue of the 1980s. The legal mandate of equal opportunity for women emanates primarily from two federal laws: Title IX of the Educational Amendments of 1972, which prohibits sex discrimination in educational programs or activities, including employment, when the school district is receiving federal financial assistance; and, of course, Title VII of the Civil Rights Act of 1964, as amended in 1972. In addition, President Carter in 1978 signed into law a pregnancy disability amendment to the Civil Rights Act. This law had the effect of eliminating unequal treatment of pregnant women in all employment-related situations.

The Age Discrimination in Employment Act of 1967, as amended, promotes the employment of the older worker based on ability rather than age by prohibiting arbitrary discrimination.

Because of their importance, four major federal influences in the manpower planning process have been presented in detail. However, personnel administrators must also become familiar with all legislation that protects employment opportunity rights.

Termination procedures, an aspect of the appraisal process that is seldom addressed, are extremely important. Because "getting fired" has such a devastating effect on the financial and emotional welfare of an individual, termination procedures must be fair and objective. Most states have statutory provisions outlining the due process that must be afforded teachers before termination. Such legislation, while applying to the professional staff, provides a model for boards of education in establishing similar procedures for all employees. The education and welfare of students is the primary concern of a school district, but employees also have rights that must be taken into consideration when developing appraisal procedures and dealing with employee dismissal.

Teachers and administrators usually work under the provisions of an individual contract; classified personnel are employed at an hourly rate or for an annual salary. Using individual contracts for teachers and administrators is a matter of tradition also mandated by law in some states, and distinguishes a professional employee's working conditions from those of classified employees.

Teachers' and administrators' contracts must meet the requirements of general contract law, state statutes, and the precedents established through case law. A contract is an agreement between two or more competent persons for a legal consideration on a legal subject matter. The five basic components, therefore, to every valid contract are: offer and acceptance, competent persons, a consideration, legal subject matter, and proper form.

IMPLICATIONS FOR SCHOOL BOARD MEMBERS

There are four implications for boards of education that emerge from this presentation of personnel management.

First, school boards should require the superintendent of schools and his or her staff to keep board members informed about new state and federal legislation and court decisions dealing with personnel issues such as affirmative action, equal employment opportunity, employment terminations, and tenure.

Second, school boards must continually review and update their policies concerning personnel management. Policies dealing with manpower planning, recruitment, selection, placement and induction, staff development, appraisal, compensation, and collective bargaining are necessary to give the administration direction and guidance in managing the personnel function.

Third, professional personnel are contracted with the board of education upon a recommendation of the superintendent. Board members have a right, therefore, to review the credentials of potential candidates, but should never make their own recommendation.

Fourth, most states have statutes setting forth the due process required in the termination of professional personnel. However, school boards have some latitude in establishing procedures to implement these statutes. It is imperative that these procedures be objective, defensible, and humane.

SELECTED BIBLIOGRAPHY

CASTETTER, WILLIAM B., *The Personnel Function in Educational Adminis-tration* (3rd ed.). New York: Macmillan Publishing Co., Inc., 1981.
HARRIS, BEN M., KENNETH E. McINTYRE, VANCE C. LITTLETON, and DANIEL F. LONG, *Personnel Administration in Education: Leadership for Improvement.* Boston, Massachusetts: Allyn & Bacon, Inc., 1979.
MATHIS, ROBERT L., and JOHN H. JACKSON, *Personnel: Contemporary Perspectives and Applications* (2nd ed.). St. Paul, Minnesota: West Publishing Co., 1979.
REBORE, RONALD W., *Personnel Administration in Education: A Management Approach.* Englewood Cliffs, N.J.: Prentice-Hall, Inc., 1982.
STOCKARD, JAMES G. *Rethinking People Management: A New Look at the Human Resources Function.* New York: American Management Association, 1980.

CHAPTER TEN
THE ROLE
OF THE SCHOOL BOARD
IN COLLECTIVE
BARGAINING

The essence of collective bargaining is compromise, which is how employees share in the decision-making process of the school district.

Collective negotiation has become a way of life in American education. The first significant collective bargaining agreement was negotiated in 1962 with the teachers in New York City. Since that time, over half of all state legislatures have enacted collective bargaining laws relating to public school teachers.[1] Personnel considerations such as salaries, fringe benefits, and working conditions constitute the major negotiable issues. Membership in teacher organizations has also increased and consequently, because of dues, so have the fiscal resources of these organizations, amounting to millions of dollars annually. Because personnel expenditures constitute approximately 80 percent of school budgets, virtually every aspect of education has been influenced by this phenomenon of negotiations.

The now famous Air Traffic Controllers strike has been misunderstood by many people who have a casual knowledge of collective bargaining in the public sector. Collective bargaining has not been abrogated by the fact that many PATCO members were fired because they refused to return to work. Collective negotiation is, therefore, here to stay. The form and style are still subject to alteration, but the basic process is irreplaceable.

Experience dictates that the underlying consideration in collective bargaining

[1] Education Commission of the States, *Cuebook II: State Education Collective Bargaining Laws* (Denver: The Commission, 1980), p. V.

is participation in the decision-making process. Teachers and administrators want to have significant input into the priorities which are established by boards of education when these affect their salaries, benefits, and working conditions. It is a natural development in our democratic life style to continually look for more significant ways to participate in governance, whether this be in the political sphere or in our employing institutions. Furthermore, as a process, collective bargaining is successfully working in the private sector and certainly can be transferred to the public sector. This chapter deals with the major components of the collective negotiations process as it operates in education.

The terms "collective bargaining," "collective negotiations," and "professional negotiations" have all been used with various nuances of meaning when referring to this process in public education. To avoid confusion and because the "process" is universal in scope, these terms will be used interchangeably in this chapter.

Also, much discussion has occurred as to whether the National Education Association and the American Federation of Teachers are labor unions or professional organizations. This distinction appears to be functional in nature. If representatives of an organized group bargain collectively over salaries, fringe benefits, and working conditions for their membership with management, they are in essence a labor union. The terms "labor union" and "professional organization," therefore, will also be used interchangeably in this chapter when referring to their involvement in the negotiations process. The same definition holds true for administrator organizations when they collectively negotiate. It appears this interchange of definitions is a burgeoning trend in public education.

HISTORICAL PERSPECTIVES

Collective Bargaining in the Private Sector

Collective actions by employees have a long history, going as far back as the medieval guilds. These actions have always been influenced by the current economic, political, and social conditions of the times. Such influences are even stronger today because the technology of the news media makes it possible to update the public daily on political, social, and economic trends.

There are four major Congressional acts providing legal guidelines for collective bargaining in the private sector: the Norris-LaGuardia Act of 1932, the National Labor Relations Act of 1932 (Wagner Act), the Labor-Management Relations Act of 1947 (Taft-Hartley Act), and the Labor-Management Reporting and Disclosure Act of 1959 (Landrum-Griffin Act).

The Norris-LaGuardia Act was the first general public policy position on labor unionization. The act supported the concept that workers have a right to organize, if they so desire, into unions. Particularly, the act restricted the U.S. courts from issuing injunctions that would restrict labor activities. It also outlawed the yellow-dog contract, which was an agreement employers required employees to sign as a condition of employment. The employee by contract stated that he was not a member of a union and would not join a union as long as he worked for that company.

The Wagner Act is perhaps the most important piece of labor legislation. This act guaranteed workers the right to organize and join labor unions for the purpose of collective bargaining with employers. The Wagner Act also prohibited employers from engaging in the following unfair labor practices: (1) Interfering with or coercing employees in exercising their rights to join labor unions and bargaining collectively; (2) Interfering with the formation or administration of any labor union; (3) Discriminating against an employee because of union activity; (4) Discharging or discriminating against an employee because he or she filed charges or gave testimony under this act; (5) Refusing to bargain with the representatives chosen by the employees. The National Labor Relations Board (NLRB) was established and given the responsibility of conducting elections to determine union representation and applying this law against the designated unfair labor practices.

The Taft-Hartley Act was passed to amend the Wagner Act and to prevent unfair labor practices by unions. It sought to protect a worker's right not to join a union and employers for mistreatment by unions. The Taft-Hartley Act specifically outlawed the closed shop, allowed the Federal government to seek an injunction preventing work stoppages for eighty days in a strike defined as injurious to the national welfare, prohibited the use of union funds in connection with national elections, required union officers to swear that they were not members of the Communist Party, required unions to file financial statements with their membership and the U.S. Department of Labor, allowed the states to pass right-to-work laws, and made it illegal for any collective agreement to contain a clause requiring compulsory union membership.

The Taft-Hartley Act also prohibits unions from engaging in the following unfair labor practices:

1. Refusing to bargain collectively with an employer,
2. Causing an employer to discriminate against an employee who was refused membership in a union or expelled from a union,
3. Engaging in secondary boycotts, an act which exerts pressure on an employer not directly involved in a dispute,
4. Causing an employer to pay for services that were not rendered,
5. Engaging in a conflict between two or more unions over the rights to perform certain types of work,
6. Charging excessive or discriminating initiation fees.

The Landrum-Griffin Act resulted from the internal corruption of some unions. This act contains a bill of rights for union members which includes: freedom of speech at union meetings, secret ballot on proposed due increases, protection against improper disciplinary action. It also established the conditions to be observed in electing union officers.

The Landrum-Griffin Act, in addition, contained the following amendments to the Taft-Hartley Act:

1. Repealed the requirement for union officials to take a non-Communist oath;
2. Gave states authority over cases outside the jurisdiction of the NLRB;
3. Prohibited picketing by a union when a rival union was recognized or an NLRB election has taken place within twelve months;
4. Guaranteed the right of a striker to vote in union representative elections for twelve months;
5. Prohibited agreements by which employees seek to bring economic pressure on another employer by refusing to handle, sell, use or transport his products;
6. Authorized union shops in the construction industry and required membership after seven days of employment rather than the traditional thirty days.

Collective Negotiations
in the Federal Government

In 1962, President John Kennedy issued Executive Order 10988, which affirmed the right of federal employees to join labor unions and bargain collectively. It required federal agency heads to bargain in good faith, defined unfair labor practices, and established a code of conduct for labor organizations. However, E. O. 10988 prohibited the union shop and banned strikes by federal employees.

In 1968 a presidential committee reviewed employee-management relations in the federal service and recommended improvement to the provisions of E. O. 10988. As a consequence, President Richard Nixon issued E. O. 11491 in 1969 to supersede the previous directive.

The objectives of E. O. 11491 are to standardize procedures among federal agencies and to bring federal labor relations more in line with the private sector. It gave the assistant secretary of labor the authority to determine appropriate bargaining units, to oversee recognition procedures, to rule on unfair labor practices, and to enforce the standards of conduct on labor organizations. E. O. 11491 also established the Federal Labor Relations Council, which has the responsibility for supervising the implementation of this executive order, to handle appeals from the decision of the assistant secretary of labor, and to rule on questionable issues.

Collective Negotiations in Local
and State Governments

Although some professional organizations, including the National Education Association, support passage of a federal teacher collective bargaining law, most educators see this as a state issue. Public school employees are, in fact, working for a state agency operating in a local unit, the school district.

Over half the states have permissive or mandatory statutes governing the right of public school employees to organize, negotiate, exercise sanctions, or strike. There are, of course, substantial differences in these state laws. In a number of states, legislation covers all public employees, while in others there is a specific law covering school employees. Because the acts of legislative bodies are organic in nature and subject to amendment, repeal, and judicial interpretation, these laws will certainly undergo some modifications in the future.

MODEL BOARD OF EDUCATION
POLICY ON COLLECTIVE
NEGOTIATIONS

> The Board of Education finds that joint decision-making is the modern way of governing school systems. If school district employees have the right to share in the decision-making process affecting salaries, fringe benefits, and working conditions, they become more responsive and better disposed to exchanging ideas and information concerning operations with administrators. Accordingly, management becomes more efficient.
>
> The Board of Education further declares that harmonious and cooperative relations between itself and school district employees protect the patrons and children of the school district by assuring the orderly operation of the schools.
>
> This position of the Board is to be effectuated by:
>
> 1. Recognizing the right of all school district employees to organize for the purpose of collective negotiations;
> 2. Authorizing the Director of Employee Relations to negotiate with the duly elected employee representatives on matters relating to salaries, fringe benefits, and working conditions;
> 3. Requiring the Director of Employee Relations to establish administrative policies and procedures for the effective implementation of the negotiations process. This is to be accomplished under the supervision of the Assistant Superintendent for Personnel who, in turn, is directly responsible to the Superintendent of Schools.
>
> Upon successful completion of the negotiations process, the Board of Education will enter into written agreements with the employee organizations.

From this board of education policy a definition for negotiations may be established as follows: Collective negotiations is the process in which representatives of the school board meet with representatives of the school district employees to make proposals and counter proposals for the purpose of mutually agreeing on salaries, fringe benefits, and working conditions covering a specific period of time.

RECOGNITION AND BARGAINING
UNIT DETERMINATION

This section is concerned with answering a basic question—"Who represents whom?" In labor history most of the violence which occurred in the private sector centered around this query. Unions fought each other for the right to represent workers against management. The price was power. In education the prize is still the same, but the contest is usually nonviolent.

Recognition is defined as the acceptance by an employer of some individual group or organization as the authorized representative of two or more employees for the purpose of collective negotiations. Without recognition, each teacher is left to make his or her own arrangements with the school board, an approach which is the antithesis of collective bargaining.

There are two basic types of recognition in education, multiple and exclusive. Multiple representation does not occur in too many school districts because of the inherent problems of having two or more organizations or unions represent a specific bargaining unit. In New York City prior to the collective bargaining elections in 1961, ninety-three organizations were accorded equal representation rights by the Board of Education.[2] Although this situation was extreme, there are school districts in which more than one organization claims the right to represent a segment of the employees.

In multiple representation, recognition is usually granted by the board of education on the basis of organizational membership. This recognition is operationalized by one of the following methods: the board's representatives meet separately with representatives of each union, the board's representatives meet in joint sessions with equal numbers of representatives from each union, or the board's representatives meet in joint sessions with representatives of the unions proportionally determined. For example, if organization A has 500 members and organization B has 250 members, A is entitled to twice as many representatives on the negotiating team as B.

Exclusive recognition occurs when a single union represents all the members of a bargaining unit. The technical designation for the union in this role is "bargaining agent." The bargaining unit consists of all the employees whose salaries, fringe benefits, and working conditions are negotiated by the bargaining agent. The paramount feature of exclusive recognition is that the employer cannot negotiate with anyone in the unit except through the bargaining agent.

Exclusive recognition is the most widely used form in education for three basic reasons. First, it is supported by both the National Education Association and the American Federation of Teachers. Secondly, exclusive recognition is mandated for the public sector in many states and widely accepted in most communities, even in the absence of state legislation. Finally, private business and industry are witness to the fact that this is the most effective form of recognition.

Recognition procedures take various forms in education. The three most commonly used are membership lists, authorization cards, and elections. If a union can demonstrate that it has 51 percent membership of the employees in a bargaining unit or if 51 percent of the employees in a unit present signatures authorizing a certain union to represent them, the board may recognize this union as the exclusive bargaining agent.

A more common practice is the "representation election," which is also a

[2]Myron Lieberman and Michael H. Moskow, *Collective Negotiations for Teachers* (Chicago: Rand McNally & Co., 1966), p. 92.

necessity in the absence of membership lists or authorization cards signifying majority support. There are a number of reasons why a school board would prefer an election as a requisite to recognizing a union as exclusive bargaining agent. Some teachers who join an organization or union may not want that union to represent them in negotiations. Also, teachers join certain unions for social, professional, or other reasons having nothing to do with negotiations. In some cases, a teacher may be a member of more than one of the local teacher unions.

The representative election poses several questions that must be addressed by both the school board and the unions seeking recognition:

Who conducts the election?
Who will pay the costs of the election?
What are the ground rules for electioneering?
Who is eligible to vote?
Who will certify the results?
What will be the duration of the certification?

There are no correct answers to these questions. Rather, they must be answered within a framework that will take into consideration the variables affecting local situations. A cardinal principle is that the board and unions must maintain credibility and, therefore, a third party is often requested to intervene in finding a workable answer to these questions. The Federal Mediation and Conciliation Service or the League of Women Voters are examples of two independent agencies with the public image necessary to act as the appropriate third party. In many states with collective bargaining laws, recognition procedures and bargaining unit determination are mandated. This discussion thus pertains to those states without legislation and to those states where the law allows latitude on these issues. A few states have Public Employee Relation Boards (PERB) that will conduct the elections and make a determination on who belongs to the bargaining unit.

It is now necessary to more closely define the term "bargaining unit." School districts not only employ teachers of many different subjects and levels but also a wide variety of specialists: psychologists, nurses, social workers, and attendance officers. In addition there are a number of classified employees: cooks, custodians, bus drivers, maintenance workers, secretaries, and clerks.

To have collective negotiations there must be a determination on what specific category of employees is represented by the bargaining agent who wins the representation election. In practice, this determination must occur as part of the recognition process because only those employees in a bargaining unit will be allowed to vote on which union will represent them. The definition most commonly accepted states that the unit is composed of all employees to be covered by the negotiated agreement or master contract.

The fundamental criteria for determining who belongs to the bargaining unit is formulated in the "community of interest" principle.[3] While sounding elusive, it

[3] Ibid., 129

is not that difficult to implement. Employees have a community of interest if they share skills, functions, educational levels, and working conditions. Elementary school teachers of all levels, secondary school teachers of all subjects, and guidance counselors clearly have a community of interest and should belong to the bargaining unit. Clerks and secretaries, on the other hand, could not be effectively represented by this unit and should constitute a separate unit by themselves. It is conceivable that a medium to large size school district might have the following units bargaining separately with the representatives of the school board:

1. Certificated educators exclusive of supervisors and administrators,
2. Building level administrators,
3. Subject matter coordinators,
4. Secretaries and clerks,
5. Cooks and cafeteria workers,
6. Bus drivers,
7. Custodians,
8. Maintenance workers.

Each of these bargaining units would have a separate agreement or master contract specifying salaries, fringe benefits, and working conditions, all of which could be quite different for each unit.

Besides community of interest, there are two additional considerations in determining a bargaining unit. Size is important because an extremely small unit of five or ten employees will have little impact acting alone. In this case employees would have a more strategic base from which to bargain if they combined with other categories or employees. In a small school district, for example, there might be two bargaining units: a certificated employees' unit including teachers, nurses, psychologists; and a classified employees' unit including cooks, custodians, maintenance personnel, and secretaries.

A final consideration in determining a bargaining unit is effective school administration. An unreasonably large number of units would be unworkable. If guidance counselors, classroom teachers, speech therapists, music teachers, physical education teachers, and safety education teachers were all covered by different agreements specifying different working conditions, a building principal would have a difficult job of supervising staff.

There are two other issues that have surfaced in recent years that will have an influence on future negotiations, the agency shop and administrator bargaining units. Agency shop is a term borrowed from industry and is used when referring to a question of equity. An employee who is a member of a given bargaining unit may not be a dues paying member of the union that is the bargaining agent. In this case, under a bargaining agreement with the school board that includes an agency shop clause or if this issue is covered by a state collective bargaining law, such an employee would be required to pay a fee, usually the equivalent of dues to the union. While the employee would not be allowed to participate in internal union affairs, he or she would be allowed to participate in unit activities such as attending meetings called by the negotiations team and voting on ratification of the agreement.

A growing number of educational administrators, particularly building principals, are organizing into unions and bargaining with school boards. The reasons why administrators are turning to collective bargaining include: decreasing autonomy and power, loss of esteem, economic anxiety, and contagion (teachers are getting theirs, we should too). It appears that this trend will continue during the next decade, and school board representatives will be negotiating with administrator bargaining units.

THE SCOPE OF NEGOTIATIONS

The "scope of negotiations" refers to those matters that are negotiated. In some school districts, negotiations are limited to just salaries, while in other districts literally hundreds of items are discussed.

Negotiations must not be limited to unimportant matters or the process will be considered a failure by teachers. What constitutes an important item is, of course, dictated by local circumstances. A school board might be willing to negotiate only on salaries and refuse to consider such items as a grievance procedure or reduction in force policy. Experience dictates that some of these nonmonetary items are just as important to teachers as salary. It is, therefore, extremely important to place only mandatory limitations on the scope of negotiations. These limitations refer to items that are illegal by reason of state and federal constitutions, state and federal laws, or those items contrary to the policies of the State Board of Education.

Most state laws on collective negotiations stipulate that negotiations must be confined to "working conditions." This phrase usually refers to salaries and fringe benefits as well as working conditions. While the meaning of "salary" is self-evident, there is some confusion over the terms "fringe benefit" and "working condition."

A fringe benefit may be defined as a service available to employees as a direct result of a fiscal expenditure by the school district. Such services might include: accident benefits, major medical insurance, hospitalization insurance, pensions, sick pay, dental insurance, and professional liability insurance.

Working conditions refer to the quality of the employment situation. Teaching for a particular school district might be more desirable because the district has equitable policies concerning: class size, duty-free lunch periods, preparation periods, sabbatical leave, or legal assistance for teachers.

A major concern in defining the scope of negotiations for a particular situation centers around the concept of educational policy. School boards are required by statute to set educational policy. While teachers are deeply interested in educational policy and believe that they should be consulted in formulating such policy, it is commonly understood that such policy is not subject to negotiations.

The following are examples of policy questions:

1. Should the school district provide a foreign language program in the elementary grades?
2. Should statistics be offered in the high school mathematics program?
3. Should extracurricular activities be sponsored or supported by district funds?

The obvious problem is that virtually all educational policy decisions have implications for working conditions. For example, funds expended to introduce a foreign language program in the elementary grades will leave less money available to improve fringe benefits for all employees. It is, therefore, often impossible to decide issues pertaining to policy apart from those pertaining to working conditions.

Lieberman and Moskow make an observation about the scope of negotiations that summarizes and clarifies this aspect of the process:

> Finally, it must be remembered that the scope of negotiations is itself negotiated or at least affected by the process of negotiations.
>
> When the parties meet to negotiate, there is no formula which prescribes what is negotiable. Good administration does not eliminate the need for negotiations, but the scope of negotiations is likely to include those matters which have been administered in an inequitable manner. The relative strength of the parties may affect the scope of negotiations much more than academic versions of what progressive school administrators or organization leaders should negotiate. Legal, personal, political, economic, and organizational factors may have some impact on the scope of negotiations as well as on the resolution of items actually negotiated. In other words, the process of negotiations inevitably affects its scope and vice versa.[4]

THE BARGAINING PROCESS

The Negotiating Team

The purpose of this section is to analyze those factors influencing the "at the table" process of negotiations. The first issue that must be addressed is the composition of the school board's negotiating team.

There is no universally accepted practice in forming a negotiating team. However, size of a school district appears to have a significant influence on the makeup of the team. In small school districts, a committee of school board members usually negotiates directly with a team of teachers. In medium to large size districts, the assistant superintendent for personnel along with other central office and/or building level administrators might be designated by the superintendent to negotiate with the teacher union. In some large districts, a chief negotiator is employed on a full-time or ad hoc basis.

[4] Lieberman and Moskow, *Collective Negotiations*, p. 247.

In keeping with the model established in chapter one, this author believes that medium to large school districts should employ a director of employee relations who has the responsibility for managing the entire process of collective negotiations and who acts as the chief negotiator on the board's team (see Appendix B).

The size of the team is relative but should have an odd number of members to avoid a deadlock in making strategy decisions. Therefore, a team of three, five, or seven members would be appropriate. Experience also indicates that a team composed of more than seven members will impede decision-making.

Membership on the team may be by job description, appointment, or election. This author prefers a team of five members. The chairperson and chief negotiator is, of course, the director of employee relations by virtue of job position. Additional membership on the team should include building level principals because they are the first line supervisors who will be managing the master agreement. Also, many principals have been critical of school boards for "negotiating away" their authority. On a five-member team, one principal from each level (elementary school, junior or middle school, high school) elected by their fellow principals would give the team high credibility among building administrators. The final member of the team should have some specific expertise and knowledge of the district's financial condition. Thus, the assistant superintendent for administrative services or the business manager would be an appropriate appointee.

This team must function as an entity over the entire academic year. As will be pointed out later in this section, the bargaining process entails the development of strategies and the construction of proposal packages, which cannot be accomplished in the short space of a few months during the year. While the major portion of work will fall to the director of employee relations, expending a great deal of time will be required of the committee. Consequently, it is advisable to provide those principals who serve on the committee with some compensation, such as a stipend or additional administrative assistance in their buildings.

The negotiating team for the teacher is, of course, usually composed of teachers. Sometimes the officers of the local organization or union act as the team, while in other situations a negotiating team is appointed by the union officers or elected by the teachers. If the local is affiliated with a national union, experts in the bargaining process are made available to advise union officers.

A final issue concerning the board's negotiating team must be addressed. What if the building administrators organize, form a bargaining unit, and elect a bargaining agent to represent them concerning salaries, fringe benefits, and working conditions? This, of course, is the current trend, especially in large urban school districts. In this case, the same structure for the board's negotiating team may be maintained with the substitution of assistant superintendents for principals. Because each bargaining unit separately negotiates a master agreement reflecting different working conditions for employees with different job positions, it is not inconsistent with good administration for principals on the one hand to negotiate for the board and on the other hand against it.

Developing Strategies

The negotiating team is responsible for the entire bargaining process, which must begin with strategy development. This entails two activities: assessing the needs of the school district and establishing goals for negotiations.

Needs assessment may take various forms, but there are certain tasks that must be completed:

1. Review the current master agreement to determine if its provisions meet the goals of the district and if they allow for effective administration,
2. Study the previous negotiating sessions to determine if the ground rules provide for effective negotiations,
3. Analyze formal grievances filed by both the union and administration,
4. Study the arbitration decisions rendered on these grievances,
5. Meet with school district administrators to gather input concerning the provisions of the current master agreement,
6. Meet informally with the union to ascertain their concerns over the current agreement,
7. Confer with the board of education and superintendent to learn their concerns and to establish fiscal parameters.

From this information, the team sets the goals and objectives for negotiations, which are reduced to operational terms in the proposal package.

Setting the Ground Rules

With the advice and consent of the negotiating team, the chairperson should meet with the union negotiators to determine the rules under which the "at the table" process will take place. Key points that must be determined include:

The time and place for the sessions,
The number of participants who will sit at the table,
The role of each participant,
How each side will present their proposals,
Setting a target date for completing negotiations,
What kind of school district data will be needed by each side,
The conditions governing caucuses,
The provisions for recording the sessions,
The method to be used in recording counter-proposals and agreements,
The policy on press releases,
What types of impasse procedures will be employed and when,
The format for the written agreement,
The procedure for agreement approval by the school board and union membership,
What procedures will be used in publishing the ratified agreement.

At the Table Sessions

There are two objectives for being "at the table." First, through making proposals and counter-proposals, the negotiating teams should be able to ascertain what issues are critically important to each side. Secondly, each team should be able to assess the other side's bargaining power. This is the ability to get the other team to agree on an item or the entire proposal package based on your terms.

Political pressures, negotiating skill, and psychological elements are important sources of bargaining power. Although it is impossible to measure bargaining power exactly, it is apparent that, at some time, the overall advantages of agreement outweigh the overall disadvantages of disagreement.

During the bargaining sessions, it is very important to keep the board and entire administrative staff informed as to progress. If this is not effectively accomplished, rumors may adversely affect the bargaining power of the board's team.

When an agreement is reached by the negotiating teams, ratification by the respective governing bodies is the final step in the process. The board's team meets with the superintendent and board of education to recommend and explain the agreement. Formal ratification is usually by signature of the school board president, president of the union, and attested to by the secretaries of the board and union.

Because negotiating is an art rather than a science, it is extremely difficult to develop a formula for success. Nevertheless, a number of practical hints may be in order. The following are recommendations made to local boards of education by the Ohio School Boards Association:

1. KEEP CALM—DON'T LOSE CONTROL OF YOURSELF. Negotiation sessions can be exasperating. The temptation may come to get angry and fight back when intemperate accusations are made or when "the straw that broke the camel's back" is hurled on the table.

2. AVOID "OFF THE RECORD" COMMENTS. Actually nothing is "off the record." Innocently made remarks have a way of coming back to haunt their author. Be careful to say only what you are willing to have quoted.

3. DON'T BE OVERCANDID. Inexperienced negotiators may, with the best of intentions, desire to "lay the cards on the table face up." This may be done in the mistaken notion that everybody fully understands the other and utter frankness is desired. Complete candor does not always serve the best interests of productive negotiations. This is not a plea for duplicity; rather, it is a recommendation for prudent and discriminating utterances.

4. BE LONG ON LISTENING. Usually a good listener makes a good negotiator. It is wise to let your "adversaries" do the talking—at least in the beginning.

5. DON'T BE AFRAID OF A "LITTLE HEAT." Discussions sometimes generate quite a bit of "heat." Don't be afraid of it. It never hurts to let the "opposition" sound off, even when you may be tempted to hit back.

6. WATCH THE VOICE LEVEL. A wise practice is to keep the pitch of the voice down, even though the temptation may be strong to let it rise under the excitement of emotional stress.

7. KEEP FLEXIBLE. One of the skills of good negotiators is the ability to shift position a bit if a positive gain can thus be accomplished. An obstinate adherence to

one position or point of view, regardless of the ultimate consequences of that rigidity, may be more of a deterrent than an advantage.

8. REFRAIN FROM A FLAT "NO." Especially in the earlier stages of a negotiation, it is best to avoid giving a flat "no" answer to a proposition. It does not help to work yourself into a box by being totally negative "too early in the game."

9. GIVE TO GET. Negotiation is the art of giving and getting. Concede a point to gain a concession. This is the name of the game.

10. WORK ON THE EASIER ITEMS FIRST. Settle those things first about which there is the least controversy. Leave the tougher items until later in order to avoid an early deadlock.

11. RESPECT YOUR ADVERSARY. Respect those who are seated on the opposite side of the table. Assume that their motives are as sincere as your own, at least until proven otherwise.

12. BE PATIENT. If necessary, be willing to sit out tiresome tirades. Time has a way of being on the side of the patient negotiator.

13. AVOID WAVING "RED FLAGS." There are some statements that irritate teachers and merely heighten their antipathies. Find out what these are and avoid their use. Needless waving of "red flags" only infuriates.

14. LET THE OTHER SIDE "WIN SOME VICTORIES." Each team has to win some victories. A "shutout" may be a hollow gain in negotiation.

15. NEGOTIATION IS A "WAY OF LIFE." Obvious resentment of the fact that negotiation is here to stay weakens the effectiveness of the negotiator. The better part of wisdom is to adjust to it and become better prepared to use it as a tool of interstaff relations.[5]

IMPASSE PROCEDURES

It is extremely difficult to define the term "impasse." Negotiators often have trouble knowing when an impasse has been reached. However, for this discussion, an impasse will be considered as a persistent disagreement that continues after normal negotiation procedures have been exhausted.

Impasse must be expected to occur from time to time, even when both parties are negotiating in good faith. There are, unfortunately, no procedures guaranteed to resolve an impasse. Some procedures have been more successful than others, and the objective of this section is to outline them. It must also be kept in mind that improperly used impasse procedures can aggravate rather than resolve a disagreement. Therefore, a working knowledge of procedures is essential to all participants in the negotiating process.

A number of the states that have passed collective bargaining laws have also established public employee relations boards. These boards are charged with implementing the law and in most cases with administering impasse procedures, which include mediation, fact-finding, and arbitration.

[5] Ohio School Boards Association, *Negotiations Hints* (Westerville, Oh.: The Association, 1975).

Mediation

Mediation is the process by which negotiators on both sides of a dispute agree on the need for third party assistance. The role of the mediator is advisory in scope and, consequently, he or she has no authority to dictate a settlement. Some mediators use the tactic of meeting with both parties separately and attempt to ascertain what concessions each party might make in order to reach an agreement. This procedure has been most effective when one or both parties considers making concessions to be a sign of weakness.

Meeting jointly with both parties is particularly helpful in assessing the actual status of negotiations and in obtaining agreement from the parties on the phrasing of the issues. Most mediators will use a combination of separate and joint meetings to facilitate an agreement.

Mediators usually refrain from recommending a settlement until they are sure that their recommendations will be acceptable to both parties. Up until the time of recommendation, the mediator acts only as a clarifier of issues and through explicit communication attempts to defuse the antagonism between the parties, which is frequently the cause of the impasse.

A mediator may be called into a dispute at any time. In some cases he or she may even practice preventive mediation by making suggestions useful to the parties early in the negotiations.

Because mediation is a voluntary process, the parties must decide who will mediate and what the mediator's role will be in the stages preparatory to the actual negotiations. In approximately one-third of the states, this issue is settled by statute and a formal declaration of "impasse" is all that is required to put the process in motion. Often a master agreement will contain provisions outlining impasse procedures to be followed in renegotiating the agreement. When mediator services are not provided by a governmental agency, the fees for a private mediator are borne equally by both parties to the dispute.

Fact-Finding

This is the procedure by which an individual or a panel holds hearings for the purpose of reviewing evidence and making a recommendation for settling the dispute. Like mediation, fact-finding is a process either governed by state statute, provided for in a master agreement, or established by both parties before negotiations begin.

The formal hearing is usually open to the public. Parties having a vested interest in the dispute are given the opportunity to offer evidence and arguments in their own behalf. It sometimes occurs that fact-finders are requested by both parties to mediate the dispute and avoid further formal proceedings.

The fact-finding report and recommendations are also usually made public. The process is voluntary and the parties may reject all or part of the report. To a certain extent the action of the parties will depend upon the public's reactions, which in turn depend partly upon the prestige of the fact-finder.

Arbitration

This is the process by which the parties submit their dispute to an impartial third person or panel that issues an award the parties are required to accept. Arbitration can be either compulsory or voluntary. Compulsory arbitration must be established by statute. The voluntary use of arbitration has gained some acceptance in the public sector for handling grievances arising from the interpretation of master agreements.

The Federal Mediation
and Conciliation Service

The Federal Mediation and Conciliation Service is an independent agency of the federal government created by Congress in 1947, with a director appointed by the President of the United States. The primary purpose of the FMCS is to promote labor-management peace. To more effectively carry out this mission, the agency has established both regional and field offices staffed by professional mediators.

Federal labor laws do not cover employees of state and local governments. However, if state legislatures fail to establish mediation services for public employees, the FMCS may voluntarily enter a dispute.

The FMCS also has an Office of Arbitration Services in Washington. The office maintains a roster of arbitrators located in all parts of the country. Upon request, a randomly selected list of arbitrators will be furnished, from which the parties may choose a mutually acceptable arbitrator to hear and decide a dispute.

In summary, it is too difficult to promote one or more impasse procedures as the most effective approach to handling all persistent disputes arising at the bargaining table or in grievances over master contract interpretation. It is more appropriate to think in terms of sequence. Mediation should be the first procedure utilized, followed by fact-finding, and then, where it is permitted by law in negotiations, arbitration. This sequence places the responsibility for resolving the dispute first on the parties themselves. Experience teaches that better and more effective agreements are reached when the parties can resolve their own disputes. However, when disputes cannot be resolved and when it is mandated by law, arbitration curtails strikes, which always have a devastating effect on school systems.

WORK STOPPAGE STRATEGIES

The Scope of Strikes

There is nothing more disruptive to a school district than a strike. As board members, administrators, teachers, and support personnel engage in heated and public argument, schisms occur that often last for years. Community groups also become divided over who is right and who is wrong.

The American Association of School Administrators consistently opposes the strike as a weapon when negotiations reach an impasse. The AASA also supports the position that the administrative team has the responsibility to keep the school open, to protect students who report to school, to protect school property, and to maintain communications among parents, teachers, and the public.

Strikes by public school employees are illegal or limited by state laws. However, their frequency and intensity appear to be increasing each year. The news media daily remind us of the magnitude of this issue. There is also no indication that strikes will go away as school employees, administrators, and teachers become more proficient in the negotiating process.

Ten to fifteen years ago, most teachers felt that striking was not in keeping with their professional status. This thinking has vanished, and the personal traumas once associated with this type of action are also gone. Today teachers strike over many issues, including: recognition of their unions, salary increases, fringe benefits, working conditions, due process, organizational threats, curriculum control, reduction in force, and community nonsupport. Teachers have also honored strikes by nonteaching personnel and have attempted to get those unions to support their work stoppages.

School Employee Strike Tactics

A strike by school employees is usually the result of failure at the bargaining table. The objective of any strike is to gain as favorable a settlement as possible from the board of education within the shortest period of time.

There are a few key issues that have been used by teacher unions to rally support for a strike, and these include: pupil-teacher ratio; planning time, particularly for elementary school teachers; and extra pay for extra duty, particularly for secondary school teachers. With decreasing enrollments and inflation, the rallying issues of the future will probably settle around job security items, such as evaluation procedures and reduction in force policies.

In a strike, school employee unions and especially teacher unions have almost unlimited resources at their disposal from their state and national affiliates. In very sensitive strikes, as many as a hundred field staff members may be available to help the local union.

A careful examination of strikes will verify the following tactics as some of the most commonly used by teacher unions.

1. Inundating the community with the reasons for the strike. Handbills, advertisements in the local press, and news coverage are the main vehicles employed.

2. Placing the blame on a specific person, such as the superintendent or school board president. This tactic will channel the pressure exerted by parents and the community.

3. Encouraging local and state politicians to become involved in the dispute. School employee groups represent a sizeable number of votes.

4. Working diligently to gain support from other unions in the community.

5. Staging a strike in the late spring because this will interfere not only with graduation but also with state aid, which is usually calculated on a certain number of days in attendance before the end of the school year.

Although some strikes do spontaneously occur because of unexpected developments, most teacher strikes are well-orchestrated. Generally, teacher unions are aware weeks or even months in advance that certain negotiation demands are strike-producing issues.

Administrative Strategies

If a school system finds itself in the middle of a strike without an adequate plan of action, the board of education has not been paying attention to the tenor of the times or the situation in their own school district. In fact, the superintendent and his or her cabinet should have a carefully developed strike plan even in the most tranquil of school settings.

This strike plan should operate at both the district and building levels. The American Association of School Administrators has developed a series of steps in a plan that can serve as a guide for administrators and school boards in establishing their own individual district plans.

BEFORE A STRIKE

District Level

1. Develop the overall district plan as well as a board policy statement well in advance of an anticipated strike (preferably, when there is absolutely no indication of a strike).

2. Provide as early as possible for the notification of news media, parents, staff, of the likelihood or possibility of a strike.

3. Notify staff members of the applicable state law and school board policy concerning a work stoppage and the legal ramifications of such action.

4. Establish provisions for a Decision-Making Center to have the overall direction of a strike and assign specific responsibilities to those key people in the Center.

5. Make contacts with police, fire, health, telephone, and other community/state agencies likely to be needed or contacted during a strike.

6. Prepare a list of names and telephone numbers for the specific individuals in each agency who can be contacted day or night in emergency situations.

7. Provide for "hot line" telephones for citizens and staff members so they may receive strike information.

8. Install a bank of unlisted telephones in the Decision-Making Center to facilitate ongoing and continual communications.

9. Obtain, or make provisions to obtain, two-way radio systems for strategic points in the district (or mobile car radios, beeper systems).

10. Develop building strike plans and reporting systems for daily status reports from each building.

11. Notify the news media of the media area and provide the time(s) and place of daily (or more often) briefings concerning the strike.

12. Have the board of education pass the necessary legal resolutions required to deal with the strike (restraining orders, injunctions, picket line restrictions, formal notification to personnel on strike, etc.).

13. Continue to seek a solution to the strike and keep such initiative on the side of the administration and board.

Building Level

1. Develop with each building principal a building Strike Plan in conformance with the overall district plan.
2. Secure back-up personnel for each building principal to act in his or her stead during the work stoppage.
3. Make provision within the building Strike Plan for a daily, early-morning report to the Decision-Making Center.
4. Make provision for a daily written report listing the names of staff who reported for duty and the numbers of pupils in attendance at the building.
5. Make provision for continuity of communications in the event that telephone lines are unusable.
6. Make provisions for each building principal to have specific guidelines and authority to close the building when the safety and health of the pupils are threatened, or when it is impossible to carry on an educational program.
7. Make provision for adequate building security (leaving lights on at night, security guards, etc.).

AFTER A STRIKE

District Level

1. Notify all groups.
2. Hold briefing session for all administrators and board members.
3. Prepare building principals for the return of teachers.
4. Issue public statement detailing strike settlement to news media.
5. Begin making plans to defuse "anticlimactic" emotions.

Building Level

1. Do not allow striking teachers to return to the classrooms until all substitute teachers are out of the building.
2. Make plans to focus major attention on the educational program and learning environment for students.[6]

When the Decision-Making Center mentioned above is established at the central office, duties are assigned by the superintendent of schools with the advice of his or her cabinet. Central office administrators are assigned specific tasks to be performed during the strike corresponding to the provisions of the above stated AASA plan. The director of labor relations could be given the task of notifying staff members of the state law and board policy concerning strikes and the legal ramifi-

---

[6] American Association of School Administrators, *Work Stoppage Strategies* (Arlington: The Association, 1975), pp. 48, 49, 58.

cations of such action while the director of public relations notifies the news media of the times and place for daily briefings concerning the strike. In like manner, the building principal and, if it is a large school, his or her administrative team are responsible for implementing the building level provisions.

ADMINISTRATION OF THE MASTER AGREEMENT

The process of collective negotiations is usually ineffective unless the agreements reached are put into writing. Therefore, written master agreements are essential because they formalize the basic rights governing the parties in their relationship and reduce controversy over the content of the agreement.

Provisions in the Agreement

Most master agreements are extremely detailed and replace board of education policies covering working conditions. There are certain common items included in most agreements that are deemed essential:

1. Recognition of the union as the exclusive bargaining agent,
2. A statement of purpose,
3. The duration of the agreement and method for renegotiating the agreement before the expiration date,
4. Incorporation of a grievance procedure,
5. Incorporation of impasse procedures,
6. Description of who is a member of the bargaining unit,
7. A statement concerning dues check-off,
8. A fair practice statement,
9. Salary schedules and guidelines for the duration of the agreement.[7]

As an example of the types of articles and appendices which operationalize these provisions, the "Table of Contents" from the Dade County master agreement is reproduced in Appendix C.

The style and format of the master agreement will sometimes be dictated by state statutes but, in the absence of legislation, school boards and unions must look elsewhere for help. In many cases, teacher associations affiliated with national unions have access to model master agreements which can be adapted to local situations. In fact, some models are complete in every detail except for filling in the blanks with the proper data.

---

[7]Lloyd W. Ashby, James E. McGinnis, and Thomas E. Pering, *Common Sense in Negotiations in Public Education* (Danville: The Interstate Printer and Publisher, Inc., 1972), pp. 59-60.

Implementing the Master Agreement

It is the responsibility of the administration to implement and interpret the provisions of the agreement. Furthermore, the administration is only limited by the specifics of the master agreement, commonly referred to as "management prerogative."

In the day-to-day interpretation of the agreement, it is certainly possible for violations to occur. Most written agreements, therefore, provide for a grievance procedure by which individuals, the union, or the administration alleges that the master agreement is being violated or misinterpreted.

Most grievance procedures contain the following common elements:

1. A careful definition of the term "grievance,"
2. The purpose of the grievance procedure,
3. A clause stating that a person making or testifying in a grievance will not face prejudicial treatment,
4. A clear outline of the appropriate steps to be taken in a grievance and the time allotments between each step,
5. In the case of arbitration, who will bear the costs and the qualifications required of an arbiter.

SUMMARY

Collective negotiations have become a way of life in American education. This is exemplified by the fact that over half the states have enacted collective bargaining laws affecting teachers. The underlying consideration in collective negotiations is participation in the decision-making process, which is a natural extension of our democratic lifestyle. Teachers and administrators want to have significant input into the priorities established by school boards when these priorities affect their salaries, fringe benefits, and working conditions.

Collective negotiations may be defined as the process by which representatives of the school board meet with representatives of the school district employees to make proposals and counter proposals for the purpose of agreeing on salaries, fringe benefits, and working conditions for a specific period of time. To operationalize this process, it is necessary for the board of education to adopt a policy giving the administration authority to implement negotiations.

Collective actions by employees have a long history in the private sector, going as far back as the medieval guilds. These actions are directly affected by the economic, political, and social conditions of life. There are four major congressional acts providing legal guidelines for collective bargaining in the private sector: The Norris-LaGuardia Act of 1932, The National Labor Relations Act of 1935, The Labor-Management Relations Act of 1947, and The Labor-Management Reporting and Disclosure Act of 1959.

Collective negotiations in the federal government are affirmed by Executive

Orders 10988 and 11491. Federal employees have the right to organize and bargain collectively but cannot strike.

Public school teachers are state employees working in a local unit, the school district. As such they are not covered by federal legislation, but rather by the acts of state legislatures. There are substantial differences in state statutes granting collective bargaining rights to teachers.

There are six aspects to the collective negotiating process: recognition and bargaining unit determination, the scope of negotiations, the bargaining process, impasse procedures, work stoppages, and master agreement administration.

Recognition and bargaining unit determination answers the question, "Who represents whom?" Recognition is the acceptance by an employer of a bargaining agent as the authorized representative of a bargaining unit. There are two types of recognition, multiple and exclusive. Experience dictates that exclusive recognition is the most effective. The three most commonly used recognition procedures are: membership lists, authorization cards, and elections. In an election, a third party such as the Federal Mediation and Conciliation Service should be engaged to handle the mechanics of the election process.

The bargaining unit is composed of all employees to be covered by the negotiated master agreement. The criteria for deciding who belongs to the unit includes: a community of interest among the members, effective bargaining power, and effective school administration.

The scope of what is negotiable usually entails salaries, fringe benefits, and working conditions. A major problem in defining "scope" is the fine line between educational policy, which is the prerogative of the school board, and conditions of employment, which are negotiable.

The "at the table" bargaining process must begin with the formation of a negotiating team. An odd numbered team composed of the director of employee relations, building principals, and a central office fiscal administrator has the greatest potential for being effective. This team is responsible for developing strategies, formulating goals, setting the ground rules, proposal preparation, and participating in negotiating sessions. Once an agreement is reached, the team makes a recommendation to the school board, which formally ratifies the agreement.

If there is persistent disagreement at the table after normal negotiation procedures are exhausted, an impasse has been reached. The three usual procedures for resolving an impasse are: mediation, fact-finding, and, where permitted by law, arbitration. Mediation is the voluntary process by which a third party intervenes for the purpose of ending the disagreement. Fact-finding is a procedure by which an individual or panel holds hearings for the purpose of reviewing evidence and making a recommendation for settling the dispute. Arbitration occurs when both sides submit the dispute to an impartial third person or panel that issues an award which the parties are required to accept.

There is nothing more disruptive to a school district than a strike, which is sometimes used by unions when negotiations reach an impasse. Although strikes by teachers are illegal in most states, the number of strikes appears to be on the increase. It is extremely important, therefore, for the administration to develop a strike plan, even in the most tranquil of school settings.

The process of collective negotiations is usually ineffective unless the agreements are put into writing, which formalizes the basic rights governing the parties and reduces controversy. It is the responsibility of the administration to implement and interpret the master agreement. Furthermore, the administration is limited only by the specifics of the agreement, commonly referred to as "management prerogative."

In the day-to-day interpretation of the master agreement, it is certainly possible for violations to occur. Most written agreements, therefore, provide for a grievance procedure by which individuals, the union, or the administration may allege that the agreement is being violated.

IMPLICATIONS FOR SCHOOL BOARD MEMBERS

There are four implications for boards of education that emerge from this treatment of collective bargaining for public school employees.

First, school board members should attend workshops, seminars, and convention programs dealing with collective bargaining. State school board associations and the National School Boards Association sponsor such programs, which are of tremendous value to board members. In addition, boards of education should encourage administrators to sharpen their skills in collective bargaining through staff development programs.

Second, school board members should be active in promoting state legislation that seeks to improve labor-management relations in school districts. This is best accomplished through participation in regional and state school board associations.

Third, school board members should require the superintendent and his or her staff to keep board members informed on a regular basis about the status of labor-management relations in their school district and throughout the state.

Fourth, school board members should resist the temptation to permit "third party" negotiations. In recent years, parents and other school district patrons have been pushing to have an active involvement in collective negotiations. This treatment has hopefully established the position that collective negotiations demand refined skills by those sitting at the bargaining table. A third party will create confusion and cloud the basic relationship between labor and management. In addition, school board members have been elected to represent the interests of parents, students, and district patrons. Third party involvement seeks to displace this responsibility.

APPENDIX A
STATE PUBLIC EMPLOYEE COLLECTIVE BARGAINING LAWS AFFECTING EDUCATION[8]

STATE	NUMBER OF STATUTES[1]	LOCAL[2]	STATE[3]	OMNIBUS[4]	PROFESSIONAL COVERAGE[5] K-12	CC[8]	PS	CLASSIFIED COVERAGE[6] K-12	CC[8]	PS	SUPERVISOR COVERAGE[7] K-12	CC[8]	PS	UNION SECURITY PROVISIONS[9]	
Alabama															AL
Alaska	2	x		x	x		x			x	x			x	AK
Arizona															AZ
Arkansas															AR
California	3	x	PS		x	x	x	x	x					x	CA
Colorado									x	x					CO
Connecticut	3	x	x		x	x	x	x	x	x		x	x	x	CT
Delaware	2	x			x	x	x	x	x	x		x		x	DE
Florida	1			x	x	x	x	x	x	x				x	FL
Georgia															GA
Hawaii	1			x	x	x	x	x	x	x	x	x	x	x	HI
Idaho	1	x			x						x				ID
Illinois															IL
Indiana	1	x			x									x	IN
Iowa	1			x	x	x	x	x	x	x				x	IA
Kansas	2	x		x	x	x	x	x	x	x				x	KS
Kentucky															KY
Louisiana															LA
Maine	2	x	PS,CC		x	x	x	x	x	x	x			x	ME
Maryland	2	x			x		x	x	x	x	x			x	MD
Massachusetts	1			x	x	x	x	x	x	x			x	x	MA

[8]Education Commission of the States, *Cuebook II: State Education Collective Bargaining Laws.*

Matrix of state abbreviations (columns) versus states (rows):

Column headers: MI, MN, MS, MO, MT, NE, NV, NH, NJ, NM, NY, NC, ND, OH, OK, OR, PA, RI, SC, SD, TN, TX, UT

State	#	MI	MN	MS	MO	MT	NE	NV	NH	NJ	NM	NY	NC	ND	OH	OK	OR	PA	RI	SC	SD	TN	TX	UT
Michigan	1	×	×			×		×		×		×				×	×	×	×					
Minnesota	1	×	×							×		×						×			×			
Mississippi	1		×			×				×														
Missouri	1	×	×		×				×	×		×		×		×		×			×			
Montana	1	×	×		×	×		×	×	×		×									×			
Nebraska	2					×			×								×							
Nevada	1	×	×		×	×	×	×	×	×		×				×	×	×	×		×			
New Hampshire	1	×	×		×	×		×	×	×		×				×	×	×			×			
New Jersey	1		×			×			×							×								
New Mexico																								
New York	1	×	×		×	×		×	×	×		×		×		×	×	×	×		×			
North Carolina																								
North Dakota	1	×	×		×	×			×	×		×				×	×	×	×		×			
Ohio																								
Oklahoma	1																							
Oregon	1						×	×								×								
Pennsylvania	1													×		×		×			×			
Rhode Island	3																					×		
South Carolina																								
South Dakota	1																							
Tennessee	1																							
Texas																								
Utah																								

STATE	NUMBER OF STATUTES[1]	TYPE OF LAWS			PROFESSIONAL COVERAGE[5]			CLASSIFIED COVERAGE[6]			SUPERVISOR COVERAGE[7]			UNION SECURITY PROVISIONS[9]
		LOCAL[2]	STATE[3]	OMNIBUS[4]	K-12	CC[8]	PS	K-12	CC[8]	PS	K-12	CC[8]	PS	
Vermont	3	x	x		x		x	x		x	x		x	x
Virginia														
Washington	4	x	CC		x	x		x	x		x	x		x
West Virginia														
Wisconsin	2	x	x		x	x	x	x	x	x	x	x	x	x
Wyoming														
District of Columbia	1	x			x		x	x		x	x		x	x
TOTALS		19	7	17	32	12[8]	24	27	12[8]	24	20[8]	5	13	26

[1] Represents the number of separate statutes summarized on the table for each state.

[2] Coverage for local-level employees only.

[3] Coverage for state-level employees only. California, Maine and Washington laws are specific for postsecondary and/or community colleges.

[4] Coverage for employees of more than one governmental level.

[5] Teachers or personnel with similar or higher status.

[6] Below the rank of teacher; non-administrative support personnel.

[7] Any or all levels of supervisors and administrators, in one or more laws in the state.

[8] This column is checked only if community colleges are noted specifically in the law. State structures vary, and community colleges may be included in the K–12 system, in the postsecondary system, or may be a separate system.

[9] This column is checked if union security provisions are present in one or more of the state laws.

APPENDIX B
JOB DESCRIPTION
FOR THE DIRECTOR
OF EMPLOYEE RELATIONS[9]

Job Summary

The Director of Employee Relations is responsible for the administration of the school district's management-employee relations program. This includes the establishment and maintenance of effective two-way communications between the various organizational levels; the formulation, recommendation, and administration of school district management-employee relations policies; and the administration of the collective negotiations process.

Organizational Relationships

The Director of Employee Relations has a line relationship with the Assistant Superintendent for Personnel and reports directly to him. He serves as the chief advisor concerning employee relations matters. He has a staff relationship with other administrative personnel. The Director of Employee Relations has a cooperative-professional relationship with nonadministrative personnel with whom he negotiates. Of course, he has a line relationship with his immediate staff and they report directly to him.

Organization Tasks

In preparing for negotiations, the Director of Employee Relations shall:

Develop negotiations strategy for school district management;
Prepare proposals and counter proposals for school district management;
Analyze and evaluate employee proposals, and advise the school district management accordingly;
Know state laws, court decisions, and other litigation relevant to professional negotiations;
Secure input from all administrative personnel prior to developing school district management proposals.

In at-the-table negotiations activities, the Director of Employee Relations shall:

Serve as the chief negotiator for the school district;
Direct the school district's negotiations team;
Keep administrative personnel informed during negotiations;
Draft negotiated agreements reached with employees;

[9]American Association of School Administrators, *Helping Administrators Negotiate* (Arlington, Va.: The Association, 1974), pp. 22–24.

Maintain records of proposals and counter proposals presented by all parties during negotiations.

In administration of the negotiated agreement, the Director of Employee Relations shall:

Serve as the school district's chief advisor in the interpretation of adopted agreements;
Serve as the school district's chief advisor in all grievance matters;
Consult with principals and other supervisors concerning their understanding of and compliance with the adopted agreement;
Initiate school district management's grievance and mediation activities.

Job Requirements

In terms of educational requirements, the Director of Employee Relations should possess:

Appropriate state administrator certification;
A masters degree (minimum);
Formal course work concentrating in the areas of educational administration with exposure to curriculum, finance, school law, collective negotiations, and personnel administration;
Classroom teaching experience and at least two years as a building principal as the minimum requirement for this position.

APPENDIX C
CONTRACT BETWEEN
THE DADE COUNTY PUBLIC
SCHOOLS AND THE UNITED
TEACHERS OF DADE FEA/UNITED,
AFT, LOCAL 1974, AFL-CIO

APPENDIX D
GLOSSARY OF COLLECTIVE
BARGAINING TERMS[10]

Agency shop. This term is used when employees who are not members of an employee organization, but who are represented by it during the bargaining process and in the administration of a bargained agreement, are required to pay a service fee to the organization.

Arbitration. A procedure whereby parties unable to agree on a solution to a problem (i.e., at impasse in a contract negotiation or a grievance procedure) will be bound by the decision of a third party.

Bargaining unit. A group of employees organized as a single unit and having the right to bargain, through their designated representative(s), with the employer.

Certification. As the term applies in the recognition process: designation, by an authorized person or agency, of the employee organization representing a bargaining unit as an "exclusive representative" for bargaining purposes.

Community of interest. As used in determining an appropriate bargaining unit: similar work, interests, salaries, concerns, etc.

Contract. A written agreement on terms and conditions of employment arrived at through the bargaining process.

Court review. The means through which a court of appropriate jurisdiction may consider and rule upon actions or findings of a labor relations board or other involved agency or individual.

Decertification. The withdrawal of authorization as an exclusive representative from an employee organization. May occur when another employee organization successfully challenges the qualifications of the first organization, or as a penalty for violation of law, rule or regulation.

Dues checkoff. Deduction of employee organization dues from member's paychecks for remission to the organization treasury. Some state laws do not permit this practice; others do. When permitted, the dues deduction procedure often is negotiated as part of the contract between employer and employee bargaining unit.

Employee organization. A group of similar employees organized for the purpose of bargaining their salaries, wages and terms and conditions of employment

---

[10]Education Commission of the States, *Cuebook II: State Education Collective Bargaining Laws.*

with their employer. Most teacher organizations are affiliated with the National Education Association or the American Federation of Teachers. Often used interchangeably with *union* in the area of labor relations.

Exclusive representation. An employee organization has exclusive representation when it is recognized by the employer, for bargaining purposes, as the sole representative of the kinds of employees who are members of the bargaining unit.

Fact-finding. The process of gathering and analyzing accurate facts, information, and testimony to be used as a basis for recommendations for the resolution of a bargaining impasse or grievance charge.

Fair share fee. An amount proportionate to members' dues in an employee organization that is paid to the organization by nonmembers who are, nevertheless, represented by the organization in a bargaining relationship. Such nonmembers are a part of the bargaining unit, but not of the employee organization that represents them. A form of service fee, based on the proportion of dues that is directly related to the services the nonmember employee receives from the organization. Often negotiated.

Grievance. An allegation by an employee or by the employee organization that the employer or one of its agents, often in the process of implementing a contract, is guilty of misapplication, misinterpretation, or violation of one or more specific provisions of the existent contract.

Impasse. That stage in negotiations at which two parties are, or appear to be, unable to achieve agreement on the issues still on the bargaining table. There is an apparent lack of agreement among state laws and among state labor relations personnel as to the point at which impasse occurs: when mediation has failed, or when fact-finding has failed.

Impasse resolution. A process aimed at resolving disagreements that occur during the bargaining of a contract. Three steps may be, but are not necessarily, involved: mediation, fact-finding, and arbitration. Also known as interest resolution.

Injunctive relief. An order by a court to perform or cease to perform a specific activity.

Intervention/intervenor. A challenge to an employee organization's right to be an exclusive representative for a bargaining unit. May be issued by a competing organization or one or more employees. Most state laws limit the times for such intervention to specific points in the establishment of a bargaining relationship, during or after the term of a contract.

Legislative body.   A policy-making body that has the authority to levy taxes and/or make appropriations.

Maintenance of membership.   A requirement that employees who are members of an employee organization that has been certified as an exclusive representative remain members during the term of a bargained contract.

Management rights.   Certain rights, privileges, responsibilities and authority requisite to the conduct of an enterprise by its management.

Mediation.   That form of impasse resolution (usually implemented first) in which a third party meets with the two parties involved in the dispute, together and/or separately, in order to perform a catalytic function in an effort to help the parties reach an agreement.

Recognition.   The accomplishment of the status, by the employee organization with the employer, of collective bargaining agent for a unit of defined extent.

Representation election.   An election held to identify an appropriate employee organization as the exclusive representative of employees in a defined bargaining unit. The employee organization receiving a majority of votes is the winner.

Scope of bargaining.   Bargainable items—the limits, if any, of the appropriate subject matter for bargaining. If such are not set by law, they are determined by the interaction at the bargaining table. If there is not agreement on the scope of bargaining, decisions may be made by a public employment relations board, other administering agency, individual, or by an appropriate court.

Service fees.   A sum of money paid to the bargaining unit by nonmember employees who are, nevertheless, represented by the bargaining unit. Some state laws permit these fees; others do not. Service fees may be equal to a unit member's regular dues; they may be a certain percentage of these dues; they may be equal to that portion of membership dues that are used to cover the expense of negotiating and administering a contract. In some states, non-members represented by a negotiating unit who have valid religious objections to the payment of service fees to an organized bargaining unit may be granted an exemption from the requirement; or their service fee may be remitted to an appropriate charity.

Showing of support interest.   Submission of evidence by an employee organization wishing to represent a bargaining unit that it has adequate support/interest/membership from personnel in the bargaining unit. This may be in the form of signature cards, petition signatures, etc.

Strike.   A concerted work stoppage, usually used as an effort at the time of impasse to accomplish a contract on terms acceptable to the union.

Union. An employee organization having as one of its purposes the bargaining of terms and conditions of employment with an employer.

Union security. A blanket term for rights, granted to a union by law or agreement, that reinforce its position as exclusive representative. Dues deduction and service fees are forms of union security, as are specified periods of time during which the union's standing as exclusive representative may not be challenged.

Union shop. This term applies when an employee is required under the terms of a bargained agreement to become a member of the bargaining unit within a short time after initial employment in order to retain the job. Membership must be maintained during the term of the bargained agreement. In rare cases, union shops are permitted under state law.

Unit determination. The process of deciding which employees will be in a proposed bargaining unit. Criteria for determination include community of interest, practicality. In some states, units are specifically defined by law.

Unit modification. A change in the composition (kinds of employees) of a bargaining unit.

SELECTED BIBLIOGRAPHY

COFFIN, ROYCE A., *The Negotiator: A Manual for Winners.* New York: American Management Association, 1973.

DAVEY, HAROLD W., *Contemporary Collective Bargaining* (3rd ed.). Englewood Cliffs, NJ: Prentice-Hall, Inc., 1972.

EDUCATION COMMISSION OF THE STATES, *Cuebook II: State Education Collective Bargaining Laws.* Denver, CO: The Commission, 1980.

KARRASS, CHESTER L., *Give and Take: The Complete Guide to Negotiating Strategies and Tactics.* New York: Thomas Y. Crowell Company, 1974.

MOSKOW, MICHAEL, JOSEPH J. LOEWENBERG, and EDWARD C. KOZIARA, *Collective Bargaining in Public Employment.* New York: Random House, Inc., 1970.

NATIONAL EDUCATION ASSOCIATION, *Negotiations for Improvement of the Profession: A Handbook for Local Teacher Association Negotiators.* Washington D.C.: The Association, 1971.

INDEX